THE FIGHTIN' TEXAS AGGIE DEFENDERS OF BATAAN AND CORREGIDOR

This book's publication is generously sponsored by the C. C. Taylor '51 Texas A&M University Corps of Cadets Publishing Fund.

THE FIGHTIN' TEXAS AGGIE DEFENDERS OF BATAAN AND CORREGIDOR

John A. Adams Jr. '73

TEXAS A&M UNIVERSITY PRESS
COLLEGE STATION

First edition

∞ This paper meets the requirements of ANSI/
NISO Z39.48-1992 (Permanence of Paper).
Binding materials have been chosen for durability.
Manufactured in the United States of America

Library of Congress Cataloging-in-Publication Data

Adams, John A., Jr., 1951–
The fightin' Texas Aggie defenders of Bataan and
Corregidor / John A. Adams Jr. '73.
First edition. College Station: Texas A&M University Press, 2016
Includes bibliographical references and index.
ISBN 978-1-623-49421-6 (cloth: alk. paper)
ISBN 978-1-623-49422-3 (pbk.: alk. paper)
ISBN 978-1-623-49423-0 (ebook)
1. LCSH: World War, 1939–1945—Campaigns—Philippines—
Corregidor Island. 2. Bataan, Battle of, Philippines, 1942. 3. Agricultural
and Mechanical College of Texas (Texas A&M University). Corps of
Cadets—Alumni and alumnae (former students)—Biography. 4. United
States. Army—Officers—Biography. 5. Bataan (Philippines: Province)—
History, Military. 6. Corregidor Island (Philippines)—History, Military.
D767.4A635 2016

940.54'259910922764—dc23 2015036488

The Texas Aggie Corregidor Memorial was dedicated on April 21, 2015, at "Topside" on the Rock. In the ceremony, members of the Corps of Cadets honor guard place the great seal of the university in front of the Texas A&M memorial surrounded by three flags—the United States, Texas, and Texas A&M. In the background is the main drill field on the Rock where in February 1945 American paratroops, including Aggies William D. Walker '44 and Charles L. Slover '44, landed under heavy enemy fire to recapture the island fortress. (Courtesy of Gabriel Pamintuan.)

CONTENTS

ILLUSTRATIONS

MAPS

DEDICATION

★★★

Army Air Corps Lt. John A. Adams and wife Martha in Manila Bay, departing for Japan in 1946. The bay was littered with sunken ships and in the background is the southern tip of Bataan. (Courtesy of the author's collection.)

PREFACE

★ ★ ★

THE LAST FULL MEASURE

After my knee wound was dressed, I returned to our bivouac for some desperately needed rest. I had lost my bedroll at Moron, and Lieutenant Cliff Hardwicke '37 kindly offered me his. It was a selfless gesture, typical of the tall, courtly young Texan, for though the days were suffocating, the nights were wet and chilly. Hardwicke stretched out on the ground beside me and pulled from his pocket a cable [telegram] he had received from his father in Texas.

It read simply, *Give 'em hell, son.*

I handed the telegram back with a nod, thanked him for the bedroll, wrapped myself up, and was asleep in an instant. Before I awoke next morning, Cliff Hardwicke was dead. He had ridden early into Moron to recover our horses. As he was leading them out, a sniper shot him through the head, killing him instantly; his body had to be left behind.

Captain Edwin P. Ramsey
Near Moron, Bataan: January 16, 1942

The family of Lt. Hardwicke '37 was posthumously awarded his Silver Star for Bravery at Fort Sam Houston, San Antonio, in 1943.

INTRODUCTION

★ ★ ★

Bataan. Corregidor. The very words are distant, hallowed, and often lost to time, yet what happened there and what was endured there should never be forgotten. On April 9, 1942, the first large-scale battle of World War II ended in the surrender of American and Filipino forces to the Japanese Imperial Army. Promised relief as soon as it could be marshaled, the defenders of Bataan and Corregidor were at first ordered to hold out at all costs when, in fact, American strategists in Washington were well aware that the Philippines could be neither effectively defended nor resupplied in a timely manner following the devastating blow to the US Naval Pacific Fleet at Pearl Harbor. Thus the operational plan on the ground in the Philippines was, if attacked by an overwhelming invading foreign force, to withdraw into the Bataan Peninsula on the west side of Manila Bay, hold there as long as possible, and then withdraw to fortified Corregidor Island, "the Rock," and fight and wait.

The US-led army at the onset of the battle was an American-Filipino force composed of some sixty-six thousand Filipinos and twelve thousand Americans. Except for one American Infantry Regiment; Army Air Corps members; and scattered tank, mounted cavalry, and antiaircraft battalions, the balance of the American forces officers and senior enlisted were divided among the nine divisions of the newly created Philippine Army. Among these defenders were eighty-ninc military soldiers—former students and citizen soldiers from the Agricultural and Mechanical College of Texas—the Fightin' Texas A&M Aggies. This deployment of these Texas Aggie officers to the Philippines represents the largest contingent of any institute in the United States providing officers for the opening campaign of World War II. Over time, some twenty thousand Texas Aggies served in all theaters of the war—with nearly a thousand lost in action.

Thus this story is about the *Fightin' Texas Aggie eighty-nine.* These Aggie men hailed from every corner of Texas and ranged in rank from major general to sergeant. All products of leadership training in the Corps of Cadets at Texas A&M, these citizen soldiers received basic military skills while in college at College Station, Texas. Following graduation, most were placed in a reserve status and returned home to work in their chosen field. Due to the federal budget cuts incurred by the military during the interwar years, forced in good part by the Great Depression, only a few Texas A&M former cadets were on active duty in early 1941 following graduation. Once the war started, the balance would volunteer and be called to active duty, trained and ordered to assignments in the Philippines. Thousands of other Texas Aggies would fight worldwide in every theater of the war. And none had any idea of what was in store for them.

War clouds had long been forming over Europe with the rise of Adolph Hitler and over Asia as the militant Japanese government during the late 1930s made it clear that they intended to expand their sphere of influence and hunger for natural resources by invading China and Korea. Only a few foreign-controlled outposts at Hong Kong, Singapore, and the Philippines stood in the Japanese path to control all the Pacific Rim. And yet few in Texas had any notion of these far-off political dynamics or of the war to come.

At the time of the first Japanese air raids on December 8, 1941, the Aggies who would be numbered among the defenders of Bataan were scattered in units ranging from those at Manila, at Clark Air Field, and at Luzon outposts; field units on the Bataan Peninsula and on Mindanao; and those stationed at Fort Mills on Corregidor, known to all as "the Rock." By mid-January 1942, most US forces and their Filipino allies who survived the initial wave of attacks were concentrated on Bataan or on the Rock. The ensuing 120 days of active combat and delaying action across the Bataan Peninsula would deplete both the strength and the ability of the American and Filipino forces to halt the swarming concentration of Imperial Japanese troops, superior air power, and fire power. The valiant defense was daily hampered by shortages of ammunition, food, fuel, medicine, air support, and good intelligence to counter the seasoned enemy. Within days of the start of the Battle of Bataan, troop rations were cut in half, fuel was in short supply, and medical supplies were near impossible to obtain.

The hallmark events of this saga include the Bataan Death March that followed the surrender, brutal imprisonment, and loss of thousands shipped in "Hell Ships" to work camps in Japan and beyond. Few events in modern history have been more horrific and subhuman. Even before the attacks on Pearl Harbor and Manila, the Imperial Japanese Army had established a bloody record of brutal atrocities and disregard for human life. Merciless brutality on such a protracted scale was never before seen in modern history. The bulk of the brutal Death March occurred in the three weeks following the April 9, 1942, surrender; segments of the hostile and gruesome movement and forced march of prisoners to POW camps continued through June 1942. Starvation and abusive conditions grew greater in the POW camps as prisoners were denied adequate food, water, or medical care. Death was a daily occurrence.

By late 1944, as the Imperial Japanese High Command was pressured and panicked by the approaching US Navy and Army, thousands of POWs from Bataan were loaded on cargo ships—Hell Ships—for transfer to labor camps in China, Japan, Formosa, and Korea. With no Red Cross markings on the decks or any indication of the POW cargo below deck, thousands of US and Allied troops were killed in the accidental "friendly fire" sinking of many of these cargo ships, including more than thirty officers from Texas A&M.

My research for this project dates back more than three decades, as I have accumulated documents, pictures, and interviews on the events on Bataan and Corregidor. Landing a small plane at the tiny Kindley

Field on the narrow eastern tip of Corregidor Island in Manila Bay in April 1991 for Aggie Muster on "the Rock" was an unforgettable experience, followed by an extended visit to the Malinta Tunnel, Subic Bay, and the Bataan Peninsula. In addition to interviews with seven of the Texas Aggie officers who were embattled on Bataan and Corregidor, I was able to draw on the personal accounts from the wartime diaries and papers of Colonel Tom Dooley '35, Cliff Danclifts, Tom Dyess, General Jonathan Wainwright, Colonel Edward E. Aldridge '16, Lt. Robley D. Evans '40, Jerome MaDavitt '33, James T. Danklefs '43, T.Sgt. John Moseley '39, Lt. William Hamilton '40, and Captain Cary Abney '34, as well as detailed after-action reports and memoirs by Generals George Moore, Douglas MacArthur, Jonathan Wainwright, Edward King, John Bebee, and Captain John Coleman '27.

I was further aided in this research by a host of experts and primary sources of information that assisted in helping the story become as complete as possible. Thanks are extended to family and friends of the Texas Aggies who served on Bataan and Corregidor for their assistance, including Linda McDavitt, William Hamilton Jr., Randy Dooley Peters, Diane Davidson Claiborne, David Evans '72, and Kay Moseley Hilliard. Also, many thanks to Marylin Routt Thomason, widow of the famed twice All American football Aggie great Joe Routt '38, for her firsthand recollections of the Depression years during the late 1930s prior to Pearl Harbor and America's response to the coming of war. Joe, one of more than a thousand Aggies who made the supreme sacrifice during World War II, was killed in action during the Battle of the Bulge in late 1944.

Those who have given assistance in this project number in the scores, yet most helpful at each turn was great friend and mentor Dr. Henry C. Dethloff, as well as Bill Page '73 and Kristin Smith of the Sterling C. Evans Library at Texas A&M University, Colonel Jim Woodall '50, Jerry Cooper '63, Colonel Donald "Buck" Henderson '62, General Tom Darling '54, General Don Johnson '55, Tom Autrey '73, Dr. Roger Beaumont, and Dr. David Hockethorn. The archives staff of the Cushing Library at Texas A&M University was a tremendous help, including Robin B. Hutchison, Anton duPlessis, and

Jenny Reibenspies. Thanks also to those at Texas A&M University Press who worked on publishing this book: Katie Duelm '06, Jay Dew, and Rachel Paul. Special thanks to Anne Boykin for creating the maps used here. I would like to thank the curator of the Santa Fe, New Mexico, Bataan Museum, Jim Smith, for his timely assistance on an exceedingly cold and icy day in December 2013. The staff at the World War II Museum in New Orleans was helpful, as well as the staff at the Army War College in Carlisle, Pennsylvania. A special thanks is extended to Dr. Jim Erickson, whose detailed research on the American troops transported on the Hell Ships and their tragic fate was invaluable in helping me understand this critical stage of the Pacific War. And, as always, my wife Sherry provided a great sounding board and encouragement throughout this project.

David Evans '71, Dick Miller '71, Malon Southerland '65, and George Hester '72 gave me great firsthand understanding of Bataan and Corregidor when they accompanied me on a staff ride that included retracing the route of the Bataan Death March and visits to the prisoner of war camps at Cabanatuan and O'Donnell. This tour of Bataan was followed by the observance of Texas Aggie Muster on the Rock on April 21, 2015, and (coordinated by Marti Holmes '87) the Association of Former Students–sponsored dedication of the Texas Aggie War Memorial to those who served during the battle and Mustered in 1942 and 1946.

A very special thank you is extended to the book's sponsor, C. C. Taylor '51, whose vision and drive pushed this project into high gear and was a positive encouragement during the entire process. He has displayed a great dedication to the Texas Aggie Corps of Cadets as well as to the memory of those who served in our nation's armed forces.

While there have been many books on the saga of Bataan-Corregidor in 1941–42, none has focused solely on the contribution and sacrifice of the citizen soldiers from Texas A&M University. This is their story: a chronicle of valor, grit, and sacrifice that has never been told and—with this testament to their call to duty—should never be forgotten.

THE FIGHTIN' TEXAS AGGIE DEFENDERS OF BATAAN AND CORREGIDOR

★ CHAPTER 1 ★

DOOMED FROM THE START

I have wanted to come here [to Texas A&M] for a great many years. I go back in my mind to the days of the World War when Texas A. & M. graduates made a greater contribution to the officer personnel of the United States than any other institution of learning in the United States, and I am proud of it.

We know another thing—that our preparation is honestly made for defense and not for aggression. We devoutly hope that other nations in the world are going to get our point of view in the days to come in order that they may spend less of their national income in preparation for war and more of it for the arts of peace.

Coming here today has been a great inspiration to me.

President Franklin D. Roosevelt
Kyle Field College Station, Texas May 11, 1937

The long black Packard limousine turned slowly onto the dark cinder track at Kyle Field—its passengers seated low in the rear seat flanked by four Secret Service agents. The clear high blue sky of the May 1937 day was a fitting welcome as President Franklin D. Roosevelt, accompanied by the president of the Agricultural and Mechanical College of Texas, Thomas O. Walton, pulled to a stop behind the goal post on the north end of the stadium. Except for a brief whistle-stop at the College Station Depot west of campus by President Howard Taft in 1909, no sitting US president had ever been to the A&M College of Texas.

President Roosevelt remained seated in the backseat of the car—few knew of his affliction of polio that limited his ability to stand—as a portable microphone was positioned for him to address the stadium crowd of more than twenty thousand, composed of cadets, college staff, and local citizens. FDR was fresh from a week-long fishing trip on the *USS Potomac* in the Gulf of Mexico and docked in Galveston. The president's special private train arrived in College Station by way of Houston. Hatless and a bit sunburned, FDR's big smile and charm was in full display as he praised the tremendous sacrifice and contribution of more than 2,200 Texas A&M former students in World War I.[1]

The honor of the president's visit was overshadowed by the lingering economic depression across the nation as well as by global events far from Texas that would plunge the nation and the A&M College cadets, staff, and former students into another world war. The sentiment across the country was to avoid war at all cost. Much of FDR's administration in the late 1930s had been geared toward economic recovery and job creation after a near decade-long depression that in spite of an alphabet soup of new federal agencies, recovery programs, and potential job opportunities—the AAA, WPA, RFC, CCC, TVA, PWA—never fully lowered unemployment, exceeding 30 percent by 1938–39.[2]

By the fall of 1937, the Corps of Cadets continued as the largest military training program in the nation, and the A&M College of Texas (hereafter Texas A&M) was one of only three institutions nationwide that offered military training and commissions in all seven branches of the US Army—infantry, cavalry, field artillery, coastal artillery, engineering, signal corps, and chemical corps. One only wonders if the president, looking over the ranks of the Corps of Cadets in review, pondered the contribution these Aggie men would make if events called them into the armed services.

FDR's visit to Texas A&M was no casual sojourn. War clouds were on the horizon with Japanese expansionist objectives in Asia and Hitler's plans for a blitzkrieg across Europe, both of major concern to the president. If America became involved in a global conflict, the nation would need a strong supply of "citizen soldiers" to fill the ranks.

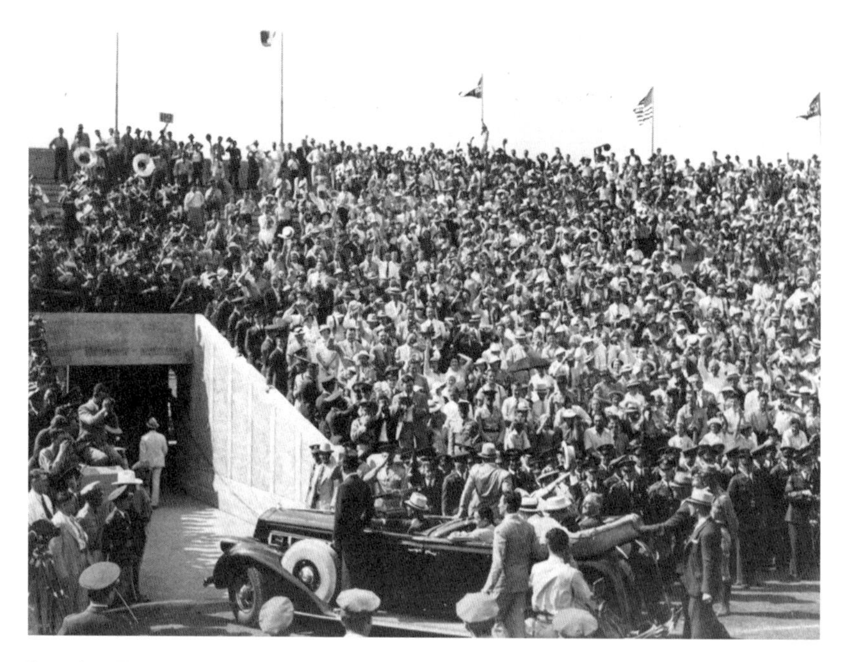

President Franklin D. Roosevelt driving out the north end of Kyle Field at Texas A&M on May 12, 1937, after delivering a presentation on national defense and praising the Texas Aggies for their contribution to the nation during World War I. (Courtesy of the author's collection.)

The potential contributions of the men of Texas A&M to the impending war were gleaned from the formal military review of the Corps of Cadets that followed FDR's visit. That day on campus, passing in review before the president, were more than three dozen cadets—from the Texas A&M Classes of '37, '38, '39, and '40—who were destined to soon fight and die at Bataan and Corregidor and in the Death March and imprisonment that followed.[3]

FDR's visit in 1937 to Texas A&M proved to be a catalyst for a decade of growth on the tiny Texas A&M campus—both in the facilities as well as through the increase in the number of commissioned officers being produced by the Corps of Cadets. In late 1937, an application for $2 million in construction funding was submitted to the Reconstruction Finance Corporation (RFC) in Washington, DC, for a grant to build twelve new cadet dorms and a mess hall to hold three thousand cadets at one sitting. The prospects for approval, following FDR's visit, were nearly certain given the fact that the president had recommended the project. The president's youngest son Elliott, whom FDR called his "small boy," was a member of the Texas A&M Board of Directors as well as close friends with the administrator and chairman for the RFC, Houstonian Jesse H. Jones. Industrialist Jones was the recipient of the second honorary doctor of laws degree from the A&M College in its sixty-one-year history—even though the college had no law school![4]

In short order, the request for funding was approved and construction of new four-story dorms began in early 1938. One irony of the massive construction of the new Corps of Cadets housing area, known as the Quadrangle or "Quad," is that the completion of the project was delayed well into 1939 because there was a shortage of bricklayers. Construction delays were finally ironed out, and in the fall of 1939,

The bugle stand and main flag pole in 1941 at the heart of the Texas A&M campus. In the back is the Academic Building and in the foreground is the Texas Aggie mascot—Reveille I, featured in the movie *We've Never Been Licked.* (Courtesy of the Cushing Library.)

more than 2,500 cadets occupied the new Spartan dorms. Enrollment in the Corps of Cadets jumped from 4,500 in June 1937 to more than 6,600 cadets in the fall of 1941.[5]

Overseeing the addition of the new cadet dorms and growth of the Corps was Professor of Military Science and Training (PMS&T) and Commandant of Cadets **Colonel George Fleming Moore '08**. Little did he know that he would become an icon of Aggie contributions and struggles on Bataan and Corregidor. Colonel Moore, a career officer, had returned to campus in the fall of 1937 at the direct-in-person request of an old 1908 classmate, captain of the '07 A&M football team and Texas A&M board member Joe Utah '08—who personally went straight to the White House to visit with President Roosevelt to request and confirm Moore's appointment as commandant of cadets.[6]

Colonel Moore, born in Austin, entered Texas A&M in 1904, majored in civil engineering, lettered in football (playing guard and tackle), and gained the nickname of "Maude"—after a wild cartoon script of the era featuring a mule always stirring up a big kick—for kicking a football like a mule over four-story Ross Hall. The former Ross Volunteer entered active duty in 1909 and received training in coastal artillery, field artillery, and ordnance. A graduate of the Command and General Staff School, he was a veteran of World War I. During the interwar period, he served two tours of duty on Corregidor and in the Philippine Islands as an expert in defense fortifications and coastal artillery.[7]

Most Americans in the late 1930s cared little about what was going on in Europe, in spite of the scattered newspaper reports, and the general public was even less concerned about Asian and Pacific events. Public sentiment across the nation was in the grip of isolationists and strongly antiwar, given most Americans felt the United States had wastefully lost 116,000 men killed in action in World War I. The rattling of swords by the Germans had little concern inasmuch as the nation was dealing with the long hangover of the Great Depression. There was even less awareness of events in the Pacific as the Japanese expanded what they termed their "Imperial Power" into

Maj. Gen. George F. Moore '08, pictured as a senior cadet, was the commander of Fort Mills on Corregidor Island and the ranking Texas Aggie officer in the Philippines. This class picture from the 1908 *Longhorn* highlights his cadet days in the Corps of Cadets. (Courtesy of the *Longhorn*, 1908.)

Manchuria, China, and Korea. In the process, the Japanese Army racked up five years of combat experience. Vivid memories of the previous Great World War during the 1920s not only fueled the isolationist American public opinion but also were reflected in no less than 170 formal US congressional bills and resolutions during the interwar period limiting any form of military buildup or funding for war production. Skimpy military appropriations, an antiwar sentiment, and the Great Depression spawned a hardened pacifist mood. Congress renewed the Neutrality Act, crafted in the hopes of keeping the nation out of any foreign entanglements. However, in the post–World War I period, one action by the US Congress, passage of the National Defense Act of

June 4, 1920, would prove prophetic and set the stage for the establishment of the Reserve Officers Training Corps (ROTC) and the reliance of the country on the mobilization and training of "citizen soldiers" in times of national crisis.[8]

Shortly after his visit to Texas A&M, FDR told reporters that Europe was a tinderbox of discourse and concern over German territorial aims. Thus, to test the degree of national tolerance in the face of what the president termed a "lawless world," he delivered what became known as the "Quarantine Speech" in the fall of 1937 to call attention to the rising arms race and growing hostilities abroad. The president's speech was panned and vocally rejected as the nation dipped deeper into depression. Public proof of disapproval of FDR and the lingering Depression was expressed in the fall 1938 off-year elections when the Republicans captured a dozen governorships, eight Senate seats, and a whopping eighty-two seats in the House of Representatives. However, in spite of growing isolationist concern, opponents known as the "interventionists" warned that if Britain fell, Nazi Germany would control the European continent. The president continued to work quietly behind the scenes to secure appropriations for "defense" and in January 1939 convinced Congress to pass his request for $525 million for "minimum" necessities for the military—the largest funding since the last Great War. Prospects for expanding the armed forces, which during the 1930s had dwindled to an aging, ill-equipped, and untrained force, remained bleak.[9]

Since 1919, the ranks of the US Army were a shell of neglect and peacetime frugality. By the summer of 1940, the armed forces numbered about 185,000 men and ranked a poor eighteenth in size on a scale of the world's fighting forces. US Army Chief of Staff and General George Marshall painted a bleak picture of the armed forces to the Congress in April 1941: "We have virtually no corps troops, almost no army troops, or what they call GHQ special troops that are not assigned smaller units. In other words, we have nothing comparable to the United States Fleet, and these troops in the continental United States were scattered throughout the country in approximately one hundred fifty small garrisons . . . we have a reasonably adequate garrison in

Hawaii, a very deficient garrison of men in Panama, and a total of ten thousand Philippine Scouts and white troops in the Philippine Island." Given only a meager annual appropriation to start with, more than one-third of annual military funding was funneled off for pet projects such as river, bridge, and harbor improvements and for the maintenance of the Panama Canal. Except in the military service academies and the traditional military colleges such as Texas A&M, the Citadel, Norwich, North Georgia, Virginia Polytechnic Institution, and Virginia Military Institute, officer training had all but ceased. Few of those who completed ROTC training during the 1930s were called to active duty, and most were placed on the rolls as "inactive reserve." And pay for the active ranks fared little better—with privates in the all-volunteer army earning $21 per month and a first lieutenant only $205.[10]

Training and readiness suffered as the tactics and equipment of the army reflected the last war fought, replete with stockpiles of old Springfield and Enfield rifles, a proud traditional mounted cavalry that had no interest in tanks and mobile combat, a fleet of old airplanes coupled with a pilot shortage, and a navy with perilous few outdated ships and armaments. There was no large-scale procurement structure because there had been no need since World War I to replenish existing inventory or pursue new equipment. The United States in the late 1930s annually spent 10 percent of the national budget on the Army and the Navy, while most nations "of the Old World" spent 40 to 50 percent of their budgets on their armed forces—a top secret report by the US War Plans Division warned it was "intolerable that the U.S. was without a single combat division!" FDR noted, "Some people think of military in terms of acute pacifism. I do not." The leadership of the army was aged and had become "fossilized" along with the outdated equipment. The ranking general and chief of staff, Douglas MacArthur, upon the offer from old friend President Manuel Quezon, retired from the US Army on December 31, 1937, and moved to Manila to assume command of the newly created Army of the Commonwealth of the Philippines. He was offered the penthouse suite in the Manila Hotel and was given the rank no other American officer, before or since him, has ever held—Field Marshal.[11]

In contrast, at Texas A&M, Colonel Moore, aided by the addition of the new dorms, made extensive changes in the military-science training program by adding new staff, renovating Ross Hall as the new military instruction center, and stressing leadership training in all levels of the Corps of Cadets. The seven branches of cadet training on campus—infantry, field artillery, cavalry, coast artillery, corps of engineers, signal corps, and chemical warfare service—were staffed by 33 officers and 55 enlisted personnel and proved very effective in training the 6,500-man Corps. In addition to training in infantry combat tactics, and in the basics of aviation and artillery, the Corps of Cadets maintained an impressive 75 mounts and trained in horse cavalry maneuvers. Saturday drills were common. Moore insisted that cadets be trained in concert with regular army standards.[12]

Following the 1940 presidential election and victory of FDR over Wendell L. Willkie (both candidates had promised to keep America out of war), National Guard units across the nation began to gradually call increased numbers of reserve officers to duty to fill their ranks. War clouds on the horizon resulted in the Texas A&M Board of Directors authorizing President T. O. Walton to offer the campus and its facilities to the national government "in any needed capacity." In September 1940, with Roosevelt's strong urging, the Selective Services Act (i.e., the draft) was passed, and in mid-October, Colonel Moore was ordered by the War Department to return to regular Army duty in the Philippines and assume command of the Fort Mills coastal artillery garrison on Corregidor. Moore was joined by more than a dozen young Texas Aggie officers he had handpicked to man the coastal artillery and antiaircraft units on the Rock. In May 1941, all dependents of American military personnel were ordered to return to the United States. While the American force in Manila began to grow, few in the United States had any understanding of the massive aggression demonstrated by the Japanese armies invading and ravaging China on the pretext that the Imperial Empire needed access to raw materials and petroleum. In Washington, DC, concerned with the rising tensions in Asia as Japan occupied Indochina, in July 1941, President Roosevelt returned General MacArthur to active duty in the US Army and federalized the commonwealth forces in the Philippines.[13]

By the fall of 1941, heightened tensions in Europe and Asia resulted in the US War Department calling more than 3,000 of an estimated 5,000 Aggie former students who held inactive reserve officer commissions to active duty. It was in this call to duty that most of the Aggie 89—destined to serve on Bataan and Corregidor—entered active duty. In addition, the June Class of '41 at Texas A&M produced another 535 commissioned officers. Nationwide, the mustering of troops expanded sevenfold as the Army grew from under 300,000 to more than 2.4 million in fewer than eighteen months, with more than 7 million men called to active duty by 1945. As the ranks were filled, American war strategists worked to address pending threats worldwide. Weary from years of Depression, the American public was slow to recognize the aggressive actions of both Japan and Germany. A nationwide Gallup poll a few weeks before Pearl Harbor indicated only 17 percent of Americans favored war with Germany—and Japan was not even mentioned.[14]

DAY OF INFAMY: "THE CAT HAS JUMPED"

Any hope of avoiding war was shattered by the Japanese surprise attack on Pearl Harbor early Sunday morning, December 7, 1941. Waves of carrier-based fighter-bombers struck the Pacific fleet anchored in Hawaii, as well as airplanes and facilities at nearby Hickam Air Field. First reports of the attack on Pearl Harbor gave no hint of the extensive carnage and destruction. In a matter of hours, the American naval force lay in ruins, with damage to some two dozen warships of which two battleships, the *USS Arizona* and the *USS Oklahoma*, sunk—grounded in the shallow harbor. The only saving grace was that the carrier fleet—the *USS Enterprise*, *Saratoga*, and *Lexington* and sup porting heavy cruisers—was out to sea and not touched. The surprise attack killed in excess of 2,200 men, with another thousand wounded. To this day, the Pearl Harbor attack is memorialized by a solemn memorial in the harbor over the sunken *USS Arizona*. The pride of the American Navy at 31,400 tons, she was the largest battleship in the US fleet—from which bunker oil still bubbles to the surface daily, a silent reminder of the American lives lost. Aviation pioneer Billy Mitchell's concept of "air power," and Japanese torpedo-bombers' ability to sink battleships, was unfortunately vindicated![15]

The first wave of Japanese bombers struck Pearl Harbor at approximately 0755 on December 7, and across the International Date Line, in Manila and the western Pacific, it was after midnight on December 8. The night was quiet except for a number of parties at the Army-Navy Club, dance halls, and large hotels in Manila—especially the Fiesta Pavilion of the grand Manila Hotel, welcoming new officers to the island and GIs returning home from the festivities. One Aggie who missed the Saturday night fun was newly commissioned **Lt. Andy Marmaduke James Jr. '41** of Dalhart, Texas, known to his friends and family as "AM," who was in the headquarters communications center at the command post. After arriving in Manila, AM had been trained in communication operations and decoding of messages. AM was the staff duty officer on the morning of December 8 and recalled, "I was the first Army person [in the Philippines] to know that we were at war with Japan. On December 8 at about three o'clock in the morning I was on duty when a message came in which said, 'QUOTE—JAPAN HAS STARTED HOSTILITIES GOVERN YOURSELF ACCORDINGLY—UNQUOTE.'"[16]

And at 0340 on December 8, across Manila Bay at Fort Mills on Corregidor, Navy Radio Intercept Installation duty officer Ensign Rudolph J. Fabian called to wake General George Moore with two back-to-back messages as follows:

> **"HOSTILITIES COMMENCED WITH AIR RAID ON PEARL"**
>
> **"AIR RAIDS ON PEARL HARBOR. THIS IS NOT A DRILL"**

When General Jonathan Wainwright received the radio dispatch on the hostilities at Pearl Harbor, he notified his staff, saying, "The cat has jumped."[17]

While the defense of the US military operations and interests in the Pacific had been in the planning stage for nearly four decades prior to the Japanese attack on Pearl Harbor, few in Hawaii or Washington could explain the total surprise and massive losses. The United States had anticipated a war with Japan for years, with General MacArthur estimating a full-scale attack in April 1942. Military planners in Washington had expected that US installations in the Philippine Islands would be one of the first attacked in order to eliminate a natural defensive position that might contain any overt action by the Japanese. At 0602, as news from Pearl Harbor spread, headquarters notified all Allied echelons in the Pacific, including Manila: "A STATE OF WAR EXISTS BETWEEN THE UNITED STATES AND JAPAN. GOVERN YOURSELF ACCORDINGLY."[18]

RAINBOW

US planners had crafted a number of color-coded documents, or "Rainbow Plans," to deal with different regional areas and nations in the event of attack. The purpose for using colors instead of code names or locations was to avoid any diplomatic embarrassment, should any plans be leaked. The plans to address an attack and hostile action against our allies from Japan were known as War Plan Orange—WPO-3. The central element of the WPO-3 was to concentrate American and Filipino troops to fight a delaying action until forces and supplies could be sent from allies such as Australia or dispatched from the West Coast of the United States. While planning is critical, and planners in Washington were fully aware of the buildup of Japanese Imperial Army across Asia, few anticipated the speed and organized process the Japanese mustered to sweep across the western Pacific. Furthermore, in only two days, the devastating attack and destruction of the US Pacific Fleet at Pearl Harbor paralyzed a rapid response. Furthermore, the Far East Air Force was crippled, and there was little likelihood of a speedy military recovery.[19]

Overnight the United States and the Texas Aggies were at war. In College Station, December 7 was a quiet and unseasonably warm afternoon when news arrived. Cadets at the campus theater were watching a rerun of *A Yank in the R.A.F.* when the theater manager interrupted to announce that Pearl Harbor had been bombed. Disbelief and wonder swept the campus, followed by yells of "Beat the hell out of Japan!" Shortly after President Roosevelt addressed Congress and called for a formal declaration of war against Japan on December 8, Texas A&M President Walton and Commandant Colonel Maurice D. Welty urged the cadets to remain focused on school. Headlines in the campus newspaper, the *Battalion*, read, "Old Army Gets the Spirit."[20]

FDR and Chief of Staff General George C. Marshall had a mammoth task of training and arming an army and navy for battle on two fronts. Their primary attention was given to the situation in Europe. The president, military leaders, and planners realized there was no way to relieve the embattled American and Filipino forces on Bataan and Corregidor. At best, they instructed General MacArthur, who had returned to active duty in the US Army in mid-1941 and assumed command of all forces in the Pacific, to fight a delaying action as outlined in WPO-3. In late July 1941, the Philippine Scouts were called into service of the US Army by executive order of President Roosevelt, yet no funding for training, no new supplies in volume, and no new American troops were on the way to relieve them. Their plight was doomed as of the first day of Japanese intensive bombing attacks at Clark Field north of Manila on December 8.[21]

By the first week of December 1941, US military forces in the Philippine Islands numbered under 20,000—to defend, along with the thousands of recently mobilized Filipino Scouts, an archipelago of some 7,083 islands with more coastline than the United States. These American-Filipino forces were spread thinly in a number of defensive positions on Luzon, in the Manila area, on Mindanao, and on Corregidor. Ten divisions of the Philippine Army, with US staff and advisor assistance, had been mobilized, yet units were not at full strength, and all were poorly equipped and poorly trained. One after-action report noted that, due to the haphazard call-up of troops, "very few of the Philippine Army personnel had actually fired their weapons prior to combat firing against an all too realistic enemy." Of the

Texas Aggies in the Philippines, a dozen were in the Manila area, two dozen on Corregidor, and the balance scattered at posts and units across Bataan, Luzon, Clark Field, Nielson Field, San Fernando, La Union, and Mindanao.[22]

The Japanese attack by more than 250 Formosa (Taiwan)-based aircraft on Manila and associated US air fields across Luzon on December 8 was devastating. Confusion reigned among the senior staff officers. With full advanced knowledge and warning following the attack on Pearl Harbor, commanders in the Philippines had left their planes parked wing to wing, thus allowing the Japanese to destroy the entire force *on the ground* in less than an hour! This most troublesome blow was the near total destruction of the Army Air Corps' B-17s, P-35s, and P-40s. The Japanese raid on Clark Field was over in fourteen minutes! The thirty-five B-17 Flying Fortresses based in the Philippines composed the greatest concentration of heavy bomber strength anywhere in the world—and more were en route. Caught in the first wave was Aggie **Lt. Arthur "Tex" Gary '40** of San Marcos, who was killed along with four of his B-17 crew attempting to get off the ground. The story of Gary's life and death, the first Texas Aggie killed in World War II, became the subject of a 1943 book, *Queens Die Proudly*, as well as a feature article in *Reader's Digest Magazine*. Tex Gary was a favorite of the unit and not overwhelmed by all the Army regulations. His crew recalls, "Good-natured, devil-may-care Tex—on hot days he would fly Old 99 [his aircraft number for his B-17] stark naked except for a pair of shorts, sweating like a mule and cussing the tropical sun. I loved the guy like a brother."[23]

Squadron commander Captain Frank Kurtz was tasked with collecting the personal effects of those airmen killed in the Japanese bombing of December 8: "So I went down the line of the dead for the last time and took from each the thing I thought he valued most [to send home to their family]. And when I came to Tex at the end of the line—it had to be his Texas A. &. M. class ring, the thing he was proudest of, and I knew he'd want to send it his mother." Kurtz recalled, "Yet at first I couldn't get it off his finger, although his big hand was warm and soft as ever. 'Okay now, Tex, come on, boy, give it up now,' I said to him and then with just a little tug it slipped right off."[24]

Lightly armed ground troops were ill equipped to respond to long-range Japanese bombers dropping from 22,400 feet as well as the wave after wave of fighter planes strafing the fields and facilities. At Clark Field alone, total casualties on the first day of the war included 189 dead (based on the after-action log book of Capt. Jerry McDavitt) and more than 150 wounded, among them pilot **Captain John August Bergstrom '29** of Austin, who was killed trying to get to his plane. A state of confusion and shock prevailed, made more distressing by the fact that the remains of the dead airmen scattered across the base would not be collected and buried until a week had passed. In the chaos, one of the few P-40s to get airborne was shot down by American soldiers mistaking the plane for a Zero—the wounded pilot was able to bailout to safety. And within days, except for a few fighter planes, all remaining US aircraft were flown to Darwin, Australia, and thus the Far East Army Air Corps in the Philippines no longer existed. More than two dozen pilots were evacuated, and any remaining air corpsmen were assigned to army infantry units on Bataan.[25]

American and British intelligence had greatly discounted any serious threat from Japanese airpower. So-called experts reported during the late 1930s that the Japanese had no skills to either build or fly aircraft. On the contrary, Japanese naval aviators were the best in the world at the time, many having flown more than a hundred combat missions in China since 1937. They were highly motivated, well trained, well led, and ruthless. Japanese aviator skills were captured on live film by Norman Alley as fighters chased and sunk the *USS Panay* in the Yangtze River on December 12, 1937. The blatant attack killed and wounded a dozen sailors, including the ship's captain. This footage of the first US warship sunk since World War I was shown by Universal Pictures in theaters across America. President Roosevelt's response to the attack was calmly, "Nations have gone to war on less provocation than this." This reality, combined with the unpreparedness of the American forces early in the war, proved devastating. As one observer noted, the "fatal hubris of the West in the face of plentiful evidence of

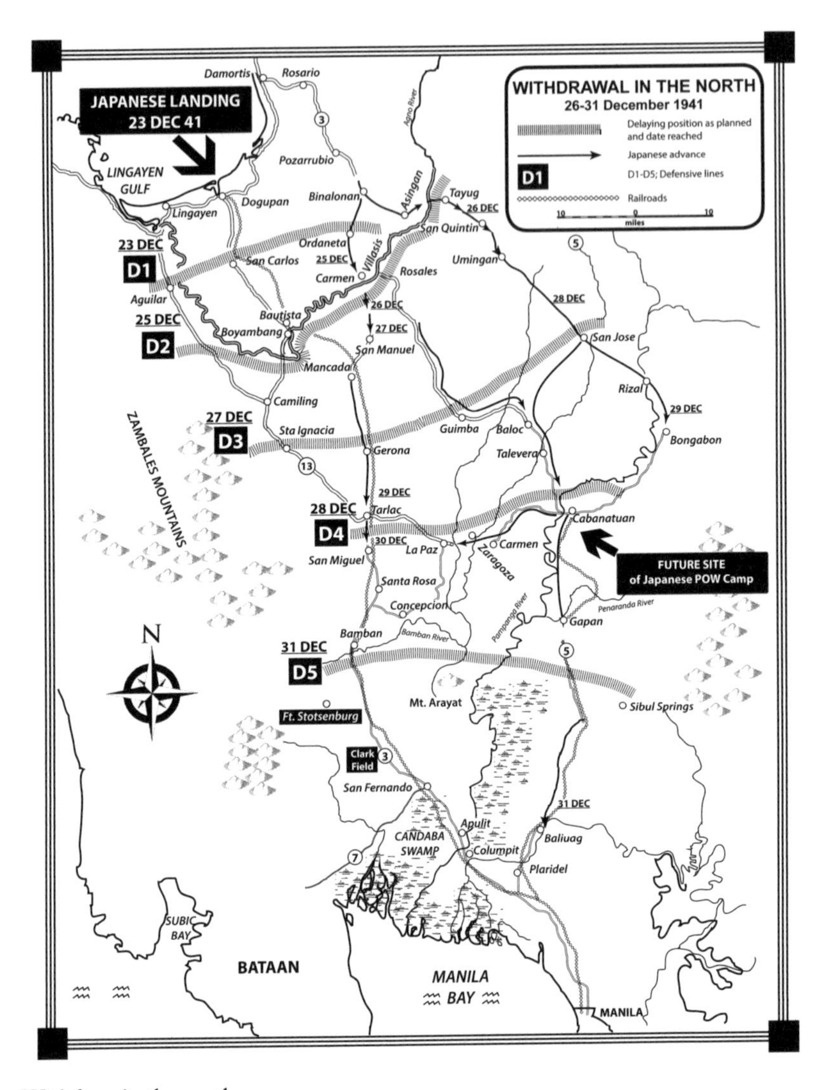

Withdraw in the north.

the Japanese threat would cost hundreds of planes and aircrews in the early months of the Pacific war."[26]

As the Japanese air attacks spread to Nichols Air Field, Nelson Field, the Cavite Naval Dock at Manila, and supply depots across the island, General MacArthur reassessed his plans. More than a thousand civilians were killed at the Cavite marine docks. Japanese spies and Filipino collaborators in Manila carried on extensive espionage activities before and after the bombings. Japanese scout planes had flown reconnaissance missions over Luzon and Manila since December 5. General Lewis Brereton recalled, "They had agents everywhere. Army G-2 knew that our telephone lines were tapped. On the second night that Nichols Field was bombed we found fires and flares [set by spies] marking the field."[27]

WAR PLAN ORANGE-3

The first plan to fight the Japanese, who were expected to land troops, was with a maneuvering defense to stop any enemy invasion at the point of landing, with orders for "no withdrawal from beach positions." This was soon scrapped and War Plan Orange-3 was invoked. MacArthur relocated his HQ from Manila along with the President of the Philippines to the Malinta Tunnel on Corregidor—known to the defenders as the "Rock." Even with the advanced warning, logistics and resupply were very poorly handled, as tons of supplies, ammunition, food, and medical items were left, looted, or destroyed in Manila warehouses. The defenders of Corregidor and Bataan were soon placed on half rations. A few supply boats and airplanes landing at Kindley Air Field (little more than a small strip on the eastern tip of the island) brought in some relief, but never enough to overcome the damage caused by the increased bombing by the Japanese.[28]

In the confusion that followed the initial attacks by the Japanese and eventual withdrawal to Bataan, General Wainwright's candid assessment of the state of forces in the Philippines confirmed the concerns to launch an active and adequate defense:

> Infantrymen had been trained on average of three to four weeks, our artillery never even fired practice shots—indeed, the first shot was aimed in the general direction of the approaching enemy, none of my divisions had an anti-tank battalion, the only communications with the various divisions was through the public telephone lines, and to top everything the main bulk of my men were not only untrained but undisciplined and lead by extremely inexperienced Filipino officers. That they lasted as long as they did is a stirring and touching tribute to their gallantry and fortitude.[29]

Scores of Texas Aggies were a part of the fight from the time the first bomb was dropped at Clark Field on December 8. **Captain Cary M. Abney Jr. '34**, who had left his family and growing insurance agency in Marshall, Texas, following his March 1941 call to active duty, was in charge of the headquarters staff of the 4th Composite Group and Post Adjutant at Clark Field. With his unit decimated, he assisted with the organization of the remaining remnants of air corps personnel into army infantry units on Bataan. **Captain Jack Kelley '29**, a member of the 7th Materiel Squadron, 19th Bombardment Group, was on the air field ramp when the bombing started. The Japanese bombing was precise and devastating. Following the death of his unit commander during the first wave of the attack, Kelley was made squadron commander. He gathered his men and departed to Bataan. At first, in all the confusion, he was reported missing in action, yet Kelley eventually was listed as a POW in October 1942. One of the few American planes that did get airborne on December 8 was a worn-out P-35A fighter from Del Carmen Field on Luzon flown by Aggie **Lt. James Henry '39** of the 34th Squadron, 24th Pursuit Group. Engaging the enemy south of Clark Field, he and a couple of other planes were hopelessly outclassed, outgunned, shot up, and thankful to be back on the ground after taking on the Japanese Mitsubishi A6M2 Zeros—superior to any fighter the Allies could put into the air during the early stages of the war in the Pacific. The American pilots referred to the never-before-seen Zeros as the "mystery ships." Henry proclaimed to his fellow pilots, after a hair-raising dog fight during which he was shot up but able to land, that he would never again go up against Japanese Zeros in an old P-35A. In spite of the outdated aircraft, the Americans were able to shoot down seven Japanese fighters.[30]

Four days after the attack on Clark Field, the 19th Bombardment Group HQ ordered six B-17s at Del Monte Field on Mindanao to attack the concentration of Japanese forces off-loading in the harbor at Legaspi. The crews planned to "fly in close formation for mutual protection" since there was no fighter escort available. In the lead Flying Fortress was AC Captain Jack Adams and Texas Aggie navigator **Lt. Harry J. Schreiber '36** from Galveston. The hastily planned raid was doomed from the start. After takeoff, four planes returned to base with mechanical problems as Schreiber navigated the remaining two planes over the target at eighteen thousand feet. As the bombs were dropped, Adams dove into the clouds to avoid five Zeros racing to attack. The crew shot down four of the Zeros but not before the last Japanese fighter knocked out two engines. Instead of bailing out over enemy territory, Adams made a wheels-up crash landing on the Island of Mashate. With the help of the Filipino natives, the crew evaded the Japanese to return to Del Monte Field in early January 1942, joining other aircrews waiting orders and/or evacuation. Finally, on March 14, 1942, Schreiber and fifteen air crew members were flown out to Australia. Upon arrival, he was selected to be the navigator on Commander of US Air Corps in Australia General George H. Bert's B-17, dubbed *Alexander the Swoose*—due to the fact the plane had been cobbled together with multiple spare parts and was thus a cross between swan and goose![31]

Houston engineer **Lt. James Richard Oppenheim '35** was called to active duty in mid-1941. The former campus boxing champion and expert marksman was also at Clark Field, having arrived on October 23, 1941, as head of the Headquarters Company of the 803rd Engineer Aviation Battalion. In the immediate hours after the first attack, the 803rd was used to construct a series of alternative air fields to handle the expected new airplanes that never arrived. By New Year's Day 1942, Oppenheim and his unit were withdrawn to Bataan and assigned to road and communications construction. In the chaos of the attack on Clark Field, **Major Clarence Reid "Buck" Davis '27** of Lufkin, squadron commander in the 7th Material Group, was killed in action.[32]

Major Maynard "Runt" Snell '21 had just arrived in Manila on Thanksgiving Day as the Executive Officer of the 192nd Tank Battalion and his unit, bivouacked near Clark Field, had not even fully unpacked their gear. Following the attack, the Battalion regrouped and was ordered to disperse around the perimeter of the field and be ready to oppose a rumored enemy paratroop landing. No such event occurred, and the 192nd Tank Battalion was moved toward Bataan;

Snell was assigned as a liaison to General MacArthur's staff for logistics. He served in this capacity on Bataan until the surrender. All three Texas Aggies, Abney, Kelley, and Snell lived through the Death March and harsh POW camps only to be placed on the first of the ill-fated Hell Ships directed to transport the POWs away from the Philippines, the *Oryoku Maru*, bound for Japan on December 15, 1944. Kelley and Snell died on this Hell Ship. Abney survived the sinking of the *Oryoku* and was placed aboard the *Enoura Maru*, which in turn was sunk off Formosa on January 9, 1945.[33]

Aggie **Captain Jerome A. McDavitt '33**, 23rd Field Artillery of the Philippine Scouts, Northern Luzon Forces, also witnessed the Japanese attack from his post near Clark Field. With much of the base still burning, personnel wounded, and the dead scattered across the field, he and the members of his battery were ordered to Clark to "sneak out the dead bodies and place them in the morgue." They worked into the night, with fires and secondary explosions continuing long after dark, until evacuation orders were given to pull back to Bataan and Corregidor. McDavitt's plan soon changed. Once at Hospital No. 2, a facility on the road from Manila, the medical unit commander Colonel James O. Gillespie requested that McDavitt and a few of his men assist with the evacuation of the nurses and ensure they were ferried across the bay to Corregidor, noting that he "did not want the nurses in the field when the Japs came in."[34]

By midnight, Captain McDavitt had commandeered a paneled van and a Hudson sedan and loaded the nurses and baggage aboard. They headed for the docks at Mariveles with the headlights out. The roads were jammed with confused Filipino civilians and soldiers going in all directions. As they approached the coast, a military checkpoint stopped the small caravan due to an attack on the ammunition dump at Little Baguio. Not able to proceed until 0400, the small group arrived at what was left of the Mariveles Navy docks at sunrise to find no boats or help—they had missed their arranged rendezvous. Japanese fighters were still strafing the docks as McDavitt and his nurses hid in a concrete culvert waiting for help. While the nurses remained under cover, McDavitt and his driver found a navy lifeboat and two oars and rolled the boat into the water. The small boat would only hold five. Three nurses, the driver, and the captain boarded the dingy. Before leaving, he made sure the other nurses were safe and explained he would row to Corregidor and then come back for them. As McDavitt recalled, "There was really nothing else to do. One of the nurses, Eunice Hatchett, a gal from near my home in Caldwell County, Texas, came up to me and said, 'Jerome'—she didn't call me captain or nothing—'Jerome, if you don't come back and get us, when I get back home I'm going to tell your Mama and Papa.' And she meant every damn word!"[35]

McDavitt and his crew rowed into the pitch dark toward Corregidor and by chance were picked up halfway across Manila Bay by a US Navy patrol boat and dropped off at the North Dock on the Rock. As the Japanese planes continued to bomb and strafe, the nurses left behind were picked up, crossed two miles under constant fire, and joined their medical unit in the Malinta Tunnel.

Heavy Japanese air attacks continued on December 9 and 10. Bases that had not been hit on the eighth were targeted on the ninth. One such base, ignored during the first twenty-four hours, was Nichols Air Field, ten miles south of Manila. **Captain John S. Coleman Jr. '29** was commander of the 27th Materiel Squadron and in charge of ground defense around the field. Knowing an attack would come soon, Coleman recalls, "We had twenty Filipino boys on duty that morning [December 8], and I put them all to digging slit trenches near our squadron HQ. I knew trenches would be of more help than shined shoes!" At four o'clock on December 9, the sky was full of aircraft: "I looked up and counted ninety-six bombers, flying at about 21,000 feet, our antiaircraft shells were exploding just below them." Within seconds, the field was carpet bombed by five-hundred-pound bombs, destroying hangers, barracks, Coleman's office, and water supply tanks. Oddly, during the first wave, they did not hit either the runway or the grounded fighter planes. They soon returned to finish the job, and the air attacks continued against every air base on the island, wiping out any hope of an American air response. Captain Coleman survived the Battle of Bataan, Death March, and POW camps and later wrote one of the most compelling eyewitness accounts on the struggle: *Bataan and Beyond: Memories of an American POW* (1978).[36]

The original objectives of the Hundred Days campaign of the Imperial Army had been achieved with stunning success. Following the Japanese attacks on Pearl Harbor and the Philippines, disaster mounted as Guam fell on December 10, 1942, and Wake Island on December 23. British operations in Malaya fell, shipping facilities at Hong Kong surrendered on Christmas Day, and the "impregnable" Singapore was attacked, defeated, and occupied on February 15, 1942. Outposts of US Marines stationed in China and British holdings at Shanghai were soon overrun and captured. No military conquest in modern history had been so quick and so far-reaching. The confusion created by these attacks on the Allies was compounded by the Tokyo blitz of psychological disinformation that flooded the airwaves—only to be repeated and embellished by reports on the US West Coast noting that there could be an invasion of California! Except for the Japanese occupation of the remote tip of the Aleutian-Attu Islands in Alaska, the mainland of the United States was never under any real peril.[37]

A major question then and now was how the American command and forces in Manila were caught flat footed and seemingly unprepared, even though they had ten hours warning following the attack on Pearl Harbor. General MacArthur had been warned by the War Department to be on "High Alert," yet did not believe an air attack by a large force from Formosa was possible. William Manchester, in *American Caesar* (1978), concluded MacArthur "was a gifted leader, and his failure in this emergency is bewildering." Others have also received criticism. Army Air Corps General Henry H. "Hap" Arnold had warned his commander in Manila, Major General Lewis H. Brereton, to be on alert and ready—yet less than a third of the three hundred aircraft under his command were combat ready. In a blistering phone call to Brereton, Hap Arnold wanted to know "How in the hell could an experienced airman like you get surprised with your planes on the ground? That's what we sent you there for, to avoid just what happened." The publication of General Brereton's *Diaries* in 1946 resulted in a sharp and defensive reaction by General MacArthur in the *New York Times*, yet to this day, the events of December 8, 1941, in Manila still appear unresolved. The US Navy fared no better. The US Asiatic Fleet based at Cavite was destroyed at the docks. Not one of the nineteen submarines successfully engaged the enemy transports, largely due to the fact that most of their torpedoes were late 1920s vintage and duds when fired.[38]

US air and naval power in the Philippines was effectively neutralized, and what few warships and airplanes that were still in operation were ordered to regroup in Darwin, Australia. With the bulk of the air power destroyed on the ground, as many pilots as possible were ordered to Darwin to wait for replacement aircraft. The escape, by sea and air, was not an easy task, yet two Aggie pilots from the 39th Bomb Group survived the bombing of Clark Field: **Lt. Henry "Pelly" Dittman '39** of Goose Creek, Texas, a standout halfback on what A&M Coach Homer Norton called his "1938 all-star football team"—many of the same group of players that won the National Championship in 1939—along with pilot **Captain James R. Griffin '39** of Blooming Grove, Texas, who had been at Nichols Field. When new aircraft were slow in arriving, they were each assigned new jobs. Dittman continued his career in the Army Air Corps, commanding a number of training bases, and Griffin remained in the Pacific and was killed in action in New Guinea on March 26, 1943.[39]

In Manila, MacArthur and American officials in Washington assured and reassured the people of the Philippines and the troops that relief was on the way. Washington quickly clamped down on all reports of casualties and damage—it would be months and even years before the full extent of the Japanese attacks of December 7–8 were known. The old adage "the first causality of war is the truth" proved as true as ever. And President Roosevelt, in his weekly fireside chat broadcast, warned the shocked nation that the news would become bleaker before it became brighter. Notwithstanding, the immediate questions and primary focus both on the ground in Manila and at headquarters in Washington was preparing for the next phase of the battle.[40]

General MacArthur, as commander of US Army Forces in the Far East (USAFFE) and his commanders had a brief few days to solidify their defensive plans—and while available as an operation option, the

WPO-3 was not yet put into motion. An atmosphere of shock, further aggravated by a massive communications breakdown, seemed to immobilize much of the high command from Manila to Washington—as one observer noted the chain of command was in a "state of suspended animation." Chaos and vacillation was compounded by President Quezon's urging General MacArthur that somehow the Philippines could declare neutrality and avoid war.[41]

As the Japanese bombers and fighters continued to attack from the air, the primary concern was where the main body of the Japanese forces would land. With no air cover or reliable reconnaissance and only meager naval patrol boat assets, the Americans depended on a string of coast watchers to relay intelligence from points around the archipelago. As Table 1.1 indicates, it may have seemed that MacArthur had a vast army at his command, but in fact he had at best a hastily assembled civilian guard that was both poorly trained and ill equipped. MacArthur overestimated the ability and readiness of his Filipino soldiers and underestimated the Japanese. General Wainwright and his aide, **Lt. Tom Dooley '35**, saddled their horses at Fort Stotsenburg adjoining Clark Air Field and rode over to see if they could assist, and wrote the following in an after-action report:

> It is only fair to explain the all Philippine army divisions were comparatively untrained and understrength. Many troops had gone through five months of Philippine military training, but some did not even have this background. Also, some of the units now moving to contact with well-trained Japanese divisions had not been mobilized until after the declaration of war.
>
> No steel helmets or individual entrenching tools were available to the Philippine troops. The uniforms these units habitually wore were light tropical hats, fatigue clothes and canvas-topped shoes. All the men were equipped with bolt-action M1917 Enfield rifles, but very few spare parts were available. This point was of concern to unit commanders due to the many malfunctions caused by broken ejectors [many rifles had broken extractors, so after the weapon was fired, the shell case had to be pushed out of the gun with a piece of bamboo!].[42]

TABLE 1.1. Assignment of Ground Forces, USAFFE, December 3, 1941

Sector Force	*US Army*	*Philippine Army*
North Luzon (General Wainwright)	26th Cavalry (US)	11th Division
	One Bn., 45th Inf. (PS)	21st Division
	Btry. A, 23rd FA (PS)	32nd Division
	Btrys. B and C, 86th FA (US)	71st Division
	66th QM Troop (PS)	
	Force HQ and HQ Co. (US)	
	192nd and 194th Tank Bn.	
South Luzon (General Parker)	Force HQ and HQ Co. (US)	41st Division
	Btry. A, 86th FA, HQ Btry	51st Division
Visayan-Mindanao (General Sharp)	Force HQ and HQ Co. (PS)	91st Division
		81st Division
		101st Division
Harbor Defense (General Moore)	Headquarters	
	59th CA (US)	
	60th CA (AA) (US)	
	91st CA (PS)	
	92nd CA (PS)	
	200th CA (AA) (US)	
Reserve Force	Philippine Division and HQ (US)	91st Division HQ
	86th FA (PS)	
	US Far East Air Force	

Source: Louis Morton, http://www.history.army.mil/; Jonathan M. Wainwright, "Report of Ops, 1941–42."

Only one unit of Filipino Scouts were at full strength and well trained, and while American units were trained in their basic branch of service (with a vast majority of the US officers called up and trained during mid-1941), they had no combat experience or tactical training to operate in the field under fire as a large force. In addition to poor training, command, control, and communications (C3) was complicated due to the fact that commonwealth troops in the PA divisions spoke as many as eleven different dialects. Most Filipino officers spoke the native Tagalog and some English or Spanish, while American officers assigned to the units were limited to English—causing confusion as well as the delayed and inaccurate relay of translated commands. The situation in the Philippines was desperate. The coming battle and retreat into the Bataan Peninsula was not one of fixed position but instead required constant maneuvering and withdrawal. The defense of Bataan would be the lynch pin of the soon to be implemented WPO-3 strategy.[43]

Luzon and the Manila Bay harbor defense were divided into three zones. The critical North Luzon Force was under the command of General Wainwright and comprised the central plains area, the Lingayen coast, and the entrance into the Bataan Peninsula. The southern section of the defensive line Luzon Force covered the area south and east of Manila and was commanded by General George M. Parker. This section was a critical staging area for reserve troops, the location of the field hospitals, and supply depots. Defense of Manila Bay and the ocean approaches to Manila was known as the Harbor Defense and was under command of Maj. Gen. George F. Moore. This force comprised Fort Mills on Corregidor as well as coastal artillery and antiaircraft artillery of both the American and Philippine Coast Artillery Command. The southern Philippine islands and alternate air fields were under the command of Brig. Gen. William F. Sharp.[44]

It was common knowledge that the Japanese had landed small reconnaissance units at Aparri, Bataan Island, and Vigan on the north coast of Luzon and reconnoitered the area around Lingayen Gulf. Any question about a Japanese landing in force ended on the early morning of December 22, when the Japanese 14th Imperial Army under the command of Lt. General Masaharu Homma, an experienced combat commander in China during the 1939 campaign, came ashore with overwhelming force. The main assault force, known as Tsuchihashi Force, quickly overran the beach defenders at La Union on the Lingayen Gulf, 135 miles north of Manila. American air support was requested, but it did not arrive. After the bombing of the US Naval Base at Cavite in Manila Bay, all American naval forces, except for a few PT boats, were ordered to withdraw to Australia. Facing little resistance, the ninety-boat flotilla on the Imperial Navy off-loaded more than forty-three thousand troops and support units composed of Japan's best divisions, most of them battle-hardened veterans of the Chinese War. (MacArthur had overestimated the landing force to be eighty thousand Japanese troops.) Between Christmas Eve and New Year's Day, the island's North Luzon defenders under General Wainwright's command established and then abandoned five separate "retrograde movements" to delaying defensive positions. Japanese air and naval superiority (Japanese naval vessels moved into the littoral water to shell the defenders), combined with the employment of increasing amounts of tanks and artillery, proved devastating to the ill-prepared Americans and Filipinos.[45]

Major Thomas Dooley '35 was a key eyewitness of the war in the Pacific, from the opening attacks at Clark Field and various POW camps through to his liberation and presence with Generals MacArthur and Wainwright at the unconditional surrender of the Imperial Japanese Army on the deck of the *USS Missouri* in Tokyo Bay in early September 1945. For his actions during the first hours of the Japanese attack on December 8, General Wainwright awarded Dooley World War II's first Silver Star.[46] As aide-de-camp for the general, Dooley was well aware of the magnitude of the situation facing the defenders and was thus dispatched to northern Luzon to prepare for the Japanese invasion. He recognized the tremendous challenge the defenders would face once the Imperial Army gained a beachhead between Agoo and Damortis, giving them direct access to Highway 3 and direct southward access to Manila. Units of the 11th Philippine Army, the 71st Division, and the 26th (horse) Cavalry engaged the enemy shortly

Cadet Tom Dooley '35 as senior cadet in 1934–35. Dooley was head Yell Leader and upon arrival in the Philippines in 1941 was assigned as the aide-de-camp to General Jonathan Wainwright. (Courtesy of the *Longhorn*, 1935.)

after their landing, but due to superior Japanese forces, the Americans and Filipinos were pushed back.[47]

Shortly thereafter, the first US tank-to-tank engagement of World War II occurred between the recently federalized US National Guard units, the 192nd and 194th Light Tank Battalions, and lightweight Japanese tanks on Highway 3. As one observer noted, "The enemy tanks were of low silhouette, had no turrets and had sloped sides, so penetration was difficult to achieve. Hits on enemy tanks with our 37mm guns had been observed during the fight, but many of the shots ricocheted off the sloping armor." Dooley, an old cavalryman by training, was witness to both the confusion and the beating of the 26th Cav received from the Japanese tanks and overhead fighters. Dooley recalls General Wainwright's concern over his beloved 26th Cav: "The Cav was in a Hell of a Spot . . . but were the only troops [unit] he could trust to fight." Lack of fuel, air cover, and good intelligence were vital limiting factors for American defenders. The American-Filipino beachhead defense to stop the Japanese landing plan had failed! The primary line of defense, known as D-1, extending from Aguilar to San Carlos to Urdaneta, failed to materialize and collapsed due to poor execution. From his HQ at Rosales, not far from the landing site, Wainwright informed General MacArthur of the critical situation and his plans to fall back about seven miles along the Agno River to a new second defensive line, or D-2.[48]

A mix of nineteenth- and twentieth-century cavalry tactics and mechanized equipment were used in the delaying action. With every order to pull back, the American lines got progressively thinner and thinner. **Lt. Cliff Hardwicke '37** led his mounted platoon of the 26th (horse) Cavalry of Philippine Scouts at a gallop past units of M3 Stuart light tanks (armed with one 37mm gun and two 30-caliber machine guns), a scout car platoon, and mechanized units, in an effort to cover the withdrawal across the Agno River at Tayug. The intense combat produced moments of valor, but the mounted scouts lacked the ability to stop the heavy enemy surge. The mix of horses and machines in battle was epochal: "A composite platoon from Troop A (26th Cav) attacked the enemy tanks with hand grenades and pistols while riding among and past the vehicles. The surprise cavalry charge allowed some members of the machine gun platoon to rejoin the regiment and the remainder of 1st Squadron to withdraw at a full gallop past the regimental CP toward the regimental lines. The cost was high to Troop A for it lost about half of the counterattacking force, but the enemy tanks halted in confusion."[49]

The losses in troops and horses continued to be staggering, yet the 26th Cav covered the withdrawal through New Year's Day and battled

Defenders of Bataan fought a delaying action against the Japanese, highlighted in this picture in which, due to poor quality and/or shortage of munitions, they responded with homemade Molotov cocktails to attempt to stop enemy tanks. (Courtesy of the author's collection.)

on until early March. The Japanese pressed their attack day and night. Spread across the line of defense, the 11th, 21st, and 91st Philippine Divisions fought valiantly but were outgunned and outmaneuvered as units were cut off or unable to establish any strong positions to defend. The speed with which the Japanese moved and their overall training, gained in years of fighting in China, was conspicuous. General Wainwright was fighting only a holding action, falling back from one defensive line to the next (five defensive lines in total), in hopes that by buying time the bulk of the army and supplies could be relocated to Bataan. The Japanese pushed the defenders closer to Manila daily, resulting in MacArthur—despite the majority of the citizenry begging the Americans to stay and defend the city—declaring the capital a free and open city, in hopes of reducing wholesale destruction and death to its citizens. Little did the defenders know, the fate of the Philippines was decided in Washington as the decision was made to send all available resources first to the European Theater.[50]

On Christmas Eve 1941, General MacArthur ordered the final evacuation of all troops and supplies into the Bataan Peninsula. By Christmas Day, Wake Island and Hong Kong fell to the Japanese. In Washington, Prime Minister Winston Churchill and his key military staff were at the White House meeting with the president, General George Marshall, Secretary of War Henry Stimson, and recently promoted Brigadier General of War Plans Ike Eisenhower. The prime minister, in his improvised map and briefing room on the second floor across from his bedroom in the White House, bluntly questioned America's near-term response to the crisis in the Philippines. Churchill's goal, despite the overwhelming American antipathy toward what seemed like an unstoppable Imperial Japan, was to ensure the European front was America's first priority. Given the distance and invasion force required to regain the Pacific, it was assumed such a campaign was impractical—the PM was assured, "Europe first."[51]

The abrupt evacuation of Manila was disorderly and confused chaos and only added to an American army already in disarray. In spite of the North Luzon Force blowing some 184 bridges between the landing beach and the outskirts of the capital, the Japanese—many on bicycles—rapidly surrounded the city. As the enemy bombed and strafed the city and port, soldiers, sailors, and civilians commandeered any floating craft (weaving past scores of partially sunken ships littering the waterfront) to cross to Bataan and Corregidor. Tokyo Radio broadcast the Japanese triumph in Manila and described the headlong retreat into Bataan as "a cat entering a sack."[52]

To the south of Manila at Limon Bay, the Japanese landed a secondary force of ten thousand troops, known as the Morioka Force, that moved toward the capital. In the confusion, MacArthur neglected to inform local naval commander Admiral T. C. Hart of the evacuation of Manila and transfer of HQ to Corregidor. Hart made it clear to the general that the failure to communicate cost his men and units the loss of extensive submarine materiel and facilities needed to defend the bay. There was no reply. While sealing the fate of Manila to Japanese occupation, the general fully invoked War Plan Orange-3 to delay the advance of the Japanese and protect Manila Bay at all cost. General Wainwright opposed WPO-3 as a "defeatist plan" and noted, "A defense must be active, dammit, not passive!" Japanese forces occupied Nichols Air Field on the twenty-eighth, cleared the runways, and began offensive air operations. Total combined American-Filipino casualties during the first three weeks of war among

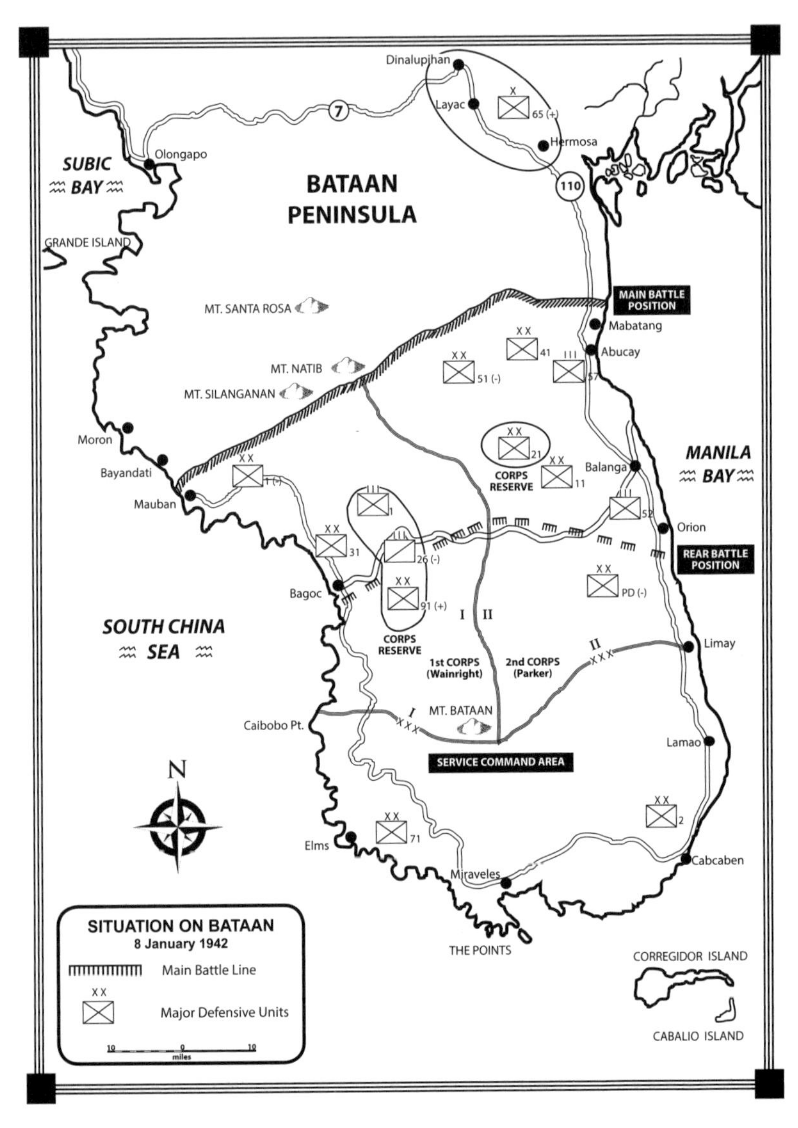

Situation on Bataan, January 8, 1942.

both military and civilians exceeded two thousand dead. Wainwright repeatedly advised MacArthur weeks prior to December 8 to preposition supplies in North Luzon, assuming there was going to be a major effort to defend against the Japanese landing, but he was ignored—with Wainwright concluding our forces "were doomed before they started to fight."[53]

And while the commanders at Pearl Harbor were considered for court martial as a scapegoat for Washington's ills and poor intelligence, MacArthur had developed a rapport with the American people (and news media)—for example, gracing the covers of both *TIME* and *Newsweek*, with the heading "MacArthur of Bataan: The War's No. 1 Hero"—as well as a close relationship with President Roosevelt. According to press releases from General MacArthur's office, his troops on Luzon had the situation "well in hand."[54] The unrealistic nature of the general's reports would soon be apparent. The eventual relocation of his HQ to Australia was promoted in the media as the general's plan to lay the groundwork for a grand Pacific counteroffensive. Thus New Year's Day 1942 ended the first phase of the World War II defense of the Philippines in northern Luzon—and as General Wainwright would recall "the peninsula of Bataan was to become a symbol of forlorn hope." The start of the next saga began—with four months of dogged resistance during the Siege of Bataan and with the defenders on Corregidor resisting for one additional month.[55]

★ CHAPTER 2 ★

THE SIEGE OF BATAAN

For forty years it has always been our strategy—a strategy born of necessity—that in the event of a full-scale attack on the Philippine Islands by Japan, we should fight a delaying action, attempting to retire slowly into Bataan Peninsula and Corregidor.

FRANKLIN D. ROOSEVELT
WHITE HOUSE FIRESIDE CHAT, FEBRUARY 23, 1942

Bushido made the sword its emblem of power and prowess. Did Bushido justify the promiscuous use of the weapon? The answer is unequivocally, no! As is laid great stress on its proper use, so did it denounce and abhor its misuse.

INAZO NITOBE

The New Year of 1942 brought no new hope to the defenders of Bataan for relief or rescue. General Homma and his troops entered Manila in a grand victory parade under limited orders that there would be no looting. Still, more than a thousand Filipinos were raped, tortured, and killed in the first two weeks of occupation, and more than three thousand men, women, and children were crowded into a concentration camp at Santo Tomas University. Any thoughts by the Japanese that the defenders flooding into Bataan had given up were premature—the real fight was just beginning! The delaying action by the Filipino-American troops was at best a temporary measure, since the defenders had little hope of making any massive counteroffensive strike. The chaos accompanying the belated decision to retreat into Bataan resulted in large stocks of food, fuel, ammunition, and medical supplies from the United States

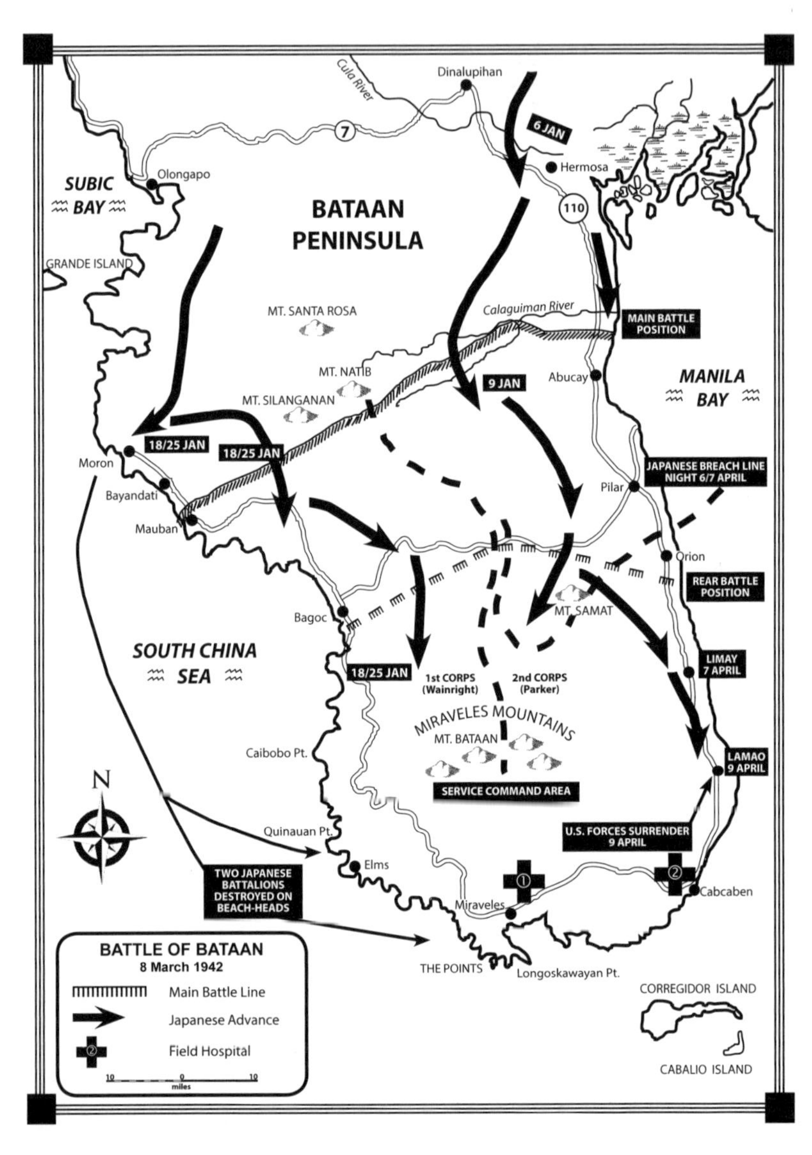

Battle of Bataan, March 8, 1942.

placed in war reserve during 1941 being left behind and lost. A delaying force was ordered by General Jonathan "Skinny" Wainwright to dig in along the eighteen-mile-long defensive line known as D-5. This final preplanned Luzon defensive position ran from Bamban, around the northern base of Mt. Arayat and the Candaba Swamp, to the small town of Sibul Springs. The main goal was to protect the main intersections into the Bataan Peninsula at San Fernando and Calumpit Bridge.[1]

Expecting a head-on attack from the Japanese, the defenders were somewhat surprised when General Homma's main strike force went around the right side of the American line down Highway 5 in order to strike a knockout blow at Manila—with the misplaced assumption that the Luzon-Bataan resistance would come to an end. If, however, the Imperial Japanese Army had remained focused on the thin, depleting line at D-5, General Homma and his troops could have encircled and cut off Wainwright and nearly the entire North and South Luzon force. Instead, the general had strict implicit orders from Tojo, the Imperial General Headquarters (IGHQ), and Chief of Staff General Sugiyama that the "main purpose of the attack was the occupation of Manila" and thus the capture of the capital in order to score political points with the Emperor in Tokyo. The Japanese thrust toward Manila allowed Wainwright and his retreating forces time to evacuate into Bataan and provided extra time for his engineers to blow the bridges.[2]

A detailed account of the retreat and near nonstop action on New Year's Eve to avoid being trapped by the oncoming Imperial Army was chronicled by **Colonel Edwin E. Aldridge '16** of Eagle Pass and the 51st Division, a career officer since graduating from Texas A&M. His broad military experience gives light to the situation encountered:

> Had a couple of light drinks to bring in the New Year. We left for Plaridel [8 miles west of Calumpit] at 3:30 AM on the 31st, arriving just before daylight. Ride up there was a nightmare, no lights and considerable traffic, ran off the road a couple of times but no accident. When we got to Piaridel we found Gen Jones in the school with action so close that our C.P. [command post] was ordered to move . . . could not get any communications. Meanwhile quite a tank battle was going

General Jonathan M. Wainwright, commander of forces on Bataan. (Courtesy of the author's collection.)

> on at Baliuag . . . it seems a bunch of tanks had broken our forces [the retreating 91st Division] through Cabanatuan and had almost cut off the Southern Luzon Force . . . not over 350 men all that was left of both the 71 and 91st Divisions between the Japs and the Calumpit Bridge. I ran into [Major Harry O.] Fischer '29, he was looking for some prime movers [artillery tractor] to take some Navy 8" guns to Bataan, he found some but could not move them all.[3]

QUITE A TANK BATTLE

By New Year's Eve, the 192nd and 194th Tank Battalions had been in constant contact with the enemy for over a week, with the primary mission being to delay the Japanese advance. The delaying action to defend the Calumpit Bridge placed the light M-3 Stuart tanks of the 192nd in a pivotal position to hold the Japanese attack at Baliuag, seven miles north of the bridge across the Pampanga River. Three of the top seven officers in the 192nd headquarters company were Texas Aggies: **Major Maynard G. Snell '21** of Lampasas, **Captain Joseph A. Revak '30** of Beaumont, and young **2nd Lt. Marshall H. Kennady Jr. '40** from San Antonio, along with **M.Sgt. William G. Boyd '27** of College Station. While Snell and Revak coordinated positioning of the unit as well as logistics, Lt. Kennady was dispatched to his additional duty as tank commander of five tanks assigned to HQ Company. He was dispatched to support C Company. Upon receipt of intelligence that enemy forces were moving into Baliuag, it was confirmed that the Japanese were massing men and tanks. The 192nd planned to spring an ambush by trapping the Japanese tanks as they crossed a narrow bridge into the village. Knowing surprise was a critical element, half of the Stuart tanks were wedged into and between the native *nipa* huts while Lt. Kennady's five Stuart tanks braced for a headlong confrontation hidden inside native huts on the far side of the village. Once trapped in the village, C Company launched the attack in a bold and bloody crossfire, dominating and winning the first tank victory of World War II. Engaged with the enemy at close range (within yards), the Japanese lost eight tanks and crews as well as hundreds of infantry.[4]

The actions of Lt. Kennady in the largest tank-versus-tank battle thus far in World War II were chronicled by Cpl. William Hauser, HQ Company, 192nd Tank Battalion:

> The Lieutenant aimed the barrel out one of the windows. About four o'clock the shit hit the fan and they began shelling our position. Tanks began coming across the bridge, coming down from the north, and reports of "Got him!" The battle lasted a while and we kept going back and forth, up and down the streets. Once we were a couple of feet from him [Lt. Kennady]. He got four goddamn Jap tanks. He radioed the colonel, "You want a goddamn Jap tank? I'll put a line on one and drag it in by the ass."[5]

General MacArthur noted in his memoir, *Reminiscences*, published in 1964 (only weeks before he died), the pivotal nature of the fight waged by Wainwright and his outmanned troops and tankers in their exodus from Luzon to Bataan:

> We would hold enough to force the Japanese to take time to deploy in full force. . . . Again and again, these tactics would be repeated. Stand and fight, slip back and dynamite. It was savage and bloody, but it won time. Driving with reckless fury, they strove desperately to cut the vulnerable road junction at San Fernando and the bridge defile at Calumpit . . . our North Luzon Force reeled back, bruised and battered . . . just by a spilt second our dynamiters blew the Calumpit bridge [at 0615 on January 1, 1942] as the Japanese were marching out upon it.

Company commander, **Captain Robley D. Evans '40**, former county agent from Fort Worth, assigned to the 2nd Provisional Battalion, 45th Infantry Regiment Philippine Scouts, was at the center of the battle to cover the withdrawal into Bataan during the last week of December. His reflection on the situation further accents the critical nature of the events:

> As company commander of A Company, I led the advance of the battalion and engaged and harassed the enemy withdrawing under severe pressure until we reach[ed] the Lucban bridge. There the entire Battalion was committed in a defensive position and with Company A in the center of the line held this bridge under heavy fire delaying the advance for three days, until forced to withdraw to Los Banos where the battalion again assumed a defensive position and held that road until it was necessary to abandon that position because of flank attack from the rear. This unit being the last organization to leave South Luzon and was the rear guard for the entire South Luzon Force, making the withdrawal mostly by foot.[6]

STAND AND FIGHT

During the first week of January 1942, Filipino-American commanders on the northern edge of the Bataan Peninsula worked to obtain an assessment of what troops and equipment had been saved in the retreat. Some eighty thousand men, sixty-five thousand Filipinos, and fifteen thousand Americans, mixed with an estimated twenty-six thousand fleeing citizens and uprooted farmers, crossed the final bridge into Bataan at Layac. The tanks of the Imperial Army proved very effective. Since there were no antitank weapons, the defenders resorted to "Molotov cocktails"—beer bottles filled with gas and wrapped in rags. While a Japanese force moved toward Manila, a rear guard pressed the desperately withdrawing 11th and 21st Philippine Divisions into Bataan. MacArthur's alternative plan to defeat the enemy on the beaches had been a total failure.[7]

The Allied retreat from the Lingayen beachhead had cost more than twelve thousand Filipino and American casualties. Manila had been abandoned. The US Army Air Corps was neutralized. All US naval piers and ships had been destroyed, and the recovery of critical supplies of food, fuel, and equipment was botched and supplies left behind—in spite of having over a two-week warning. The neglect and confusion resulted in the abhorrent abandonment of tons of critical foodstuffs and supplies. At one location alone, more than ten million pounds of rice in government warehouses in Cabanatuan was abandoned (ironically the future site of a major POW camp). Tons of fresh meat was left in the San Miguel Cold Storage Plant in Manila, and supplies of sugar could not be transferred from one province to the next without overcoming red tape (bureaucratic paperwork). In addition, someone in US Army Forces Far East (USAFFE) HQ had prohibited the seizure of large quantities of Japanese-owned food stocks near Manila. Captain John Coleman remembers vividly how members of his Air Corps material group left Manila empty handed, leaving depots of C-rations and staple goods untouched. Under War Plan Orange-3 (WPO-3), detailed prewar plans called for supplies for only about 43,000 men for up to six months; these supplies were to be staged and prepositioned in holding areas at the outbreak of war. However, by early January, more than 106,000 wedged into the Bataan Peninsula needed daily food. The Imperial Navy was able to interdict the sea lanes around the Philippines to cut off communications and almost completely halt the critical resupply of food, ammunition, and medicine. Now only the remote dense jungle of Bataan and the rocky heights of Corregidor stood between victory or defeat.[8]

The Bataan Peninsula is of varied volcanic terrain, forty-five miles long, and fifteen miles at the widest point. Thus it was surrounded on three sides by shark-infested waters, and Japanese patrol boats at sea and overhead Zeros harassed every move. The mountain peaks of two huge ancient volcanos on the peninsula range from three thousand to five thousand feet; these played a major role in the defensive positions that General Wainwright's troops attempted to hold. The Bataan Province had historically been a military reservation and training area, affording many of the defenders some advanced knowledge of the battlefield. Under the plans outlined by WPO-3, a series of three defensive positions running the width of the peninsula had already been established. Roads along the coast of Bataan were improved, but those across the peninsula were little more than dusty cobblestone paths and carabao trails through dense bamboo thickets and dense *ipil-ipil* trees, all tangled with rattan vines. The luscious, green tropical jungle is most deceptive, rising to brutally hot temperatures in the dry season, January to May, made even hotter by the high humidity.[9]

THE ORDER OF BATTLE

As the defenders of Bataan continued their cut to half-rations to below two thousand calories per day, and thus incurring more sickness in the ranks, the Imperial Japanese Army continued to land more fresh troops and heavy artillery as well as fly hourly harassing air attacks. From the foxholes and recovery hospital in the jungle in the southern part of Bataan, the troops received a steady dribble of news over the Radio Freedom broadcast from Corregidor as well as the nightly program of propagandist Tokyo Rose—whose falsified reports and nostalgic music reminded the troops of their hopeless condition. Both broadcasts failed to offer any good news. The full damage of the Pearl Harbor attack and a threat of a submarine attack on the West Coast soon convinced the defenders that help was not on the way—and yet morale is reported to have remained high. The Japanese broadcasts and daily leaflet drops proved more irritating than effective, as the enemy promised the Filipino troops safe passage and the good life in Manila.[10]

Generals MacArthur, Wainwright, Moore, and King continued to assess the defensive situation yet were faced with fewer options as time passed. The Japanese had total air and sea superiority. A combination of artillery fire and high-altitude bombing, followed by daily harassment by the Japanese Zeros, constantly kept the defenders pinned down and allowed few avenues of escape. To pull back all eighty thousand defenders to Corregidor was a dismal option, given the fact that the tiny island could not support and feed such an influx and no sea craft were available to ferry the troops in significant numbers. Notwithstanding, plans were drafted to slowly transfer nurses and key medical personnel to the Rock. This decision became more urgent as the Japanese began to purposely bomb the field hospitals as they moved south down the peninsula.[11]

War plans outlined in WPO-3 called for the forces to withdraw into Bataan and defend against a superior Japanese force for at least six months until the US Navy arrived with convoys of reinforcements and supplies. Except for the plans to stand and fight, given the inability to resupply food, fuel, and ammunition into Bataan, WPO-3 was largely obsolete. What the plan did not fully anticipate was the total loss of air cover and support as well as a limited naval coastal reaction force able to harass and delay enemy landings and resupply. Given the rough geography of Bataan and the mountains that ran down the center of the peninsula, the defensive lines were split into three areas. The main battle line was only ten miles south of the Layac Bridge. The western side of the Abucay line, named for an old banana hacienda in the area, was manned by I Corps under the direct command of General Wainwright and ran from the South China Sea at Mauban about five miles to the base of Mt. Natib. The center part of the line was Mt. Natib, about four miles wide, the volcano ranging up to 4,222 feet and seen as impassable by large numbers of men and equipment. The final stretch of the eastern defensive line of 15,000 yards, or about 8.5 miles,

Japanese propaganda notice dropped from the air to encourage American and Filipino soldiers to surrender. (Courtesy of the author's collection.)

Site of American field Hospital No. 1 on southern Bataan. Built to hold five hundred patients, the hospital was soon filled with more than two thousand casualties. (Courtesy of the author's collection.)

running from Mt. Natib to Manila Bay at Mabatang was defended by II Corps and commanded by General George Parker. The southern tip of Bataan, below the Mariveles Mountains, contained untrained reserves (a mix of airmen from Clark Field, navy support personnel from Cavati Naval Yard, and raw untrained Filipino cadets) and the service command area for excess equipment and the field hospitals.[12]

The defenders were dug in. In spite of waves of Japanese bombers and artillery bombardment, the Japanese advance at Abucay Hacienda was repelled and a victory for the Filipino-Americans. The defenders held their ground and devastated the attackers. Japanese bodies piled three and four deep in the front of the Scouts' foxholes, as the Japanese kept coming in a bloody banzai attack. To overcome the Abucay minefields, the Japs stampeded a herd of carabao through the mines and attacked in the tracks of the animals and over their dead carcasses. The line was briefly breached at the center, but defenders swiftly

TABLE 2.1. Order of Battle on Bataan, January 1942[13]

I Corps: General Parker
11th, 21st, 41st, 51st Divisions
Philippine Scout, 57th Division
American artillery, tanks
Effective troops: 25,000

II Corps: General Wainwright
1st, 31st, 91st, 71st Divisions (PA)
26th Cavalry (PS)
Battery each of field artillery and SPM
Effective troops: 22,500

Service Command Area: General Selleck
24th Pursuit Group; Constabulary and Philippine troops
Mixed units of reserve/coast guard troops
Effective troops: 20,000

counterattacked, reclaiming the lost ground. This was more than just a probe—it was a true test of the defenders.

The delayed offensive by the Japanese against the forces dug in on Bataan along the Abucay line was partly due to the misconception by the enemy that the campaign was in a mop-up stage, involving only the remnants of the Filipino-American troops. Under pressure from the Imperial General HQ command in Tokyo to conclude operations, General Homma agreed to transfer a large part of his crack troops for a new mission to capture Java. In return, he received twelve thousand less experienced replacements of the 65th Brigade, intended only to be used for occupation duties. The troop exchange did not reduce the overall Japanese fire power or air superiority, and in fact, more fresh troops were fed into the battle until early April 1942.[14]

To get a firsthand look at the situation on Bataan and to confer with his senior officers "in the field," at first light on January 10, General MacArthur and a few of his senior staff crossed the choppy bay from Corregidor to Bataan. In spite of sniper fire and occasional artillery, the general visited the HQs of Generals Parker and Wainwright and gave a brief inspection of I Corps installations. The tall, confident, field-tested veteran of World War I and the Philippine Uprising of 1903–4, with his soft cap (no helmet), dark sunglasses, riding crop, and pipe, walked around the area inspecting and talking with rank and file troops and then returned to the Rock. Captain Tom Dooley recorded in his diary that General MacArthur was firm in his assessment to the troops that the tide would soon turn; his general "points" were simple and straightforward: "1) we would stop the Jap attack and would counter-attack; 2) Jap air superiority was only temporary; 3) 20,000 troops were [preparing] in Mindanao; 4) we will soon re-occupy Manila;" and given that the major item of concern was when relief was coming, "5) we have caught the imagination of America." This was the last time the general would set foot on Bataan. And by coincidence, General Homma on the same day made his first demand to MacArthur for the immediate unconditional surrender, declaring, "Your prestige and honor have been upheld." Homma was answered with salvos of artillery throughout the night.[15]

Although Homma exploited General MacArthur's "prestige and honor" to appeal to the general, MacArthur received mixed reviews for his actions in the immediate hours after the first Japanese attacks on December 8; yet by and large he worked with the hand he was dealt. Among most career military officers, the general was already a legend. Among the rank and file soldiers surviving day to day in the field, he became a handy target for their frustration and scorn; they nicknamed him "Dugout Doug." MacArthur would retain his lofty mystique among the men, who had hoped that somehow he would save them from looming defeat by pulling off an eleventh-hour miracle. Still the songs and poems that filled the troops' free time and lonely nights came in course, as they penned a number of ditties and tunes, such as these verses set to the "The Battle Hymn of the Republic":

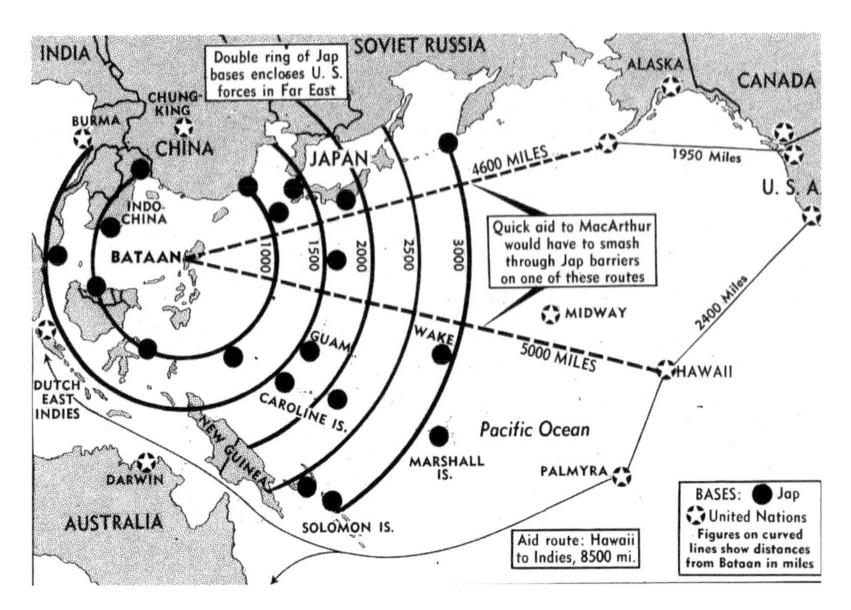

This map was drafted by the US Army and published in papers across America, with the caption, "Gen. MacArthur must fight on unaided on Bataan Peninsula; map dramatically indicates how the defenders of Bataan are cut off from US supply or bomber help." (Courtesy of the author's collection.)

Dugout Doug MacArthur lies ashakin' on the Rock,
Safe from all the bombers and from any sudden shock.
Dugout Doug is eating of the best food on Bataan,
And his troops go starving on . . .

Dugout Doug's not timid, he's just cautious, not afraid,
He's protecting carefully the stars that Franklin made.
Four-star generals are as rare as good food on Bataan,
And his troops go starving on . . .[16]

GIVE 'EM HELL, SON

The first full-scale attack in the Battle of Bataan followed a fierce Japanese artillery barrage begun on January 11, 1942, against the Abucay position. General Parker, along with Texas Aggie officers

Colonel Edwin Albright, Captain McDavitt, and Captain Coleman (rearmed airmen turned infantry spread among the Filipino units), had prepared for such an onslaught and waited until the last minute following the Japanese shelling to open fire with his artillery on the advancing Japanese troops and tanks down both sides of the Layac, or East Road, into Bataan. Surprised by the heavy return fire, the Japanese were forced into adjacent sugar fields where they were then attacked by crack elements of the Philippine Scouts. The fierceness of the fighting increased as attack and counterattack continued for the next forty-eight hours. The prime defender at this point was the 57th Infantry—Philippine Scouts comprising 1,914 Filipino enlisted men commanded by American officers. Charging Japanese soldiers would impale and sacrifice themselves on the double-apron barbwire to allow advancing troops to run or climb over their bodies pinned to the wire; many became human grenades, and others repeatedly attacked headlong, yelling, "Banzai!" The Philippine Scouts on the Manila Bay side of the defensive line held their ground and pushed back the Japanese advance.[17]

Realizing they were up against a more formidable force, the Japanese (reinforced with fresh troops that had landed at Port Binanga) reverted to guerrilla tactics in an attempt to infiltrate American lines. As Wainwright noted, "They came silently as snakes . . . infiltrating our flanks." This change of tactics in mid-January proved effective in causing confusion and some panic in the rear of the defenders' lines. Moving down the line toward the Mt. Natib volcano, the reinforced enemy marshaled a direct frontal attack on the Philippine 41st Division and effected the "disintegration" and rout of the 51st Division (PA). It also allowed time for a larger Imperial force to skirt the rugged volcano, attacking and enveloping the exposed left flank, resulting in a two-mile-wide hole in the Abucay defensive line. American-Filipino troops fought against heavy odds with inferior equipment and weapons: 70 percent of mortar ammunition proved to be duds, there were few accurate maps, and no field radios and thus no communications between units and the command post. Their Enfield rifles were defective, and they had no replacement parts. With few entrenching tools,

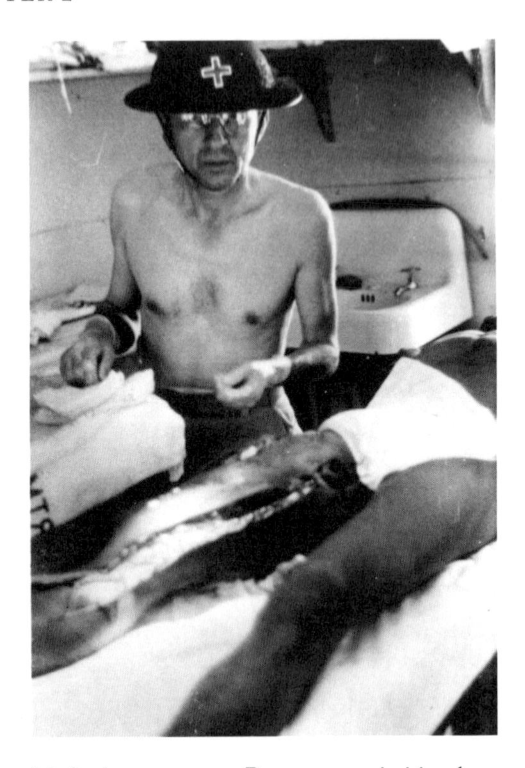

Medical treatment on Bataan was primitive, here with doctor Lt. Col. Frank Adamo, clad in "operating clothes," treating a case of gas gangrene. (Courtesy of the author's collection.)

troops resorted to the use of bayonets and meat can lids to dig trenches and foxholes. Soon the US Army engineers improvised bamboo grenades to replace the World War I vintage duds. After only thirty days in the field, most of the Filipino troops, according to General Parker, "were barefooted and ragged."[18]

The major role of American officers was to serve as trainers and advisors in the Filipino units. However, many times, the advisors stepped in as active line commanders to rally the Filipino troops. Such is the case of Aggie **Lt. Col. Eugene T. Lewis '27** and his staff of American officers and noncommissioned officers. After nearly being surrounded by the enemy, they took operational leadership of the

43rd Infantry Regiment (PA) on January 16 after the rout of the 51st Division. While Lewis "had no command authority," he, in fact, exercised immediate command in this dire situation to prevent being overrun. Lewis at once repositioned his troops on the exposed 43rd's flanks and ordered artillery support to pin down the enemy. Such close-in fire was dangerous, as the poorly trained Filipinos often misdirected fire over friendly troops.[19]

Lt. Col. Lewis ordered the resupply of the frontline troops, deployed his American officers among the units, and ordered a gradual "pivoting action" to draw in and trap the enemy piecemeal. By January 17, reconnaissance patrols reported the destruction of the Japanese infiltrating units. Louis Morton in *The Fall of the Philippines* noted, "Under the calm guidance of Lt. Col. Lewis, regimental instructor, [the 43rd] held against repeated onslaughts." By January 19, the main line of resistance (MLR) of the 43rd had been weakened due to repeated Japanese attacks by fresh reinforcements. With their objective of holding in place accomplished, the 43rd was ordered to pull back on January 20–21. This may have been the high point of the defense of Bataan. Had the defenders had reinforcements, improved artillery, and air power, they might have halted the 14th Imperial Army in its tracks long enough for a counterattack.[20]

The 26th Cavalry, composed of American officers and Filipino Scouts, was ordered forward by Wainwright to strike in the enemy's rear in hopes of delaying and disrupting Japanese operations. From the far left side of the Abucay line, the 26th was ordered to push up the South China Sea coastline three miles to the tiny village of Moron (or Monong). D Troop led by **Lt. Clifford G. Hardwicke '39** of Sherman, Texas, engaged the enemy on January 16, slowing their advance. The unit was regrouped around midnight on January 17, following evacuation of the wounded, which included Hardwicke's close friend, Lt. Edwin P. Ramsey. After conferring with Ramsey about his wound, Hardwicke led a small contingent back to Moron to recover horses lost in the earlier battle. Entering the village under continuous enemy fire, he secured the release of seventeen horses but was shot from his saddle by a sniper upon departure. Ramsey was shocked to learn of his friend's demise and recalled Cliff's pride over the one-line telegram he had received from his father back in Texas—"Give 'em hell, son." Tom Dooley recorded in his wartime notebook, "The ugly part of the day was announcement of Cliff Hardwicke's (Sherman, Texas) death. He had gone up for some horses that were lost . . . and a sniper, 'a Jap in Filipino uniform' killed him. Our patrol got him . . . the Japs are a treacherous group of vandals." For his brave actions that night, Cliff Hardwicke's father was posthumously presented his son's Silver Star for gallantry in March 1943 at Third Army Headquarters in San Antonio.[21]

Numerous pockets of gallant action occurred up and down the defensive line, but the overall ability to defend the Abucay position dwindled as men grew tired and were low on food and ammunition. Panic and piecemeal retreat followed the devastating envelopment and isolation of the center of the Abucay-Mauban line, with Wainwright's HQ nearly surrounded and cut off. On January 22, Major General Sutherland, Chief of Staff for General MacArthur on Corregidor, visited General Parker's command post west of Limay. After a discussion of the situation, he concurred that a withdrawal was essential to being able to hold on as long as possible. One battalion commander in the 41st Division recalled in his after-action report, "The order to 'hold at all cost' was more idealistic than realistic."[22]

Fort Mill, P.I.
Jan. 15, 1942

Subject: Message from General MacArthur

To: All Unit Commanders

. . . Help is on the way from the United States. Thousands of troops and hundreds of planes are being dispatched. The exact time of arrival of reinforcements is unknown as they will have to fight their way through Japanese attempts against them. It is imperative that our troops hold until these reinforcements arrive.

> *No further retreat is possible. We have more troops in Bataan than the Japanese have thrown against us; our supplies are ample; a determined defense will defeat the enemy's attack. . . . I will call upon every soldier in Bataan to fight in his assigned position, resisting every attack. This is the only road to salvation. If we fight we will win; if we retreat we will be destroyed.*
>
> *MacArthur*

Captain John Coleman and his men of the Army Air Force, 27th Material Squadron, remained in the heat of the action:

> We had 163 men of which an average of about 100 were on the front line near Orion. We had about 44 back in the rear, some on crash boat crews, some driving half-tracks and tanks. We had on the front line 3 machine guns, of which 2 were water cooled Brownings and one Marlin machine gun. We had two BARs; the rest of the enlisted men had 30 caliber rifles and officers had 1 pistol each. We had two grenades each. Some carried 4 each on patrols. About 2/3 of the machine guns were taken off wrecked airplanes, and too heavy to carry.[23]

Thus a change of position was ordered under cover of darkness for frontline units on January 24–25, covered by a rear guard comprising a small force of infantry and US tanks. Confusion continued as the message to withdraw was not decoded by some units, and what valuable supplies were on hand were left behind as traffic congestion clogged all roads southbound. A Japanese counterattack with concentrated artillery, which fortunately did not occur, could have led to the collapse of the entire I Corps position. Once again a new defensive position was established to run across the bottom third of the peninsula from Limay on the Manila Bay across and around the south side of Mt. Bataan to Caibobo Point on the South China Sea. With the ocean on three sides and the enemy at the front, this was indeed the last defensible line.[24]

Texas Aggie Captain John S. Coleman fought until the last hours of the defense of Bataan and was captured after efforts to escape to Corregidor. (Courtesy of the author's collection.)

The plight of the Bataan defenders was captured in numerous poems and songs, but none was more pungent than the verses penned by United Press International reporter Frank Hewlett in early 1942:

Battling Bastards of Bataan

We're the battling bastards of Bataan;
No mama, no papa, no Uncle Sam;
No aunts, no uncles, no cousins, no nieces;
No pills, no planes, no artillery pieces;
And nobody gives a damn.[25]

Behind the final Limay-Caibobo line were a mix of some twenty-six thousand to twenty-eight thousand trapped civilians and two army hospitals packed with the wounded. Communications were poor, and there was no relief in sight. At least 60 percent of all troops had malaria, beriberi, or dysentery. By late January, it was decided that only high-priority personnel such as doctors, nurses, and intelligence personnel would be evacuated to Corregidor. Conditions in the field steadily deteriorated under harsh pressure from both the enemy and the exposure to jungle conditions. One company commander recalled:

> So close were the two lines that automatic weapons of the enemy were thought to be friendly guns unless the "pound" of the Jap 7.7 could be detected or the "slip-slip" of the machine rifle could be distinguished.
>
> The men lived in their foxholes for approximately eleven days. If killed, the man was covered in his hole. Evacuation of the dead was nearly impossible due to the intensity of enemy fire. Malnutrition had sapped the strength of the Filipino soldiers so that the evacuation of the wounded turned out to be a problem of physical strength. Feeding was a laborious and extremely dangerous process.
>
> Food was always a problem. The soldiers grew weaker by the day. The men were fed twice daily. Their ration consisting of a canteen cup of rice and a spoonful of salmon gravy.[26]

THE POINTS: INFANTRY AIRMEN

As the advance on the Filipino-American line at Abucay continued, General Homma, weeks behind schedule, came under increasing pressure from Tokyo to mop up the Bataan Peninsula in order that the troops and planes could be used in other parts of the Pacific. In mid-January, Homma ordered an "Inchon" type landing behind the American line at a location on the South China Sea just above the critical supply base and reserve forces at Mariveles on the southernmost tip of the peninsula; if Mariveles fell, Bataan was lost. The "Points" was a landing site where a series of finger-like projections jutted out to sea. The enemy objective was to secure the beachhead, infiltrate and cause mass confusion in the rear, link up with advancing Japanese forces, and cut off or surround the retreating enemy forces. While at first surprised, the defenders reacted quickly by sending two fast torpedo boats and four patched-up P-40 fighters that had been hidden at a crude jungle strip near Cabcaben to attack the enemy landing barges. Despite heavy losses, the Japanese force was able to land more than half its troops at Quinauan and others at a second landing at Longoskawayan Point. To counter the Japanese attack, Wainwright ordered in a mix of Philippine Scouts, Constabulary troops, navy seamen, and a handful of "planeless" Americans fliers from the 24th Pursuit Group.[27]

When Clark Field was destroyed on December 8, these Army Air Corps men were left in limbo. The few remaining US Army Air Corps planes were flown to Australia, but the majority of the pilots, crews, and mechanics were ordered to Bataan and integrated into infantry units and placed on beach defense. Still expecting replacement planes from the United States or Australia, the commander of the 24th PG was assured his pilots and crews were "only on loan to the infantry." The 24th PG and the units of the 3rd, 17th, 21st, and 34th Pursuit Squadrons as well as the 27th Materiel Squadron were assigned to the Service Command Area (located in the far southern third of Bataan) as the provisional Air Corps Regiment that was effectively formed on January 7, 1942. The pilots, airmen, and support personnel were not enthusiastic about their new assignment, with Major General Lewis H. Brereton recalling, "Some of the fighter pilots are fuming mad about all the prominence given Hawaii on the radio while little attention is made of the Philippines, even though the Japs have landed here."[28]

Little did they know that a secret communication in late December to MacArthur from Chief of Staff George Marshall made it clear help was not on the way: "It now appears that the plans for reaching you quickly with pursuit plane support are jeopardized." General Marshall, always the realist, was very influential in advising President Roosevelt not to send more troops and equipment to MacArthur, "since it would detract from the cross-channel European project." The troops in the field and the airmen were not given this information. The replacement planes never arrived and the status of the airmen never changed; these new air corps infantrymen included four Texas Aggie pursuit pilots: **Lt. Willis Powell Culp III '38** from Elgin, **Lt. Charles E. Gaskell '41** from Dallas, **Lt. Howard P. Hardegree '39** from Ben Wheeler, and **Lt. James M. Henry '39** from Kingsville.[29]

The newly armed infantry airmen of the 24th PG were sent to duty along a rocky ten-mile sector from Caibobo Point to Mariveles. With no infantry training and little or no support, they dug foxholes and persuaded the engineers to string barbwire along the beach. They were armed with an assortment of virtually antique weapons, including defective Enfield rifles, obsolete mortars, a 37mm cannon, and a Marlin machine gun. More than two-thirds of the outdated mortar rounds fired were duds. Upon unpacking the Marlin, it was noted it had been wrapped in grease and newspapers dating from the early 1920s! With no tripods for mounting the guns, the airmen used tree stumps. Grenades were made from bamboo tubes stuffed with TNT or dynamite. As the enemy began concentrating on Longoskawayan Point, General George Moore of Corregidor was requested by the Bataan forces to provide artillery fire until a solid defensive position could be established. Moore recalled, "We answered at 1213 hrs. on the 26th by Battery Geary (12-in Mortars). Sixteen rounds of 700 lb. each, point detonating, instantaneous fuse, personnel shell were used [fired a distance of over six miles] and proved most effective. According to observers, some fragments flew 500 yards and a large fire was started. The next morning 24 rounds were fired with another 16 on the 29th. This was the first firing by major caliber coast artillery guns at an enemy since the Civil War [Fort Sumter, 1861]."[30]

Holding the high ground above the beach was a key factor in stopping and containing the Japanese landing force from moving inland. Lt. Gaskell was involved in action on January 22 as the enemy attempted to move inland. On the twenty-fifth, the commander was relieved of command—replaced by the hard-charging Colonel Clinton Pierce, commander of the 26th Cavalry (PS)—and promoted to brigadier general. He assumed command of the 71st Division. The seesaw battle along the Points continued through January 29, when the 17th Pursuit Squadron, Lt. Culp's unit of about two hundred men and reserves from the Philippine Constabulary as well as the 2nd Battalion, 45th Philippine Scouts flanked the Japanese, pinning them on the beach and in caves along the shoreline. A handful of ill-armed airmen and Scouts had isolated the Japanese in a four-thousand-square-yard area, with their backs to the sea and cut off from supplies. The Japanese planned to fight to the death, with their commander reporting to HQ, "The battalion is about to die gloriously."[31]

By early February, the remaining Japanese stragglers trapped on the rocky beach received explicit orders dropped in bamboo tubes by planes to retreat. Instructions included time of tides, hour of moon rise, and orders to make rafts or swim north to Morong along the coast. The instructions were of little use to the small force remaining. The American and Filipinos had annihilated two entire enemy battalions—1st and 2nd Batt, 20th Imperial Infantry, about 2,500 men—with only about a few dozen holding out. However, to the Japanese commander's relief (and surprise), he was eventually ordered to retreat by slipping through the thinly manned line above the beach covered by dense jungle. Before retreating, the Japanese buried their heavy weapons and "killed those of their comrades who were too badly wounded to walk." Those who did break out of the beachhead (some tried to swim out to sea) in an attempt to infiltrate northward were tracked and killed or captured by the Scouts of the 26th Cavalry.[32]

Army historian Louis Morton's classic work on Bataan, *The Fall of the Philippines*, documents the savage nature of the fight around the closing days of the Points that would prove a harbinger of the future: "There was a reluctance and disinclination to take prisoners. The Scouts had found the bodies of their comrades behind Japanese lines so mutilated as to discourage any generous impulse toward those Japanese unfortunate enough to fall into their hands. Some bodies had been bayoneted in the back while the men had had their arms wired behind them, one rotting body had been found strung up by the thumbs with the toes just touching the ground, mute evidence of a slow and tortured end."[33]

ON BORROWED TIME

Following the total rejection of the Japanese invasion at the Points, the Imperial Japanese Army slowed offensive operations to assess their strategy. The brief halt came as a welcomed surprise to the defenders. American morale was further improved, and there was a glimmer of optimism when—erroneously—rumors spread that General Homma had committed *seppuku*, better known as *hara-kiri*, in MacArthur's former elaborate penthouse suite in the Manila Hotel, due to his failure to capture Bataan. In fact, given the swift defeat of the British in Malaya, Hong Kong, and Singapore, Homma was under tremendous pressure from commanders in Tokyo to wrap up the costly operations on Luzon and Bataan. Homma alone had failed to make his objective on time.[34]

A brief Japanese offensive was launched on February 15 (coinciding with the same day Singapore fell) to probe the American defensive positions but soon halted due to stiff American opposition. The cost of the delay took a toll on the Japanese 14th Army. From January 6 until March 1, casualties included 2,700 killed, more than 4,000 wounded, and some 12,000 sick with malaria, dengue fever, hookworm, diarrhea, dysentery, and beriberi. Entire battalions were disbanded. For a brief moment, according to Homma's testimony during the postwar trial, the Japanese army was so weakened by late February that a large-scale Filipino-American counterattack would have crushed the 14th Army.[35] This assessment is confirmed in Dooley's diary:

> In captured documents, etc. it is rightfully believed that First Corps (commanded by Wainwright) has not only repelled a main, coordinated attack of the Japs, but inflicted heavy losses. We killed about 2,500 Japs and do not know losses from artillery or wounds. The General impressed on division commanders a warning not to relax. Most probably the Japs have realized that we cannot be driven out with forces they have here, so they will pull back and sit, while we sit . . . and additional forces brought in from China to polish this place off.[36]

Yet reality soon set in. The loss of the British strongholds at Hong Kong and Singapore broke any hope to be relieved—if for no other reason than Prime Minister Churchill's realization there was no way to mount a counterattack in such a distant location. So long as the Japanese controlled the air and sea, the American defenders were doomed to a slow battle of attrition as they clung to the tip of Bataan. The actual material losses of the bombings were not severe, but the effect of the constant air-artillery attacks on troop morale and combat readiness of the troops was pronounced. Low supplies of ammunition, clothing, shelter halves, fuel, and a chronic shortage of food along with poor communications and mounting numbers of wounded and sick in the two overcrowded jungle field hospitals precluded any reasonable hopes of a counterattack. Despite the fact that the Philippines lies close to the greatest quinine-producing area in the world, very little quinine was provided to troops. A large supply of quinine to calm the spread of malaria would possibly have made a significant change in the levels of casualties and resistance. As Morton concludes, "It was for these reasons that all proposals for an offensive, while feasible tactically and desirable for reasons of morale, were strategically unsound."[37]

The starving troops steadily received a diminishing amount of food. By March, with rations cut from one half to one quarter, one combatant observed, "The ration at this time consisted of 4 ounces of rice and 1.6 ounces of salmon, which becomes very nauseating as a steady diet and is definitely not enough to sustain life." Virtually all the troops suffered serious malnutrition—resulting in chronic fatigue, reduced immune systems, and in many cases night blindness and edema. Ordered to dig in opposite the newly reinforced Japanese frontline, the defenders prepared for the final battle. There were two primary field hospitals, one located at Limay and the second south of Cabcaben, holding more than seven thousand wounded and sick combined. Another four thousand were treated at provisional field hospitals. The declining health of the command gradually had a disastrous effect on combat efficiency. The combination of jungle diseases and malnutrition left the combat efficiency of most of the defenders at a little below 50 percent by March 1942.[38]

The Japanese used many crude attempts such as lewd propaganda leaflets, calls for Filipino troops to attack the Americans, and broadcasts from the Manila radio station KZRH with a Tokyo Rose–like host backed by the theme song for her nightly program, "Ships That Never Come In." The troops also received *The Voice of America* shortwave radio broadcast by American stations, which drew mixed reviews from the soldiers who had little faith in pledges of the timely arrival of reinforcements, supplies, and food. Famed radio broadcaster Walter Winchell remarked in a national broadcast picked up by the defenders on Bataan, "To hell with this hero stuff; let's send them some HELP!" And Army nurse Lt. Juanita Redmond remembered with some irony when a report came in that Santa Barbara, California, had been shelled by the Japanese, someone at the field hospital cracked, "So MacArthur wired the US officials that *if they can hold out* for thirty days we'll send 'em help [from Bataan]!"[39]

There was no shelling of Santa Barbara, only hysterical reporting, and there was no help bound for Bataan. President Roosevelt's fireside chat in honor of Washington's Birthday, broadcast on February 23, conclusively signaled there was no prospect of relief for Bataan. Roosevelt dared to say what Secretary of War Henry Stimson and the War Department would not utter after the Arcadia War Planning Conference with the British, speaking of duty and sacrifice: "This generation of Americans has come to realize . . . that there is something larger and more important than life of any individual . . . something for which a man will sacrifice . . . not only his association with those he loves, but his life itself." As morale on Bataan dipped to a new low, American and Filipino defenders dug in for the next battle.[40]

On March 10, Tom Dooley accompanied Wainwright on a rough barge ride across Manila Bay to Corregidor to confer with General MacArthur. While waiting at the entrance of Malinta Tunnel, Dooley ran into Major John King, formerly a regular Army master sergeant stationed at Texas A&M when Dooley was a cadet in the mid-1930s. General Moore had given King (who while not a graduate of Texas A&M was considered a member of the Texas Aggie cadre) a field promotion when he accompanied the former A&M commandant to the Rock. As Dooley and King talked "over old and better days" at Texas A&M, General MacArthur abruptly appeared. Aware of Dooley's

Silver Star award, the general stuck out his hand, "I was just talking with your chief outside and just wanted to shake hands with you." Surprised by the brief encounter, they would not see each other again for three and a half years until the surrender ceremony on the deck of the *USS Missouri* on September 2, 1945, in Tokyo Bay. Upon Wainwright's return to Bataan with secret orders to prepare for a change of command upon MacArthur's departure to Australia, General Homma sent Wainwright an airborne demand via messages stuffed in empty beer cans dropped over the battlefield. Calling for surrender and an end to the needless bloodshed, Homma extolled, "We have the honor to address you in accordance with the humanitarian principles of '*Bushido*,' the code of the Japanese warrior." After reviewing the general's message, Wainwright, a dedicated scotch drinker, quipped, "The bastards could at least have sent a few full cans of beer."[41]

In late March 1942, as conditions became direr, Wainwright sent a number of detailed urgent messages to Washington. The War Department and General Marshall insisted that all efforts be made to smuggle food and medical supplies in, but numerous blockade runners and submarines delivered only a fraction of the food and ammunition needed to hold out. In a strange exchange of messages with Washington, the War Department seemed confused when Wainwright responded to a question on his current combined troop and civilian strength, noting there were 90,000 on Bataan and, with the inclusion of the forces on Corregidor as well as naval elements and civilian refugees, total strength (or, better stated, those needing to be fed), 110,000 total. The cause for the surprise at the numbers of defenders is perplexing, with Marshall's only reply to Wainwright, "Your recommendations always receive my immediate personal attention." Disaster was imminent.[42]

ALL HELL BROKE LOOSE

In spite of General Homma's brush with the disgrace of being relieved of command, new fresh troops from Singapore landed for the final push. More leaflets demanding the surrender were dropped to at once "accept an honorable defeat." If not, Homma declared his army was "at liberty to take any action whatsoever." This no-quarter message would greatly impact the troops and their treatment on the Death March. After days of heavy bombing of American positions—and the plainly marked field hospitals (claiming it was an accident)—the Japanese concentrated fresh troops between March 28 and April 1, and Homma boldly boasted over Manila radio that an all-out offensive would be launched on April 3, Good Friday. The massive Japanese artillery barrage, accompanied by intense aerial bombing of more than sixty tons of bombs, lasted for six hours and was considered the most intense shelling since the waning days of World War I. **Captain John F. Coleman '27** vividly recalls the fierce bombings, "We received an extremely heavy bombing from five-hundred pounders. It uprooted trees that were forty to seventy feet high. I was very nearly covered up in my foxhole. Blood ran out both my ears from the concussion."[43]

Communication lines were knocked out, defensive redoubts were made useless, the bamboo thickets and cane fields along the battle line were set ablaze, and smoke was so thick it blotted out the summit of Mt. Samat. Coleman prepared his unit for the oncoming assault: "We had been told several weeks before that the Japs would not take prisoner. It looked like it was going to be another Alamo, a fight to the finish. With no food, no artillery, no machines guns or planes, something had to happen fast if we were to hold out."[44]

The bombardment, which included shelling from Japanese warships offshore in the China Sea, had been concentrated on the center of the defensive line, as artillery and bombers "carpet bombed" the American-Filipino positions, effectively knocking the fighting will out of the 41st, 42nd, 21st, and 22nd Divisions, rendering the soldiers choked by dust, dazed, and demoralized. As the Japanese troops attacked—nearly unopposed into the center of the defenders—the shattered forces were in full withdrawal, allowing Homma to secure his first object, Mt. Samat, to prevent the Americans from holding the high ground. As dawn broke on Easter Sunday, April 5, the Japanese resumed the combined air and artillery bombardment. The shelling was followed by a massive assault with tanks, launched in an attempt to turn the flank of the defenders and push them into Manila Bay.

The Americans considered a counterattack on April 6 but could not make the necessary arrangements, given the continuous pressure of the enemy to prevent the defenders from regrouping. While a brief counterattack was organized, the defenders could not counter the overwhelming enemy odds.[45]

The psychological impact on the troops grew grimmer daily. General King's chief surgeon reported to the general that the combat effectiveness of the men "was rapidly approaching the zero point." Nearly 80,000 troops, including 12,500 Americans and 8,000 Philippine Scouts, were wedged into the tip of Bataan with their backs against Manila Bay. Depleted units were cobbled together to fill in the dropping numbers due to sickness: "our food was gone," recalled Colonel Ed Aldridge '16, "and the orders and counter-orders only added to the confusion." To gain firsthand information on the situation on Bataan, General Moore '08, accompanied by aides Tom Dooley and Bob Brown, crossed Manila Bay under enemy fire on April 6. Greeted at the dock by a dirty and tired group of soldiers, it was clear the situation was dire. The final line of defense stretched around the base of the two-thousand-foot-tall Mt. Samat, from Orion on the east to Bagac on the west, or bayside. To seal the victory, the Imperial Army sent in fresh troops of the 4th and 21st Divisions from China. The terrain was harsh. Numerous freshwater streams radiated from the sides of the mountain covered in dense jungles, swamps, and few roads larger than foot paths.[46]

Much has been written about General King's sudden surrender, with some implying he failed to follow orders. Events to the contrary were underway, as plans were already drafted at Wainwright's HQ on Corregidor to evacuate a large number of units from Bataan to the Rock. Orders created, in spite of MacArthur's attempted long-distance management of the situation from his office in Australia, late on April 7 and issued by General Lewis C. Beebe and Colonel C. L. Irwin on the early morning of April 8, predate any action taken by General King. The "secret" order outlined the "plan for movement of units to Corregidor"—to include elements of the 31st, 57th, and 45th Infantry; the 26th Cavalry; the 88th, 86th, and 24th Field Artillery; and one battery of 37mm antiaircraft guns of the 92nd Coastal Artillery. Units were to bring all weapons, equipment, field ranges, and cooking equipment, and a "full complement of American officers if possible." According to documents held by Captain Robley "Bob" D. Evans '40, his unit, the 45th Infantry, received authority to "activate plan at about 7:15 p.m., 8 April." However, it was never to be—and was confirmed in General Beebe's postwar published diary entry of April 8: "We tried to pull some units out of Bataan," but "all our troops there are doomed." As thousands of men crowded at the far southern tip of the peninsula near Mariveles, it soon became apparent there was not any seaborne transportation to evacuate the troops and equipment to Corregidor.[47]

By April 8, a state of chaos existed under the heavy air and artillery. Communication was reduced to runners. Frontline commanders lost all contact with many of their units. Roads to the rear became jammed and easy targets for the strafing fighters. All command and control had broken down. Wainwright notified MacArthur that his troops had "no power of resistance" and are "fast folding up." In spite of this, MacArthur sent orders to Wainwright and relayed to King for a counterattack. Due to the near total exhaustion, there was no unit capable of advancing. General King ordered the prearranged code word, "CRASH," be sent to all commanders to be prepared to destroy all tanks, artillery, and heavy equipment. In spite of the chaos, one shortsighted order was that none of the few remaining tanks were to be transferred to Corregidor. Most of the men had lost more than thirty to fifty pounds of their body weight, were sick with malaria, and were too weak to bear arms. In the waning hours of the battle for Bataan, Captain John Coleman recalls, "Every man in the 27th Material Squadron but 1st Sgt. Boston had malaria before the surrender. I had only 47 men [out of the original 163] able to walk when the surrender came. Starvation and malaria were contributing factors."[48]

On Wainwright's desk were "standing orders" from MacArthur's HQ in Australia that prohibited surrender under any condition. In his memoir, *Reminiscences* (1964), MacArthur bluntly noted, "I was utterly opposed to the ultimate capitulation of the Bataan command. If Bataan was to be destroyed, it should have been on the field of

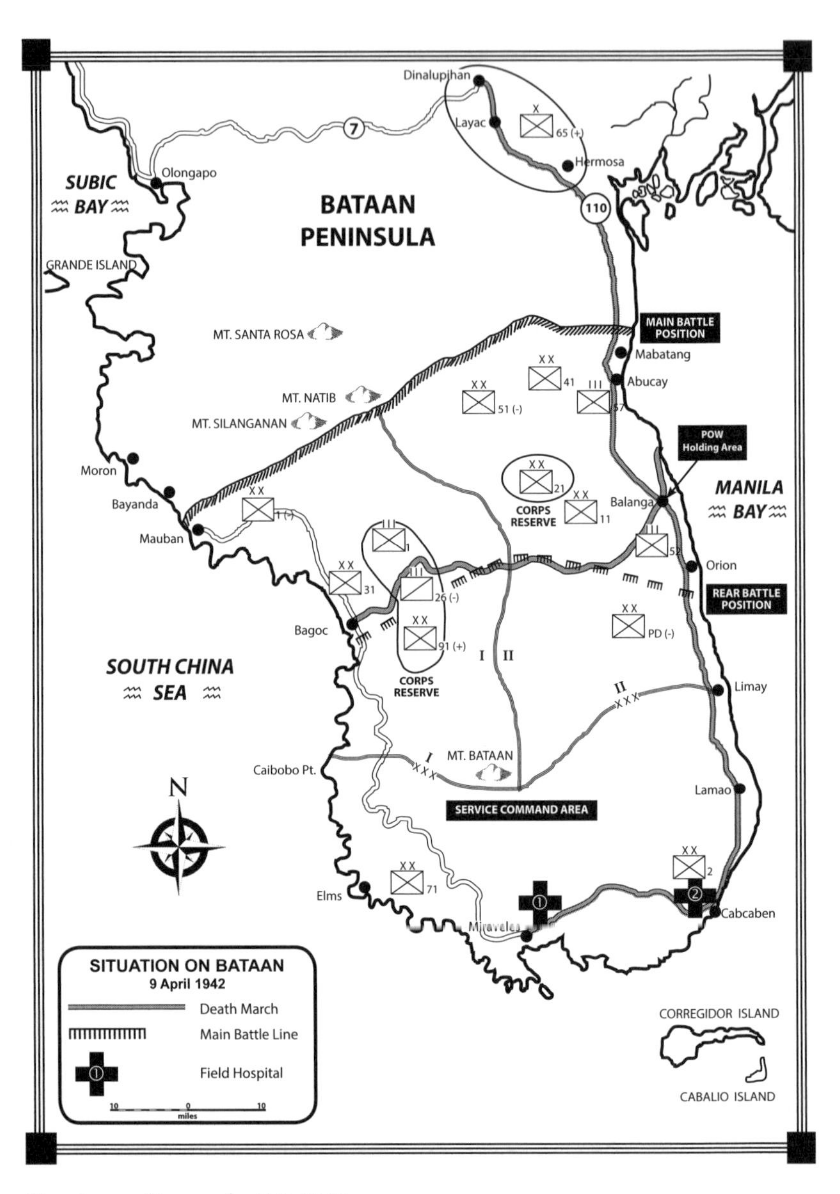

Situation on Bataan, April 8, 1942.

battle in order to exact full toll from the enemy." In spite of this new information on the deteriorating conditions, MacArthur did not change the orders. General King was under constant pressure from Wainwright at HQ on Corregidor to attack. However, in the field of battle, King contacted his unit commanders still engaged with the enemy or in retreat, and all stated they did not have the manpower or physical ability to attack. Command and control had evaporated. Texas Aggie **Captain Cary Abney '34** lost nearly his entire unit between April 3 and April 8, recording in his notebook the final hours for the fight of Bataan, "Pushed out of Orion Sector 4/8/42. Fought a disastrous rear guard action to line between Limay and Lamio—on Alonga River. Line completely shattered by Japanese Infantry the following day at 4:00 p.m. The attempt to form a line at Cabcabon was a total failure!—S. N. A. F. U."[49]

The *Ballad of the Bastards* captured the fate of the defenders during the final hours:

All our reserves from rear and flanks,
Were rushed to fill our broken ranks.
Too weak, too sick, to late were they to have
A chance to save the day.
We did our best to hold the shore
That overlooked Corregidor.
The enemy, the place overran
And we surrendered on Bataan.[50]

SILENCE OVER BATAAN

For weeks the fate of the Bataan defenders was well known. The fact that the sick and hungry troops had held out so long is tribute to their courage and will to fight. The jig was up. For three months, against heavy odds, the defenders had slowed down a corps-sized contingent of the Japanese Imperial Army onslaught. Back home newspapers carried the bare minimum of information from Bataan, with sweeping headlines like "Bataan Line Broken" and "Japanese Forces Pound

New Line on Bataan"; all the while the White House and War Department knew the end was near. The Japanese took full advantage of the confusion, dropping leaflets in Bataan: "Your US convoy is due in the Philippines on April 15th but you won't be alive to see it. Ha! Ha!" The end was near. As the bloodiest battle engaged by American forces in some seventy-five years drew to a close, the US Army Chief of Staff General Marshall was not at the War Department to monitor events but instead landing in London with presidential aide Harry Hopkins to discuss the American "expansion" of troops and materiel in Europe—the Battling Bastards of Bataan seemed for the moment truly forgotten.[51]

Tom Dooley, the generally jubilant former Aggie yell leader, entered a curt diary entry on April 6, 1941: "morale has gone down noticeably in past 2 weeks due mostly to the much talked of 'help' that never arrived. Never has anyone thought that Americans would be in a position in which the United States would be termed 'impotent.'"[52]

Accurate numbers are still hard to determine, but it is estimated that, in the fighting on Bataan, ten to twelve thousand American and Filipino forces were killed and more than twenty thousand wounded, while Japanese casualties are estimated to be more than seven thousand killed and twelve thousand wounded. Homma's orders and high-level commands to take the Philippine Islands in "50 days" instead led to the fall of Bataan on day 125, and he still had to take Corregidor. In the case of the Americans, General King had no other choice. He held the fate of some seventy-eight thousand emaciated men on Bataan in his hands as he approached the Japanese for surrender terms, the largest single surrender of American soldiers since General Stonewall Jackson captured Harper's Ferry eighty years earlier. While the fateful decision to surrender occurred on April 9, as early as April 7, plans were under way to evacuate medical personnel and antiaircraft units for redeployment on Corregidor. Dooley's diary entry notes the deplorable condition of the two-thousand-odd men swimming from Bataan: "'Those who came out of Bataan [to the Rock] during the night, upset, tired, jittery, dirty survivors of the catastrophe and most merely sat in a stupor—men temporarily out of hell!'"[53]

General King's overture to surrender the largest force in American history to succumb to an enemy was a fait accompli and at first rejected by the Japanese area commander, Major General Kameleichiro Nagano, who referred him to a lower-ranked officer and demanded to deal only with General Wainwright. King informed the Japanese general he had no means of contact with Wainwright but his reasoning went unheard; thus no American formal surrender by King ever took place and nothing was signed. As King attempted to secure safe passage for his troops, United Press correspondent Frank Hewlett in his last Bataan dispatch penned the following after the surrender: "The great fires and explosions that I saw in the Philippines are still vivid in my mind, but I remember even more vividly the little flashes of light I saw on Bataan the night of April 9, after the surrender. They came from soldiers hidden on the shore, and were from flashlights. They all repeated patiently to Corregidor, five miles away, and flickered the distress code: '. . . - - - . . . (SOS) . . . - - - . . . - - - . . .'"[54]

Instead of a formal surrender, General King and his staff were interrogated by a hostile group led by Colonel Motoo Nakayama, senior operation officer for the 14th Army. Nakayama refused to discuss terms with King and demanded, like his first meeting with Nagano, to only talk with General Wainwright. The main aim of the Japanese was to clear the Americans and Filipinos out of the tip of Bataan and press the battle on Corregidor. After King laid his pistol on the table as a sign of total surrender, he rebuked the colonel, asking if he surrendered in person, would his troops be treated well—as outlined in the Geneva Convention.[55]

The curt Japanese colonel tersely replied, "We are not barbarians!"[56]

> Courage is a quality God has seen fit to dispense with utmost care.
> The men of Bataan were His chosen favorites.
>
> MAJ. GEN. EDWARD P. KING JR.
>
> 1942

★ CHAPTER 3 ★

WE ARE NOT BARBARIANS!

> Bataan has fallen. The Philippine American troops on this war-ravaged and bloodstained peninsula have laid down their arms—with their heads bloody but unbowed—they have stood up uncomplaining under constant and grueling fire of the enemy for more than three months—our men have fought a brave and bitterly contested struggle . . . until the last in the face of overwhelming odds.
>
> General Jonathan Wainwright, April 9, 1942

> I slipped back as if in mud. It was human flesh that we were walking on. We could smell decaying human flesh all along the road where men had been killed, their bodies left where they had fallen. The columns of tanks, trucks, and cavalry had run over them, pulverizing their bones into pulp.
>
> Captain John S. Coleman '27

The situation was grave. The uncertainty of surrender set the stage for the next chapter in the fight for survival—to withstand the Death March, internment, the Hell Ships, and savage treatment by the Japanese soldiers. One of the most barbaric, sadistic, and inhumane episodes in modern wartime history was carried out by the Japanese Imperial Army against the prisoners of Bataan and Corregidor. The Japanese Army had a long legacy in their murderous dealings in China, especially the depredations inflicted on both troops as well as noncombatants in Manchuria (1931), Shanghai (1937), Nanking (1938), and Hong Kong (December 1941), followed later in the Malaya Peninsula and Singapore (1942). An aggressive militarist's war faction was fully ingrained in positions of influence at all levels of the Japanese government. Thus the pattern of the Japanese "war of aggression," blatantly sanctioned torture, and the mutilation of prisoners of war and noncombatants and was condoned by "a common plan and conspiracy" at the highest level of the Japanese military and government in Tokyo.[1]

Claiming to be the superior race and destined to "free" Asia from colonial powers and thus preside over the region, known as the Greater East Asia Co-Prosperity Sphere, for military control and to harness strategic resources, Japan found solace in years of atrocities, brutality, and cruelty to support their claims as the masters of Asia. This air of superiority was first directed on a large scale against the Chinese in the early 1930s and by the late 1930s at American and British interests and possessions in Asia. Since "particularly white foreigners," according to Edwin Hoyt, "had been maligned and mistreated in Japan from time immemorial," the level of hate was reflected in repeated policy statements and articles, such as the *Japan Times* feature "Anglo-Americanism Must be Wiped Out: Japan Fighting Ideological War to Manifest Lofty National Interest":

> The breaking down of the so-called Washington structure and Anglo-American self-centered ideology and *the complete destruction* of the same pernicious, selfish interests is our ultimate objective in this war. We were compelled to enter this war for our self-protection.
>
> *After this annihilation* an equitable order will be installed in the world. Thus the War of Greater East Asia is being waged as a grand ideological campaign to advance our national conceptions in both spiritual and material ways. The essence of ideological war should be as such.[2]

The "institutionalized" brutality and inhumanity was a mix of ingrained feudalism espoused in the so-called *Bushido* tradition—an ancient Japanese cult-like warrior code—and pure barbaric cold-blooded "sport." The evidence of brutality is overwhelming. Tokyo newspapers routinely carried front-page stories of the honor and glory of beheading their Chinese enemies. One group of Japanese officers were profiled in the news media with a series of articles for committing more than one hundred beheadings in China, accentuating the thrill of such an achievement and lamenting only that "their blades had, of course, been damaged [dulled]." Such reports of torture, beheadings, and rape were known to the American, British, Australian, and Filipino authorities. Compassion for the captured was forbidden—a fundamental tenant of Japanese military training and doctrine. Stories appeared periodically in the Manila newspapers. Furthermore, such news was also in papers across America. On the eve of the fall of Bataan, April 8, 1942, the *Boston Herald* published a story, "Jap Slaughter of Prisoners Described by Escaped Fliers," detailing the appalling cruelty of the Japanese—how they captured sixty Australian soldiers after the fall of Rabaul, lined them up, and tied their hands behind their backs. Each captured Aussie soldier was given a revolver and ordered to commit suicide. In response, they fought back, and all but two of the Aussies were shot or bayoneted to death. One wounded escapee told the press in Melbourne, "The Japs will pay for this when our chaps get them." On Java, an officer requested the commander of the Imperial Army 36th Division to supply American prisoners of war "to kill for practice." Two Americans were sent for, blindfolded, repeatedly bayoneted for sport, and then decapitated with shovels by the Japanese soldiers. No means of bloody mistreatment or torture, including cannibalism of captured American pilots, was disallowed.[3]

For the prisoners of Bataan, the Japanese rose to a new level of brutality. All forms of food and drink were denied, as well as medical care. During the first few days, hundreds of American and Filipino troops were randomly bayoneted, beheaded, and executed. General Hideki Tojo's senior staff emissaries on an inspection of troops on Luzon, days before the surrender, stressed to their fellow field officers, "The Pacific war was a racist clash . . . the 'white devils' must be wiped out." This was interpreted by the Japanese officers as a logical kill-all-prisoners edict. This sentiment of no quarter was equally applied to the Filipinos. Japanese revenge, aggravated by heavy combat losses as well as a protracted campaign that was weeks behind schedule, was a major motivation. The first mass atrocity by the Japanese Army on Bataan—with direct orders from Imperial superiors, not some rogue event—occurred within hours of the surrender, when some four hundred Filipino officers and noncommissioned officers of the 91st Division were herded together in a ravine near the Pantingan River, hands tied behind their backs with phone wire, and executed one by one in cold blood, by sword and bayonet. Much has been written on the reasons for such atrocities based on Japanese traditions that abhor those who surrender and do not face an honorable death in battle. Others claim it was an aberration by a small group of untrained troops, which is totally discredited given the widespread brutality by seasoned combat troops. In spite of the fact that large amounts of Japanese records were burned before the Americans could siege them, ample records, testimonies, research, proceedings, and first-person interrogations of both Japanese and Americans were cataloged and used in the postwar criminal trials. The atrocities extended for more than four years, from the Bataan Death March to the POW camps to the Hell Ships—and to the mainland slave-labor mining and factory camps in China, Korea, and Japan. And dozens of Texas Aggie officers were victims of this treatment.[4]

These brutal events in the Philippines as well as across Asia during the war are chronicled in detail in the international military tribunal documents, compiled with evidence and testimony during the criminal trials from 1946 to 1948. Additional war crimes documents, details, and research can, for example, be found in Major William E. Dyess, *The Dyess Story: The Eye-Witness Account of the Death March from Bataan* (1944), Edward Hoyt, *Japan's War* (1986), Bernard Edwards, *Blood and Bushido: Japanese Atrocities at Sea 1941–1945* (1997), Gregory F. Michno, *Death on the Hellships: Prisoners at Sea in the Pacific War* (2001), and Tonaka Yuki, *Hidden Horrors: Japanese War Crimes in World War II* (1996). This scourge of organized atrocities and inhuman brutality should long be remembered.[5]

The Japanese cruelty meted out across the Pacific during the war years exceeds any previously documented treatment in modern history of POWs and civilians. During the course of the Japanese Imperial hostilities across Asia, they captured, killed, or wounded more than three hundred thousand Allied soldiers—this does not account for the tens of thousands of civilian casualties and troops' disregard for human life. These prisoners of war were interned by the Japanese in hundreds of locations in Asia. Exact data on the numbers of POWs on Bataan were not compiled until months after the soldiers were marched to the internment camps—and even then, with the hundreds that died weekly, many are unaccounted for. The Japanese army was first surprised at the number of POWs, estimating there would be only about twenty-five to forty thousand men on Bataan. (This estimate is strange given the fact that Homma and staff were convinced by March 23, 1942, he was up against and should prepare for sixty thousand defenders in the southern tip of Bataan.) Second, they were completely unprepared to deal with the influx of the prisoners, which resulted in poor planning and gross miscalculations, further heightened by Japanese visceral disdain for those who surrendered. General Homma was faced with a massive logistical problem, having captured more POWs than he had men under his command. Numbers vary, but the official US Army number for captives on Bataan was seventy-five thousand soldiers (about twelve thousand American and sixty-five thousand Filipinos)—the greatest capitulation to an enemy force in US military history.[6]

General Homma had anticipated the upcoming POW situation on Bataan and assigned his staff to draft a grossly flawed plan, completed on March 23, for evacuating the prisoners. Homma approved the plan on the eve of the Good Friday offensive. The plan was simple and in its first phase concentrated on the collection of POWs and second on the transfer of the soldiers to camps. As Bataan Death March historian Stanley L. Falk noted, the 14th Imperial Army plan was based on a number of "gross miscalculations"—most notably an underestimation of the number of prisoners; furthermore, the Japanese did not realize the extremely poor physical condition of the defenders on Bataan. The plans made little or no arrangements

Captured Japanese picture of thousands of hungry and ill troops at Mariveles at the southern tip of Bataan on April 9, 1942. This is mile-marker one of the Bataan Death March. The Japanese had reported there were no trucks to move the wounded or prisoners, yet in the background are scores of vehicles that went unused. (Courtesy of the author's collection.)

for transportation or food and medical care for such a large group of haggard men—thus, more than 80 percent of the captives were expected to walk to the internment camps. The Japanese trained hard for forced marches and assumed the march of POWs would be based on their norm at twenty to twenty-five miles per day. The Geneva Convention Relative to the Treatment of Prisoners of War set the daily march distance at 20 kilometers, 12.5 miles—however, when General King (who never met General Homma in person) conducted talks with senior Japanese officers on the use of the Geneva Convention, the enemy had already concluded as early as February 1942 that they would not be bound by the covenants of the Convention. Homma, in orders to unit commanders, noted that captives "should" be treated with a "friendly spirit," telling one US officer, "Japan treats her prisoners well." The ensuing rush and pressure from Imperial headquarters in Tokyo to wrap up the Bataan campaign and attack and capture Corregidor did not bode well for the safe handling of the captured American and Filipinos. The stage for disaster and death on Bataan was thus set.[7]

Bataan Death March, April 9–21, 1942.

MUTATIS MUTANDIS

The disregard for the covenants of the Geneva Convention, the most complete international code of laws of war, was a calculated decision by the Japanese, who viewed American and European pressure to agree to the code as anti-Asian. Their disregard for human life and inhumane treatment of prisoners was based on their formal rejection of the Convention, which was first signed by forty-seven nations in July 1929. While Japan had token representatives at the conference that approved the Convention, the Japan Diet declined to formally ratify the agreement prior to December 1941. There were those in the Japanese civilian government that wanted to accept the Geneva covenants in principle, but the military authorities, immersed in the Bushido concept of kill or be killed, rejected any reference to the Convention. Thus in early 1942 the United States, Great Britain, and other powers sought assurances from Japan as to her attitude toward the Convention. The response from Shigenori Togo, then serving as foreign minister, was that Japan was not formally bound by the Geneva Convention and would apply the terms of the Convention *mutatis mutandis* toward prisoners of war; in essence, Japan would only respect and comply with those aspects of the Convention they considered in their best interest. For nearly two years, the Japanese were able to limit the International Red Cross, outside observers, and the media from gaining access to the atrocities rained down on tens of thousands of Allied prisoners. Only through the International Military War Crimes Tribunal for the Far East of 1946–47, along with the graphic stories by the returning POW veterans, was the full magnitude of the brutality documented.[8]

The capture of the large numbers of Bataan POWs was further complicated by the fact that they were very malnourished—having been on less than quarter rations for more than two months—and in very bad physical shape, riddled by tropical diseases and generally shell shocked from the intensive combat. Thus this combination of near nonstop combat and malnutrition, poor shelter, limited medical care, and disabling diseases increased the death rate during the war well beyond those killed in action. Homma, during his war trial in 1946, claimed he was preoccupied with the siege of Corregidor and did not realize the extent to which the POWs were famished or the harsh treatment during the march to the POW camps. A plan was considered to move the POWs by trucks to the camps, and a few prisoners were transported eight hours via truck. However, due to the fact that so many American vehicles had been sabotaged and there was a shortage of Japanese trucks, with a majority of supplies going to southern Bataan for the assault of Corregidor, there was no transportation for the POWs. By the end of the war, the death toll in the Pacific was staggering. One-third of all American POWs held by the Japanese were killed or died in captivity, compared to only 4 percent interned by the Germans and Italians. And percentage loss among Texas Aggie former students in the Pacific was a lofty 62 percent.[9]

TABLE 3.1. US/Allied Prisoners of War by Captor

	Total captured	*Deaths while POWs*	*Percentage deaths*
Germany/Italy	235,473	9,348	3.9
Japan—Total	132,134	35,756	27.1
Japan—Only Americans	21,580	7,107	32.9
Japan—Only Texas Aggies	79	49	62

Total Texas Aggies on Bataan and Corregidor number eighty-nine: one escaped from Corregidor by plane on May 4, 1942, and another Aggie from Mindanao on May 17, 1942; two were picked up by American submarine after their Hell Ship was sunk; and six were killed in action prior to final surrender, May 6–17, 1942; 79 were deemed POWs or MIAs.

I FELT LIKE KILLING HIM

For those captured on the Bataan Peninsula, the Bataan Death March would be, in fact, a series of "marches" that in their first phase lasted more than three weeks between April 9 and early May 1942. It took more than twenty-four hours for the final fighting to calm down by sunrise April 10, yet pockets of resistance held out for nearly a week across the battlefield. The exhausted defenders had little contact with their commanders—with all communications lines cut and most runners killed—as word of the surrender spread piecemeal among the troops. The Japanese aggressors were likewise slow to halt attacking, as they also awaited orders. It would take General King's representatives more than eight hours to establish firm contact with a Japanese commander, and even then, confusion continued. Destruction of American equipment and arms larger than .45 caliber started as early as April 7. Ammunition and fuel dumps lit up the smoky night across southern Bataan as every effort was made to lay waste to critical supplies. And an ominous sign of the cease-fire was an enormous late-night earthquake that rumbled the length of Bataan.[10]

The Americans and Filipinos were ill prepared to surrender: sick and battle weary, most without food for four days, with low water supplies and only the ragged uniforms they wore. The Japanese were even less prepared, having expected the Filipino-Americans to fight until the end of April. The rush of combat spilled over as the Japanese troops continued to kill and bayonet prisoners at random. One soldier recalled, "Grinning guards plunged bloody bayonets into lifeless or dying men again and again. Some they dragged off, and only agonized screams came back to their helpless comrades." Officers in particular were tied to trees, used for bayonet practice, and left hanging for days. Soldiers found with war booty, such as Japanese documents or Japanese pistols, Japanese currency, or items made in Japan, were shot on the spot. Captain Robley Evans '40, captured near Mariveles with his unit of Philippine Scouts, confirmed that all personal belongings—watches, rings, gold-framed glasses, cigarettes, gold teeth, rings, canteens, and any items of value—were stripped from the POWs, along with all hats and helmets. During the march, Texas Aggie **Lt. Urban C. Hopmann '39** buried his ring where he slept each night to protect it and **T.Sgt. John J. Moseley '39** of Quanah hid his Aggie ring in the sole of his shoe to keep it safe—he was lucky, as many prisoners were left barefoot.[11]

Lt. Robley D. Evans '40, 45th Infantry Regiment, prior to surrender at Mariveles, as a commander of a mounted recon unit and later as a POW in Japan. (Courtesy of the Robley Evans family collection.)

Many of the defenders in the far south tried to obtain boats or swim to Corregidor. Swift currents and sharks limited this route of escape. A few hundred escaped into the jungle, yet within days were found or turned themselves in. For example, Captain Cary Abney '34 "took to the hills" and was among those captured at Orion. With no food or shelter, there was no place to run to or hide. Furthermore, due primarily to the withdrawing tactics and poor roads, there was no unit cohesion as POWs were mixed among service branches. An effort was made to separate the officers, yet most below colonel were left to march and suffer with their men. Among the thousands that were forced into the Bataan Death March were some fifty-seven Texas Aggies from combat units scattered across the peninsula.[12]

Two Texas Aggies, **Lt. Roy H. Davidson '40** of El Paso, formerly a supply officer with the 19th Bombardment Group, and **Lt. Edgar B. Burgess '38** from Fort Worth and also in the 19th BGp. (both armed with old Enfield rifles after the fall of Clark Field to fight with an

Army line infantry unit), escaped during the first hours of the surrender by following a stream to the sea coast and commandeering an outrigger canoe. Once in the canoe, they paddled south, taking a big risk to evade the Japanese blockade by night at the entrance to Manila Bay. However, their escape was foiled the next day by a Japanese observation plane that dispatched a corvette to pick them up at gunpoint. Davidson recalled, "They ordered us on board at gunpoint, then four or five Japanese sailors held us down and tied our hands and feet. The Japanese sailors just made signs of slitting our throats and throwing us overboard—probably just to see our reaction." Davidson and Burgess were among the lucky few to avoid the Death March to Camp O' Donnell as they were dropped off in Manila and marched a short distance to the old Spanish Bilibid Prison. Within weeks, both Aggies were moved to Cabanatuan Prison.[13]

Captain John Coleman '27 and friend Captain Walter Dorman of the 19th Bomb Group were ordered near midnight on April 8 to attempt to get to Cabcaben on the coast (behind enemy lines) and cross to Corregidor to report the status of their position and their reduced strength to General Wainwright. Having fought for three days straight, wounded, and with a high fever from malaria, Coleman and Dorman headed southeast to avoid Japanese patrols. Before they could get to Cabcaben, the docks had been captured. They turned down the beach, looking for another way to cross the bay. Swimming was out of the question. Dorman went for help and Coleman never saw him again. Unable to find a boat, Coleman hid in tall grass for two days until he was surrounded and forced to surrender on April 11 and moved into a POW holding area. His first encounter with the enemy set the tone for the next few years in prison: "A ragged slouchy [Japanese] soldier dragging alongside the formation, scavenging and pointed at my canteen as if asking for a drink of water. I had to give him my canteen. He unscrewed the cap and smelled of the water. He turned up his nose, then held my canteen upside down and poured out every drop of water. The he threw it down at my feet in dirt. I felt like killing him."[14]

In the confusion, **Captain Paul R. Gregory '40**, a civil engineer from Cristobal, Panama, where his family worked as missionaries, escaped during the march to the POW camp with three fellow officers assigned to the 14th Engineers. They traveled south through the jungle and evaded the enemy for more than three weeks when Gregory became ill with a high fever. Although he was assisted by a local Philippine doctor, he died of double pneumonia on May 13, 1942, and was buried by his comrades at Batangas.[15]

HOSPITAL NO. 1 AND NO. 2

Lack of medical support was a tremendous problem throughout the Bataan campaign. The shortage of supplies along with the overwhelming number of sick and wounded were staggering. There were two primary large field hospitals, built to accommodate a thousand patients, and a number of small medical forward aid stations that quickly evaporated or were overrun by the enemy. Combined patient population in Hospital No. 1 at Little Baguio and Hospital No. 2 near Cabcaben grew from ten thousand in late March to more than twenty thousand patients by April 8. Conditions under treatment ranged from cerebral malaria to massive combat wounds. By late April 10, Hospital No. 1 was surrounded by sixteen Japanese tanks, and once the Japanese confirmed that their forty-two wounded POWs had been treated well, they allowed hospital operations to continue under American medical corps supervision. At Hospital No. 2, the Japanese were much more harsh and deadly, as patients were killed and there were a number of rapes. An artillery battery of twenty-three pieces surrounded the hospital, all aimed at Corregidor in hopes that the Americans would not fire on their own hospital. After a few days, guns on the Rock began to respond with most of the shells "overs" and "shorts," yet there were several casualties from shell fragments that sprayed the hospital.[16]

The Japanese were consistently unpredictable. While Hospital No. 1 was allowed to function, at Hospital No. 2, doctors and corpsmen were abruptly ordered out. All water, food, and medical supplies were looted. The wounded were driven out of the ward at bayonet point, many postoperative cases with unfinished amputations and gaping superficial wounds, as well as hundreds suffering malnutrition and

Prisoners were marched day and night with brief intervals of rest. Little or no water, food, or medical care was provided by the enemy. There was no Japanese recognition of the Geneva Convention with regard to treatment of prisoners. Pictured in this captured Japanese photo are POWs carrying the wounded in improvised litters. (Courtesy of the author's collection.)

dysentery. There was no transport. Thrown into the heat of the Death March, weeks later, scores of patients—who either died or were killed by the Japanese—lay along the East Road. Some patients were cared for at Hospital No. 1 until May 26, 1942, when the few remaining cases and doctors were transported to Bilibid Prison in Manila. They were confined for a week on a concrete slab with little water and then transferred to Cabanatuan POW camp.[17]

Coleman and thousands of other defenders were collected in the area from Mariveles to Little Baguio on the East Coast Highway. On April 11, prisoners remained in southern Bataan as a human artillery shield against incoming fire from the Rock—despite the fact that it is a gross breach of international law to hold POWs in a combat zone. Yet for two days the POWs were placed in harm's way to prevent the guns of Corregidor from firing on the Japanese troops moving equipment in place to shell the Rock. As soon as they were to march out, the Japanese artillery started a near nonstop pounding of Corregidor. Spotters on Corregidor had located the prisoners and fired over the POWs and guards, gradually getting closer to the enemy artillery. Coleman recalls that as incoming shells began to hit all around the POWs, he warned the lone guard that spoke a little English, "We had better hit the dirt!," with the guard responding, "Hell no! If you didn't want to die, why did you join the army?"[18]

Many of the Japanese soldiers and officers on guard duty who force marched the POWs to the camps were newly arrived troops from the Shanghai and Singapore divisions. They had firsthand knowledge and experience with the harsh cold-blooded treatment given first to the Chinese soldiers and civilians and then the British and Australian POWs. On April 12, one group of prisoners, under the informal command of the former commanding general of the 31st Filipino Division, the feisty Brigadier General Clifford "Blinky" Bluemel, age fifty-six (not all general rank officers were removed from the march), were lined up in columns of fours with the wounded and sick near the front of the column to slow the pace. The beating and torture of the men as they walked started almost at once. The guards, who spoke no English, bayoneted at every opportunity, wanting them to speed up and move faster, yelling, "Speedo! Speedo!" Coleman recalls them "shouting as though they were on a cattle drive, headed for the cruel slaughter pens."[19]

The dusty, uneven, shell-potted roads, temperatures exceeding one hundred degrees, no water, and constant exposure to the blistering sun began to take a toll. When asking permission to get water, POWs were beaten, although some Japanese guards allowed the troops to drink the infested water from green, scum-covered carabao (water buffalo) wallows—which soon triggered diarrhea, dehydration, and for some, death. Captain Robley Evans '40 noted that during the forced march to POW camp, when many POWs "became exhausted and fell out, they were bayoneted or shot on the spot." The first leg of the forced march up the East Coast Road was a fifty-five-mile stretch from Mariveles to San Fernando en route to the prison camp at Camp O'Donnell, a few miles north of Clark Field. John Coleman recalls, "I looked back on the column at the men's faces. They were glassy eyed, expressionless, and stunned looking. They had gone unshaved for days, they were dusty, and their cloths were caked from salty perspiration and dirt." The march was in its fourth day and the prisoners had yet received no food.[20]

Filipino and American troops gathered from the west coast of Bataan began to fill the roads as the columns of fours numbering about three hundred for each group slowly headed north. Among those who marched to the first checkpoint at Cabcaben in hopes of food and water was **Colonel Edwin E. Aldridge '16**—at age forty-three, he was the chief of staff for Brigadier General Luther Stevens, commander of the 1st Philippine Corps, and the oldest Texas Aggie captured on Bataan. Aldridge arrived at the gathering point with General Stevens in his staff car and was abruptly yanked from the car and kicked in the face. Reaching to get his possessions, he was shoved to the rear of the group. Chaos reigned, and with each mile, the guards were more confused and brutal. Aldridge and Stevens, along with twenty other officers, were tied together two by two and ordered to sit on the ground. After the tied officers were beaten, they were forced to march. Passing Limay without a rest stop or water, the mass of the first POWs reached Balanga. Here they received their first meal, a handful of rice and salt, and a cup of water.[21]

Captain Coleman was soon joined on the march from Mariveles by fellow airmen from Clark and Nichols Field who had been reassigned to infantry and coast watching duties after their planes were destroyed on December 8 and 9. Of these eighty-three pilots of the 24th Pursuit Group, only thirty-four returned home. Seventeen died in POW camps, and thirty-two perished on Japanese Hell Ships. Texas Aggie aviators on the march included **Lt. Howard P. Hardegree '39**, 3rd Squadron, **Lt. Willis Powell Culp III '38**, 17th Squadron, as well as **Charles E. Gaskell '41** and **James M. Henry '39**, both in the 34th Squadron. Only Lt. Culp returned home; the other three Aggies, after being transferred to various camps, were listed as lost at sea and MIA—all lost in the sinking of infamous Hell Ships.[22]

Following the attack on Clark Field, only three of the twenty-two B-17s of the 19th Bombardment Group had survived the first wave of Japanese bombing. Those planes that survived were flown to Australia. As with the 24th PG, the pilots and crews left behind were converted to infantry and fought gallantly on Bataan. The Texas Aggies had seven airmen in the 19th BG captured and marched northward to Camps O'Donnell and Cabanatuan: **Captain Jack W. Kelley '29**, **Lt. Roy H. Davidson Jr. '40**, **Lt. Roy D. Russell '42**, **Lt. Edgar B. Burgess '38**, **Lt. James B. Whitley '38**, **Captain George C. Brundrett '33**, and **Lt. Maxey C. Chenault '37**.[23]

GO AHEAD AND SHOOT

At points along the route, some men were stripped and ordered to stand naked for the "sun treatment." April, with temperatures exceeding one hundred degrees, was the hottest and driest month in the Philippines before the arrival of the monsoon season. Filthy and suffering malnutrition, more than half the men had dysentery and the balance suffered from malaria. Ordered to march again, the POWs stumbled along the roadside ditches dotted with the beheaded bodies and severed heads of POWs in the dirt, swollen to monstrous size in the high heat and humidity and turned a blackish hue. Crows tore apart the bodies as swarms of green blow flies and maggots covered the grim corpse remnants. Some of those who fell were beaten with bamboo clubs until their heads were pulp and then bayoneted on the spot. Skulking along, Japanese "buzzard squads," as they were known, trailed the march procession eager to shoot or bayonet the fallen.[24]

Resting on the roadside nearly cost **Captain Joseph Revak '30** of Beaumont his life. As he was sitting with a group of Filipinos and Americans, guards ordered the group to get up—no rest. The Filipino sitting next to Revak tried and could not get up, whereupon a Japanese guard pulled a pistol and, to Revak's horror, shot the soldier dead. A guard turned his rifle on Revak, who was also having difficulty rising. The exhausted Aggie looked him in the eyes, "Go ahead and shoot." Dodging sure death, he struggled to his feet and rejoined the march.

Revak survived the ordeal, returning to Texas and retiring as a colonel in the army.[25]

Bodies of decapitated and bayoneted soldiers were often mangled in the center of the dusty road. Both the corpses of these troops and men lying half-dead along the edge of the roadside were run over by trucks and tanks heading south for Corregidor and flattened beyond recognition. Captain Coleman soon realized that the "mud" he thought he had slipped and walked on was in fact human flesh. This brutal process would continue for weeks. The smell of the dead is something the survivors carry in their nostrils to this day.[26]

BALANGA

The first major stop along the march was on the East Coast Highway at the small village of Balanga. General King and his immediate staff were the first to arrive in the village and were once again subjected to interrogation and propaganda pictures taken by both military and civilian photographers. The Japanese were very interested in the extensive underground facilities at Malinta Tunnel and pressed King to disclose the assumed location of the secret underground tunnel from Bataan to Corregidor. The general could hardly keep from laughing—there was no such tunnel! Looting of the POWs continued as new groups of guards stripped the insignia of rank from the officers and demanded money, watches, razors, and rings. More high-ranking American and Filipino officers were collected at Balanga, and the other POWs did not arrive until the evening of April 12. The rush to move prisoners northward was confused and disorganized. As disorderly groups of between one to two hundred men stumbled into the town, the numbers grew to more than ten thousand POWs in a few hours. Guard shifts were often changed every three miles; thus there was little halt in the often frenzied prodding by the Japanese to keep up the pace of the march. Some POWs were buried alive in the ditches along the road as their comrades were ordered to shovel in the dirt at bayonet point. And many who stopped to relieve themselves were shot on the spot.[27]

En route to Lubao, due to his wounds and lack of water, Captain Coleman '27 became weaker and drifted to the rear of the column. Nearing the last leg into town, he blacked out from fever and was dragged into the stopping place by two captains, one of which was Cary Abney '34, a senior cadet in an infantry company of the Corps of Cadets years after Coleman attended Texas A&M. Abney filled Coleman's canteen and bathed his face to cool him off. The officers watched him through the night as he improved slightly. By morning, Abney, who most probably saved his life, whispered to Coleman, "If you can't make the march past one o'clock, you had better not start because they are not leaving anyone alive on the road." Coleman was able to blend in a day longer to rest. Arriving a few days after Abney at Camp O'Donnell, the young officer once again helped Coleman get settled and regain some strength. Once he was better, Coleman was assigned as executive officer of the camp's ad hoc Air Corps Regiment.[28]

Prisoners were herded into open treeless fields around the village. General Homma was headquartered a few hundred yards off the main highway but later claimed during the postwar crimes tribunal that he was occupied with the offensive on the Rock and neither saw nor heard of any of the cruel and harsh conditions. There was little water and only a third of the POWs received a cup of *lugao*, a watery, bug-infested rice gruel. The edgy guards harassed the POWs during the night. There were no latrines and the filth piled up as new groups arrived in the quagmire holding area. By morning, dozens of bodies of those men who died overnight littered the ground—grotesque and bloated shapes that quickly blackened in the heat. There was no attempt to bury them. At intervals, prisoners were ordered to their feet and marched on to Orani, eleven miles north, and then to Lubao, an additional sixteen miles. Once on the road, passing Japanese trucks headed south played a cruel sport of trying to hit the POWs with bamboo poles as the trucks sped by. Many of the men were knocked senseless into the oncoming traffic and killed. There were a few trucks for the badly wounded, but most walked or died on the spot.[29]

At Lubao, a town of about forty thousand, the Filipino residents did all they could to help the POWs but risked the wrath of the Japanese if

General Masaharu Homma, commander of the Japanese 14th Imperial Army, center, at Manila Hotel shortly after the fall of Bataan. While the general's headquarters was less than a mile from the route of the Bataan Death March, he claimed no knowledge of the brutal treatment of American and Filipino troops marched to the POW camps in Luzon. (Courtesy of the author's collection.)

they were caught giving aid. The public spectacle of the sick and hungry American and Filipino prisoners shocked the local villagers. While many of the Filipino soldiers were able to escape at Lubao by fading into the local population and being hidden by sympatric supporters, the Americans were hard to hide even in the crowded streets and huts. By nightfall, the POWs were packed into an old rice mill with no ventilation or water, in suffocating heat, which soared to over one hundred degrees. This proved too much for many of the sick POWs, and again by morning the floor of the mill was covered with the dead. Soon the march continued to the railhead at San Fernando where the troops were packed into small-gauge World War I vintage wooden railcars for the final leg of the Death March to Camp O' Donnell. The horror and brutality had only seemed to begin as between 100 and 120 men were jammed, standing shoulder to shoulder, into the seven-foot-high, eight-foot-wide, and thirty-three-foot-long narrow-gauge wooden boxcars, with no air, no ventilation, no water. The smell inside the steamy boxcars as men vomited and could not control their diarrhea was unbearable. Many fainted and many died of suffocation during the journey that took up to three or four hours. Once the doors were opened, Captain Coleman reflected, "We got off the train at Capas and the guards made us leave the dead in the boxcars. From here we made an eight-mile hike to Camp O'Donnell. I had lost a lot of weight. This was April 21, 1942. It was Texas Independence Day."[30]

The horrors of the last few miles of the march to the camp continued as stragglers were repeatedly beaten or killed in cold blood. Bodies of those killed or who died of exhaustion and wounds littered the East Coast Highway every few feet, from the tip of Bataan to the front gates of Camp O'Donnell. During the deadly march, **Lt. James B. Whitley '38** was killed, his body never recovered and officially listed as MIA by the US Army on January 1, 1946. And the brutality of the Japanese continued behind the barbwire.[31]

Numbers are hard to confirm, but the best estimates are that some seventy-eight thousand men started the Death March in southern Bataan and only forty-four thousand reached Camp O'Donnell. No one knows exactly how many men died. Many of the Filipinos escaped into the countryside, along with a few dozen Americans, yet the best count indicates that more than nine thousand died during the Death March, including some six to seven hundred Americans. And upon arriving at the camps, the brutality and killing continued by the thousands.[32]

In this captured Japanese photo, prisoners at bayonet point are herded into groups for a brief rest. Anything of value was stripped from the POWs, including hats, watches, rings, and glasses. (Courtesy of the author's collection.)

HEARTBROKEN

There was a near complete news blackout after the surrender. Family and friends back in Texas and across America were given no updates and no encouragement about the fate of the sons, fathers, and husbands. Families across the nation contacted their elected representatives in Washington and military commanders at local bases but were given no hope or information. In College Station, the front page of the May 1942 *Texas Aggie* newspaper, the primary statewide publication with updates on Texas A&M former cadets, simply noted, "No Philippines News." It would be months before America learned of the horrors of Bataan and the POW camps.[33]

POWs, in this captured Japanese photo, with hands tied behind them on the Bataan Death March. Nearly a thousand American troops died on the march or immediately after arriving at Camp O'Donnell on Luzon. (Courtesy of the author's collection.)

The angst of the families awaiting news from the unaccounted for POWs boiled over, first into a local statewide campaign by Aggie families and the Association of Former Students in College Station and then growing into a near national scandal for the inadequate way the War Department handled information and relations with the families. "No report" was not an acceptable excuse by the government, who many times deflected responsibility by referring questions to the International Red Cross. After more than fourteen months with no confirmed information and concerned with the delays and misinformation from the War Department, Mrs. George Moore launched a campaign to get information, writing to close family friend, Walter W. Evans in Fort Worth, father of Bataan POW and Texas Aggie

Lt. Robley D. Evans '40. Evans, a former employee of the college extension service, was older brother to Claude Maxey Evans '08—General Moore's roommate in college—the pair known famously on campus as "Maude and Claude." The following letter from Mrs. Moore to Walter Evans describes the first letter she received from her husband since the fall of the Rock on May 6, 1942:

Tuesday July 27th [1943]

Dear Mr. [Walter W.] Evans:

I was on my way to the Red Cross this morning to try and get from them a few facts about the rules for sending cables [telegrams] etc., when your letter was handed me. I know it was useless to try to accomplish anything through the Red Cross for many of us have made repeated trips and never yet any accurate information. In June 42 a friend wrote me that I could send letters to George through Geneva. That was before his name was on a prisoner list. I visited the Red Cross head here and was told that I could not do it. And when I was notified that George was a prisoner I was told to address the letter via New York.

My friend sent hers [letter] to her husband Col. Cottrell anyway and it reached her husband. George spoke of it in a short wave Tokyo message in January and in his letter which came yesterday morning. I am heartbroken that I did not send my letters to Geneva the past months and think it is cruel that everything has been managed in such a hopeless manner.

George's letter was written November 16th [1942] and came thru Geneva: It is as follows;

"This is the first letter I have been able to write you since May 3rd [1942]. I hope you got that one and that this one reaches you also. I received your radio [telegram] the first of May which assured me that you were well at the time so that I entered my period of captivity in a more tranquil frame of mind than I would have otherwise. On October 31 a letter arrived here from Adelaide in which she stated that she had received a long interesting letter from you the day before and that you and Anne were well. This was good news for me for although I have no doubt you have written, no letter from you has reached me

to date. I am of course starved for word from you and it is my daily prayer that you are both safe and well and that we will soon be reunited for many more happy years together. Sorry we had to miss a celebration of this November 5th and sincerely hope we can celebrate the next one in a big way.

Last week through courtesy Domei I sent a message to be broadcast and another to reach you thru news channels. Hope one or both got through. I have no doubt you listen to the Japanese broadcasts. I have been at several different Prisoner of War camps since I was taken from Corregidor May 23. I hope I am located now for the duration of my captivity. This camp is in a beautiful spot and the climate is fine. We are allowed to make gardens and some plots are now beginning to take shape. We are furnished newspapers, printed in English, from time to time [to] keep up with news from that viewpoint. We have religious services each Sunday have a good choir helped considerably by one officer who plays the violin. There are lots of things I would like to write about, of course, but naturally rules of censorship forbid.

You have no doubt received instructions about addressing letters through the Red Cross. When permitted to send packages, which will no doubt be limited as to weight, send articles in the following order: vitamin tablets, concentrated foods such as bouillon cubes peanuts candies, in tins; ointment, toilet soap, shaving cream, undershirts with half arm sleeves size forty, four shorts size thirty, six light wool sox, one sweat shirt, one army field jacket or letter zipper jacket. I hope the war will be over before you get around to the winter clothing but if not I will be able to use them as my present stock will be getting low by that time.

One item of business. I don't know what the Texas laws are covering joint accounts being tied up in case anything should happen to one of the parties. Consult Travis Bryan as it might be better if you open a separate account for you and Anne and transfer funds to that account. Do not worry about me or the situation in general. As you know I have a strong constitution and a temperament which permits me to adapt myself to difficult situations and I am cashing in on them now. I know you and Anne have plenty of courage and will meet conditions as they arise with your chins up.

All my love, etc."

I can read between the lines of the letter and I know they have had a bad time of it and of course this was written eight months ago. I don't know where to turn now in trying to appeal to someone to get this thing out in the open. It is maddening to go on this way. It is my opinion that the Red Cross, State Dept. and War Dept. are just hoping that the others are doing the job and that no one is taking the responsibility.

There is a large group of wives here who are organized and have tried ceaselessly to bring the matter to someone's attention who can really do something about it. There is a large organized group of the families of civilian internees in Manila and the Far East who get out a pamphlet every month with what news they can gather. It is sent out from New York and you may have received some of their literature. All of us have the same thought, just to get some word to them. It must be next to impossible for our men to keep up their wonderful courage when no word of cheer ever reaches them.

I was glad to get your letter. If I get more news of any kind I will let you know.

Lucille G. Moore

IMPOSSIBLE TO RATIONALIZE

It is difficult to fully understand and grasp the magnitude of the isolation and premeditated brutality that was inflicted on the American and Filipinos prisoners following the surrender of Bataan on April 9. Mail and packages were either held or destroyed. As with General Moore's letter, some letters and usually only brief notes on three-by-five cards were allowed to be delivered. Details and evidence have been documented both in the proceedings of the postwar crimes trials and more important in the memory and stories brought home by those who survived the ordeal. Fully one-third of all American prisoners held by the Japanese died in captivity—and some 62 percent of Texas Aggie officers died while in Japanese captivity—far exceeding the low losses of POWs in the European Theater. While there can be no plausible excuse, one author has concluded:

> The countless acts of bloodlust and deliberate savagery committed by the Japanese during and after the Death March are impossible to

> rationalize, much less justify. Yet several strong underlying factors apparently served as triggers for these acts and may help to clarify why they occurred with such sickening regularity.
>
> Hatred for Americans and other Westerners had been deeply instilled in the Japanese soldiers as part of their military indoctrination; and their fury toward Bataan's defenders, in particular, had been whipped to fever pitch by the severe losses they'd suffered during the three months of fierce combat. Nowhere else in Asia or the Pacific had the Japanese Army encountered such tenacious resistance or incurred such heavy casualties. A combination of resentment for those who had killed friends and comrades, coupled with propaganda, and racism also influenced the Japanese behavior—driven and impacted strongly by the warrior's code of Bushido.[34]

And thus, prior to the capture of General Moore and his forces, the final phase of the defense of the Philippine Islands would be the desperate final twenty-seven-day Battle of the Rock—Corregidor.

★ CHAPTER 4 ★

THE ROCK

Although the account nowadays says that they—the Texas Aggies—gathered on April 21st [1942 on Corregidor], it was impossible to congregate because they could not be spared from their [defensive] position. So, we had a roll call, and *a Muster is a roll call.*

Colonel Tom Dooley '35
1978 Texas Aggie Campus Muster

Corregidor needs no comment from me. It has sounded its own story at the mouth of its guns. It has scrolled its own epitaph on enemy tablets. But through the bloody haze of its last reverberating shot, I shall always seem to see a vision of grim, gaunt, ghostly men, unafraid.

General of the Army Douglas MacArthur

The peaceful windswept Island of Corregidor, a natural fortress at the entrance of Manila Bay, is among the most ingenious fortifications in the annals of military history. And like the Maginot Line, Verdun, and other fixed position, highly fortified structures, the power of this fortress has since been lost to the fate of new advanced technology—most notably airpower—relegating its very strengths into crippling weakness. Notwithstanding, for centuries Corregidor commanded

The Island of Corregidor, January 1942, with Bataan in the distance. On the left is "Bottomside" and dock leading to the Malinta Tunnel; at the top of the picture is the "tail" of the island and location of the small McKinley Airfield. (Courtesy of the author's collection.)

the access into one of the most important seaports in all of Asia at Manila.

The Rock had a long history as a defensive trade isle long before the American occupation in 1898 following the Spanish-American War. As a key defensive position at the entrance of Manila Bay, it became critical to the ornate Manila-Acapulco Galleon "silver and silk" trade once the capital of the region was located in Manila in 1571. The annual silver fleets from Mexico and Peru delivered their cargos in exchange for silk, spices, cotton, and wax as well as other "curiosities" of the orient. Thus the galleon trade subsidized the fledging Philippine government and local trade as well as generated revenue to build fortifications and signal towers erected on Corregidor to ensure the security of the local maritime fleet. Except for storms and occasional raids by the Moro pirate activity, the Rock was the beacon of stability for inbound trades from 1565 through 1898.[1]

The four-square-mile island gained more attention in the 1650s when docks were built along with housing and a naval convalescent hospital. Following the establishment of a permanent lighthouse in

1875, with a beam range of thirty-three miles, the Spanish set up port-of-entry offices to verify shipping import documentation as well as a place where the local magistrate, or "corregidor," corrected and approved shipping visas—hence the name Corregidor. The harbor defense communicated by a system of semaphore signals that alerted forts in and around the bay. By the time of the Spanish-American War, the Castilians had added three large rifled, muzzle cannons, manufactured in Britain and able to fire hull-piercing projectiles more than a mile. American entry into the Philippines began in late April 1898, when marines of Admiral George Dewey's Asiatic Squadron landed and captured both Corregidor and Manila without the loss of a single sailor. What started as "a splendid little war" over Cuba resulted in the Treaty of Paris on December 10, 1898, with the Philippines Islands formally ceded by Spain to the United States.[2]

The roots of decades of ill feeling and empire building in the western Pacific region thus date first from the American occupation of the Philippines and second from the growing militarization in Japan at the

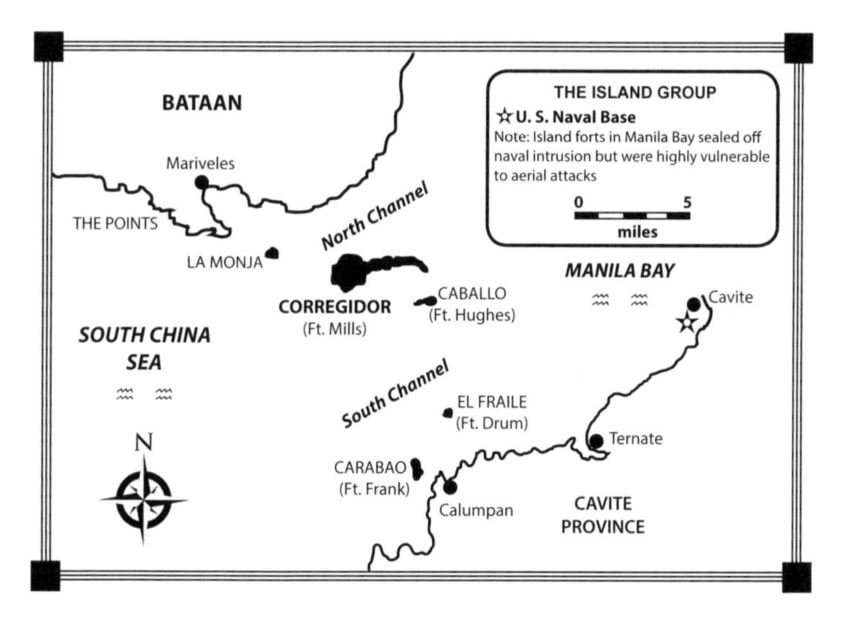

Corregidor and defensive islands in Manila Bay.

turn of the nineteenth century, who deemed over time it was in their area of interest to control all aspects of the region in their sphere of influence. Emboldened by the late nineteenth-century strategic writings of Alfred T. Mahan on the global role of sea power and fresh from the spectacular naval victory over the Russians in their defeat of the Czar's navy in the Straits of Tsushima in May 1905, the struggle for power in the western Pacific began. The American response included Teddy Roosevelt's dispatch of the US naval fleet on a round-the-world cruise, lasting from December 1907 to early 1909. However, most Americans, including Roosevelt, failed to perceive the growing threat of Japan; yet there were published concerns of Japan's eventual intentions, as is noted in this pre–World War I analysis in February 1914:

> The general feeling in Washington is that if we ever do have trouble with Japan, it will come to us not via any other country, but on straight ocean paths which run from Japanese navy yards to our possessions and to our western coast line. An enemy bent on taking the Philippines, however, probably would try to approach along a path leading by Corregidor. The attack would be by troops landed from transports at another part of the island and Manila would fall as the result of an overland attack.[3]

After decades of planning, the Japanese imperial planners concerned with their regional interest—which included securing vital raw materials and oil, the occupation of all key seaports, and the exclusion of all American and European influence—set a course that resulted ultimately in the attack on Pearl Harbor and Manila on December 7–8, 1942, and the lightning attack across the Pacific to control all in their reach.

In 1941–42, the pollywog-shaped rock isle would soon become the final lynch pin for the defense of Manila and the Philippine archipelago. The highest elevation of the near solid rock is 640 feet. The US Army and Navy during the 1920s embarked on an extensive plan for the total fortification of Corregidor, as well as for arming outlying islands to form a barrier to seaborne attacks. In excess of $50,000,000 was spent on defensive works and a thirteen-mile electric railroad system on the Rock to connect "Bottomside" near the arrival dock in the little village of San Fernando, "Middleside" at the mouth of Malinta Tunnel, and "Topside," the upper level occupied by the barracks and artillery batteries. Supporting the defense of Manila Bay were the fixed-place "concrete battleship" style islands of Caballo (Fort Hughes), Fraile (Fort Drum), and Carabao (Fort Frank). The eight long-range fourteen-inch guns (only on the three small-island fortress) and twenty-two twelve-inch mortars and batteries of guns bunkered on the network of the four islands cast a twenty-six mile protective curtain and striking distance around Manila Bay and naval facilities. In total there were 50 batteries with a total of 105 guns. Designed primarily to withstand attack from the sea, the majority of the elaborate defense system and "impregnable" fortress in the bay was completed in 1914—causing many to coin the sobriquet, "Gibraltar of the East."[4]

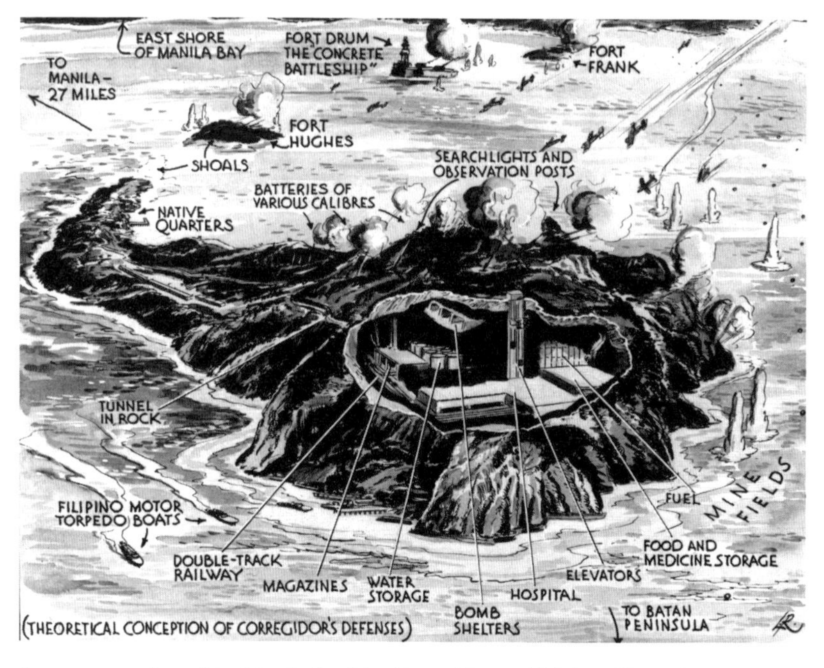

Artist conception of the labyrinth of the Corregidor and Malinta Tunnel complex and surrounding waters. (Courtesy of the author's collection.)

The Malinta Tunnel on Corregidor was a complex underground operations center for the headquarters of the Harbor Defense commanded by General George Moore. The project was started in the early 1920s and completed in the late 1930s. The underground fortress became the last command post for both Generals MacArthur and Wainwright following the fall of Bataan in April 1942. MacArthur was evacuated to Australia, leaving Wainwright in command to surrender the Rock on May 6, 1942. This diagram appears at the entrance of the tunnel. (Courtesy of the author's collection.)

Notwithstanding this massive investment in the defense of Manila Bay, concerns on the rise of Imperial Japan and the ability of the forces in the Philippines to address any threat were known as early as 1905.

LT. DOUGLAS MACARTHUR

Major General Douglas MacArthur was the first overall US commander and military governor of the Philippines in 1900 and was joined by his newly minted West Point son, Douglas, in the fall of 1903 for his first duty assignment in the 3rd Engineering Battalion on Luzon. In addition to the young lieutenant's exposure to the defenses

TABLE 4.1. Armament on Corregidor

Number of batteries	*Caliber*	*Number of guns*
	Seacoast artillery	
2	12-inch mortars	10
5	12-inch guns	8
1	10-inch gun	2
1	8-inch gun	2
2	6-inch guns	5
8	155mm guns	19
4	3-inch guns	10
Total: 23	—	Total: 56
	Antiaircraft artillery	
2	Sperry 60-inch	10
7	3-inch gun	28
4	.50-caliber	48
Total: 13	—	Total: 86

Source: Moore, Harbor Defense Report of Operations.

of Corregidor, he was dispatched to survey the downward operations on the Bataan Peninsula.

In addition to young Doug MacArthur (who had additional tours in the Philippines, 1922–25 and 1929–30), there would follow a list of future commanders and officers that were stationed on the Rock and in the Philippines—some multiple times during the three decades prior to Pearl Harbor. General George Moore '08, who assumed overall command of the Manila Harbor defenses and Subic Bay in 1940, had a total of four military tours at Corregidor. Others with tours of duty and substantial early knowledge on the defensive structure of the Philippine Islands included future general officers Edward P. King, 1915–17; Henry "Hap" Arnold, 1913–14; and George C. Marshall, 1902–3 and

1913–1916, all of whom would soon be questioned about the lack of preparedness during the years before and during the early days of the outbreak of the war.[5]

Lt. MacArthur, after recovery from a bout of malaria contracted in the Bataan jungle, was ordered by the War Department in the fall of 1905 to join his father, reassigned as military attaché in Tokyo as his aide-de-camp and an official observer of the Russo-Japanese War. He was to accompany the general and his staff for a tour and inspection of the Orient. Starting and ending in Tokyo, the group toured military bases, shipping facilities, and industries in Japan, China, Burma, Malaya, Singapore, Ceylon, India, Thailand, and Saigon. The extensive trip left a marked impression on both father and son. The ambition of the Japanese coupled with their aggressive militarization at this early date was evident. The general reported that Nippon's growing imperialist ambitions posed a potential "problem for the Pacific." In what would be a premonition of the future course of events in Asia, he warned the secretary of war in 1906 that the Philippines needed stronger defenses "to prevent the archipelago's 'strategic position from being a liability rather than an asset to the United States.'"[6]

These firsthand observations would be buried in the War Department files, even as the US Army War College began an extensive planning cycle to develop an Army plan and strategy, War Plan Orange-3, in the event the old general's observations became reality. As one observer noted, only time would dictate a rush to reality:

> The [War] Orange Plan assumed the Philippines to be the principal target for the Japanese. The grand strategy, as simple as it was naive and more an article of faith than a cogent plan of war, envisaged that Japan would send its fleet against Lingayen Gulf, the most obvious bay for an amphibious invasion of Luzon and a descent on Manila. Thence the battleships of the U.S. Pacific Fleet would sally forth from their "sanctuary" at Pearl Harbor to succor the Philippines. In the unlikely event that the fleet should be delayed, then the garrison made up of American and Philippine Scouts would retreat into the mountain fastness of

> Bataan and onto the island forts until the Navy won through. America, after all, was an optimistic nation that had never known defeat.[7]

No one in authority in 1941 in Washington or in Army-Navy planning remotely envisioned Pearl Harbor as being even threatened; the harbor at Manila was determined to be the key to American interest in the Far East. And, more important, even if Manila was attacked first by the Japanese, the dark, closely held secret was that no one believed a rescue would be possible. The cold facts are that the deep cuts in the defense budget, coupled with Japan's increased naval and military preparedness, led the War Department planners, as early as the mid-1930s, to question and doubt whether the Philippines could be defended or quickly relieved in the event of attack. In the pre–Pearl Harbor days, both FDR and General Marshall repeatedly supported the defense of the Philippines—with General MacArthur recalling in early December 1941 that one evening, as he returned from the cinema in Quipa after a screening of *They Died With Their Boots On*, he received a top-secret radio cable from the War Department "that help was on the way."[8]

At the minimum it would take a fully complimented naval force at least two years to assemble, train, and travel to the South China Sea, and this would only be possible if there was no secondary threat from Europe. Manila was five thousand miles from Honolulu and more than seven thousand miles from San Francisco—it took three full days for the Pan American China Clipper to fly from California to Manila. Any doubt of priorities was settled at the top secret June 1941 high-level US-British joint military conference, which adjourned with only ONE plan—"the Atlantic and European area is considered to be the decisive theatre." Thus Europe was the first and only priority. Any and all responses to hostile threat or action in the Far East against the United States and its allies would be defensive in nature only, with what was available to those units in the theater and with no resupply or support. The American public as well as American troops in Manila knew nothing of this "abandonment" strategy, since they and the defenders on Bataan and Corregidor were repeatedly told, even in the darkest hours, that help was on the way.[9]

GENERAL GEORGE MOORE

Much has been written about and attributed to Generals MacArthur, Wainwright, and King, yet none knew more about the defense of Corregidor, Manila Bay, and the advantages and limitations of the fight facing the defenders on the Rock in early 1942 than General George Moore. A distinguished graduate of the US Army Artillery School, he held a number of assignments across the United States, including duty in the office of the Chief of Ordnance at the War Department in Washington. Shortly after the conclusion of the Washington Naval Treaty of 1922, which limited modernization of existing forts worldwide, Moore's first assignment to the 59th Coast Artillery Regiment in the Philippines was from 1923 to 1925. During this period, the army was limited to expanding the Malinta Tunnel on Corregidor and adding antiaircraft positions. In addition to improving the tunnel infrastructure to hold ordnance, a command center, and hospital, there was a major upgrade to the water supply, utilities, and road/rail system across the Rock. It was very clear following the rise of airpower in World War I that the development of military aviation in the 1920s would pose a significant threat to Corregidor's fixed artillery positions. As one observer noted, "It struck a sharp blow at the effectiveness of this carefully wrought and vastly expensive system of defenses and nothing could be done to remedy the weakness of the forts."[10]

Moore returned to the United States in 1926, attended the Artillery Advanced Course in 1927, and attended the Command and General Staff College in 1928. Upon completion, he was returned to Manila to conduct a thorough assessment of the harbor defense plans for both Manila Bay and Subic Bay. Following his evaluation, he returned to the office of the Chief of Coast Artillery in Washington, with a brief tour at the Army War College in 1934. Review and modification of War Plan Orange-3 for the defense of the Pacific was a prime topic at the War College. Moore and his classmates, who included Colonel Jonathan Wainwright, were fully involved in the planning and assessment of Japanese militaristic activity in the region. The focus of their preparation was on the far western Pacific and the defense of the Philippines. There was no mention of Pearl Harbor. Returning to

Internal lateral of the Malinta Tunnel, pictured here in the Finance Section. More than a hundred underground tunnels were dug during the 1920s and 1930s for the headquarters, supply depot, sleeping quarters, hospital, and mess hall. (Courtesy of the author's collection.)

the War Department staff after completion of the War College, Moore—much to his surprise—was recruited by his fellow Texas Aggie classmate Joe Utah '08 in a White House visit and personal appeal to President Roosevelt to return the up-and-coming army officer to Texas A&M as the Professor of Military Science and Tactics and Commandant of some four thousand cadets in the fall of 1937. The separation from nearly three decades of frontline active army duty seemed, at the time, a possible career-ending move.[11]

Fresh from his construction experience building the defenses of Corregidor, Colonel Moore would take charge of the largest construction project to date on the Texas A&M campus. In 1937, following the request and approval from FDR and the Reconstruction Finance Corporation to provide federal funding, planning began to add a dozen new Spartan cadet dorms and a mess hall large enough to seat at least

2,500 cadets per meal. Construction began in 1938 and was completed for occupancy prior to the commandant's recall by the War Department to return to Corregidor in 1940 for a third tour of duty. In preparation for the growth of the Corps of Cadets, Moore increased the number of active duty Army officers assigned to Texas A&M, reorganized the Corps of Cadets to align with active duty norms and standards, and stressed excellence in all endeavors of the Corps. Training in tactics, leadership, and maneuvers was extended to Saturday duty.

All were aware of the war clouds on the horizon, as Germany invaded Poland on September 3, 1939, followed by a declaration of war by both England and France on the Nazi aggression. Within months, the high seas were declared active areas for attacks on shipments to and from Europe by the German Navy. For the Moore family, still living in College Station, the coming war was indeed close at hand, as their only daughter, Anne, was aboard the *S.S. Athenia* on September 3, 1939, returning from visiting Scotland to New York City, when it was sunk by a Nazi submarine U-boat 30. After being stranded some eight hours in a lifeboat in the cold waters of the North Sea, she was rescued and returned home to Texas in October to a near hero's welcome.[12]

In the fall of 1940, Moore arrived back in Corregidor for his third tour as a general officer and Commander, Harbor Defenses of Manila and Subic Bays, with his headquarters at Fort Mills on the Rock. One former officer serving with General Moore described him as "the exemplification of the officer and the gentleman." Many of the young graduates from Texas A&M "flocked to join him on Corregidor." Moore's primary task was to prepare the island for a defensive stand. With no new funding available for basic improvements such as the addition of pill boxes, the army concentrated on improving the beach defensive positions and the addition of antiaircraft defenses cannibalized from training units around Manila, transferred to the Rock and refitted on individual swivel mounts. Only twelve of these outdated "practice weapons" became serviceable.[13]

Refitting a dozen antiaircraft batteries did little to overcome the state of unpreparedness found by Moore upon his return to the Rock.

The famed "concrete battleship," Fort Drum, in Manila Bay south of Corregidor was a key part of the defenses of the harbor. Manned by more than 150 men and with walls more than thirty feet thick, the fourteen-inch-long range turret guns were of no use in defending against Japanese aerial bombardment. This fort was one of the last positions to fall in the Battle of the Philippines. (Courtesy of the author's collection.)

In his detailed after-action report, drafted while in postwar recovery at Fort Monroe, Virginia, in the fall of 1945, he was candid regarding the strategic liability and state of affairs in 1941:

> Successive commanders of the Harbor Defense had repeatedly called attention to conditions and recommended remedial action. The fact that little had been done since the original installment of armaments in the forts to improve conditions to meet the threat of attack from the air and land can be laid solely to our traditional policy of unpreparedness, our limited peace time appropriations, limitation of armament as imposed by treaty restrictions [i.e., the Arms Treaty of 1922], and the disinclination to expend funds on installations in the Philippines due to their imminent independence [from the United States].[14]

In sum, the armaments of Corregidor and the surrounding islands in Manila Bay could by 1941 be termed obsolete but still formidable. The Order of Battle, the military means to list units engaged in an operation, and strength of major units in January 1942 under General Moore's command at Fort Mills on Corregidor included a mix of Army-Navy-Marine and Philippine Scout units (Table 4.2).

KEEP THE FLAG FLYING

After being warned to be on alert by the War Department (without any specific details of action) for a hostile Japanese incident since November 29, when news reached the Harbor Defense Command Post and HQ in Lateral No. 2 of the attack on Manila, the soft-spoken, self-possessed General Moore was not surprised. The bombing of the air fields on December 8 and 9 around Manila placed the defenders on the Rock on high alert, yet no offensive action was taken. Following the evacuation of General MacArthur and his staff to Corregidor at Christmas, the active defense of the island fortifications began in early January 1942 as American and Philippine troops were pushed back into the Bataan Peninsula. From MacArthur's HQ, it became increasingly clear by late January that Bataan forces could not

TABLE 4.2. Corregidor: Order of Battle, January 1942

60th Coast Artillery, Anti-Air	US Regular Army
91st Coast Artillery	Philippine Scouts
92nd Tractor Coast Artillery	Philippine Scouts
59th Coast Artillery	US Regular Army
1st Coast Artillery	Philippine Army
2nd Coast Artillery	Philippine Army
4th US Marine Regiment	US Marine Corps
Headquarters: Harbor Defense	General Moore[15]

All include civilian support staff who were under arms / in combat.

stop the increasing intensity of the Japanese attack. As bad news was reported from the battlefield, it became apparent that reinforcement of Corregidor would be the last line of defense. MacArthur ordered Moore to transfer food and supplies from Bataan to Corregidor, thus depleting the meager supplies available to the starved Bataan defenders. MacArthur ordered that there be enough rations to feed twenty thousand men on Corregidor on half rations until June 30.[16]

In response to the shortage of food, Wainwright ordered the slaughter of the last of their cavalry horses, starting, he ordered first, with the general's prize-winning show horse, "Joseph Conrad." Tom Dooley recalled, "The 26th Cavalry horses are being slaughtered at a rate of about 30 each week for food. I have not yet been forced to eat any." The disease-ridden troops on Bataan were reduced to eating dogs, lizards, monkeys, and carabao. Hunger had no bounds: "That monkey meat is all right until the animal's hands turn up on a plate."[17]

The pivotal moment in the fate of Bataan would eventually come via a fireside chat delivered by President Roosevelt from the White House on the evening of February 23. During his talk to the nation, for the first time, everyone learned details of the devastating attack on Pearl Harbor. Up until this time, information had been kept secret and out of the media so not to reveal to the enemy the full success of their raid. The second item of bad news was that, in so many words, there would be no hasty relief for Bataan and Corregidor. FDR confided that the news would become bleaker before it became brighter. In fact, in a meeting called by General MacArthur on January 24 in the tunnel on Corregidor with his key staff, it was deemed Bataan was doomed. Due to the weakening situation on Bataan, supplies of food and ammunition were ordered to be withdrawn for Bataan and stockpiled on Corregidor to eventually support an estimated twenty thousand defenders (troop numbers never exceeded eleven thousand), and MacArthur predicted Bataan could fall as early as mid-February. Concerned with the inevitable fate, MacArthur told General Moore, "Never in history has a force of this size been left out on a limb."[18]

The situation on the Rock was very bleak, with no promise of improving. During the day prior to FDR's broadcast, the president ordered MacArthur and his family—wife, Jean; four-year-old son, Arthur; and the child's Chinese nanny, Ah Cheu—to leave Corregidor for Australia. Originally he planned to be evacuated by submarine, yet the exodus was delayed and the plans changed to leave on March 12 by four high-speed navy PT boats to Mindanao and then by two B-17s to Brisbane. The general's departure was bittersweet and viewed with mixed emotions by the embattled soldiers remaining on Bataan and Corregidor.[19]

General Moore escorted MacArthur, his family, and a group of seventeen officers from his staff to the North Dock of Corregidor to board four waiting boats. In his last words on the dock, MacArthur shook Moore's hand and said, "George, keep the flag flying . . . hold Corregidor until I return . . . I am coming back." The PT boats faded into the dark of the China Sea to evade the minefields and Japanese patrol boats that surrounded the island. The exodus and details of the general and his key staff to Australia would be kept a secret for months until W. L. White's 1943 book, *They Were Expendable*. The dramatic account was followed by a Hollywood box-office hit in 1944 starring John Wayne, highlighting the daring escape. Although the General was ordered to leave the Rock, the departure of MacArthur was a blow to morale, especially to the Filipinos who idolized the general—there were numerous accounts that "the heart went out of them."[20]

Following some confusion in the change of command between MacArthur and Wainwright, the president and the War Department interceded and overall command of the forces in the Philippines was transferred to General Wainwright, who moved to Corregidor HQ, US Forces in Philippines (USFIP). Wainwright turned his Luzon field command over to Major General Edward P. King. General Wainwright hoped to restore some level of lost morale, reminding his staff, including aide Tom Dooley, "Lee marched on Gettysburg with less men than we have here. We're not licked by a damn sight."[21]

Following Wainwright's arrival on Corregidor, Moore gave him a tour of the defensive situation on the 1,735-acre Rock. The tour was but an omen of things to come, as both generals were nearly killed in a bombing raid, escaping only at the last minute by diving into a shallow shelter.

The Japanese would gradually intensify both aerial bombing and artillery shelling from Luzon as they aimed their heavy artillery at the Rock's defenders. One of the island's greatest deficiencies was the lack of an adequate water supply. Notwithstanding, Wainwright's primary objective was to coordinate the withering defense of the troops on Bataan.[22]

THE FIGHTIN' TEXAS AGGIES

The Texas Aggie defenders on Corregidor were spread across the island in Marine units, composite Army Air Corps units assigned to the infantry, regular US Army troops, Philippine Scouts, as well as coastal artillery and antiaircraft units. General Moore was the senior Aggie on the Rock, Class of '08, followed by the second most senior Aggie, his HQ staff assistant **Major John V. King '27** of College Station. King had been on the staff of the commandant at Texas A&M and accompanied Moore when he was reassigned to Corregidor in 1941. King would survive the siege and more than three years in POW camps only to die in 1945 on the Hell Ship *Enoura Maru*.[23]

The largest concentration of Texas Aggies was assigned to the coast artillery and antiaircraft batteries. The two most active units were the 59th and 60th Coast Artillery Regiments, Harbor Defense. There were six Aggies in the 60th CA, all involved with antiaircraft operations and targeting. The regiment was divided into three battalions with the 1st Battalion composed of the HQ battery, along with Batteries A, B, C, D; 2nd Battalion, Batteries E, F, G, H; and the 3rd Battalion, Batteries I, K, L, M. These batteries were spread from the tip of the island at Kindley Field, known generally as Bottomside, across the heights of Malinta Hill, Way Hill, and Morrison Hill, as well as units at Topside near the golf course, all supported by special support units (composed of both military and civilian personnel) that handled the ammunition, searchlight and radar equipment, and sound locators.[24]

Texas Aggie members of the 59th CA and 60th CA included **Captain Willis Scrivener '37** from Taft, **Lt. Lewis B. Chevaillier '39** from Marshall, **Lt. Carl H. Pipkin '40** from Beaumont, **Lt. John B. McCluskey '36** from Anderson, **Lt. Clifton H. Chamberlain '40** from Wichita Falls, **Lt. William A. Hamilton '40** from Dallas, and **Lt. Stanley Friedline '40** from Grand Saline.

All these Aggies served for the duration of the fight on Corregidor in exposed positions that daily became more dangerous and deadly with each round of enemy shelling and bombing. Positions on the hills were particularly exposed and targeted by the enemy. Platoon leader Lt. Stanley Friedline, on April 28, 1942, was caught in a bombing raid while on top of Malinta Hill defending the entrance, a gun pit, and searchlight facility. He and a squad of men took a direct hit by a 240mm shell that came down the ventilation shaft and exploded the gas tank of the 25KV generator—spreading fire through the tunnel. Friedline and five soldiers died that afternoon and many more were wounded. The commanding officer of Battery M60th CA wrote in the after-action report, "The deaths and injuries that day was a distinct shock to all of us . . . the officers of Battery Mobile were deeply grieved over the loss of such an excellent and promising officer."[25]

As the Japanese increased the shelling from Bataan, casualties mounted, one by one the big gun batteries on the Rock were leveled, and ammunition dumps went up like fireworks, covering the island in a veiled haze of smoke and dust. A few days following the death of Lt. Friedline, Battery B, in an exposed position on Topside near the Wheeler Battery, came under intense shelling, causing **Lt. Lewis B. Chevaillier '39**, the Range Officer for the battery, to leave his protected position to evacuate several severely wounded men left lying in exposed dangerous positions. He assisted in the evacuation of the wounded to a first aid station several hundred yards away. For his brave actions on April 30, 1942, he was awarded the Silver Star. Chevaillier would survive the battle and be shipped to a POW camp at Camp Zentsuji, Shikoko, Japan, until 1945.[26]

Lt. William A. Hamilton Jr. '40 arrived in Manila on November 1, 1941. A recent graduate of Texas A&M, he completed artillery school and was posted with the 60th CA at Fort Mills. He was assigned Battery F on Topside near Battery Cheney, the site of four 12-inch-long range cannons, to command three 3-inch antiaircraft guns. By late April 1942, his guns had been destroyed by the constant Japanese bombing. During

Japanese troops landing ashore on the "tail" end of Corregidor on May 5, 1942, in their final assault on the Rock. Supported by tanks, the enemy soon moved inland and the final surrender was given by Generals Wainwright and Moore. This captured photo was released multiple times in 1942 and 1943 in Tokyo to celebrate the fall of the Philippines. (Courtesy of the author's collection.)

the final days before the surrender, his unit was given rifles and ordered to be prepared to assist the beach defenders. Before they were deployed, the island surrendered and he was shipped to the POW camp at Cabanatuan for three years and then to Camp Fukouka on Kyushu Island. He is one of only a handful of the thousands of POWs to survive three separate sinkings of the POW Hell Ships—the *Oryoku Maru*, the *Enoura Maru*, and the *Brazil Maru*. Awarded the Bronze Star, he was released in August 1945 and returned home to work for the Santa Fe Railroad and on Army Reserve duty, retiring as a Lieutenant Colonel.[27]

Hamilton's Texas A&M classmate and close friend, **Lt. Clifton H. Chamberlain Jr. '40** of Marlin, Texas, also arrived in Manila in early November 1941 and was posted with the 59th CA on one of the satellite islands near Corregidor that had been converted to what the men called "a concrete battleship." Eight miles from the Rock, the small isle of El Fraile was converted into Fort Drum. The armaments, including four massive 14-inch-long range guns in armored turrets, were positioned on the battleship-like structure built of concrete and steel with 36-foot-thick walls and deck, 350 feet long and 144 feet wide at the beam. Known by the two-hundred-man garrison as the "USS Drum," the small isle took a tremendous pounding from the Japanese who tried but never succeeded in disrupting their near self-sufficient operations. After the surrender, he joined Hamilton at Camp Cabanatuan and remained there for three and a half years until freed in the spectacular US Army Ranger raid in January 1945, which liberated 511 POWs.[28]

In the heat of the battle for the Philippines and shortly after being awarded the Distinguished Service Cross by General MacArthur, General Moore received a "radio" cable from Texas A&M President T. O. Walton that the college board of directors had dedicated and named a new dormitory on the campus in his honor—Moore Hall. It was a fitting honor, yet those back in Texas and across America, due to the fact the federal government maintained a near total news blackout in hopes of not alarming the public with the impact of the disastrous Pearl Harbor attack and the desperate status of conditions across the Pacific Theater, had no idea of the deplorable conditions on Bataan and on the Rock.[29]

INTOLERABLE SITUATION

The Bataan defenders fought on as the bombing and terrific artillery fire from the Japanese guns on Cavite Pointe pounded Corregidor and intensified. While the Americans had no planes to defend the Rock or attack Japanese positions, the Japanese with total air superiority were able to use airborne observers to provide accurate target data and damage assessments. Antiaircraft guns on the island were able to shoot down more than a hundred Japanese bombers and fighters, yet this did little to stem the aerial attacks. Attacks were targeted on the water supply, roads, and the power plant. When the power plant was knocked out, empty twelve-inch powder cans were improvised to store water. As the raids intensified, food was stacked by the gun emplacements due to the inability to safely cross the island. On April 4, on the eve of Easter

Sunday, the enemy began to firebomb the island with explosives that burst into flames before hitting the ground. Within twenty-four hours, the Rock was a mass of rolling fire and was covered in smoke. And as one observer noted in an after-action report, "The situation of Corregidor was intolerable but on Bataan it was altogether hopeless."[30]

The fate of Bataan and ultimately of Corregidor was sealed on April 6, 1942. Over the Easter weekend, MacArthur, three thousand miles away in Australia, sent a detailed cable to Wainwright ordering King to prepare a desperate offensive and "sudden surprise attack" against the Japanese along the Olongapa Road with the aim of breaking through the Japanese lines and escaping into greater Luzon to conduct a guerrilla war! Wainwright and his staff were incredulous at the general's total escape from reality. The American and Philippine warriors on Bataan were beat. A suicidal attack against the strength of the Japanese line was no solution. Nonetheless, Wainwright from his HQ on Corregidor—knowing full well the deplorable conditions of the American and Filipino

Surrender of American forces on Corregidor at the Malinta Tunnel. Prisoners on the Rock were held for three weeks on an open concrete slab before being moved by boat across Manila Bay to Cabanatuan and Tarlac POW camps. (Courtesy of the author's collection.)

troops, ordered General King to organize, rearm, and launch a full frontal counteroffensive. The defenders were little more than a scarecrow band—sick and malnourished, with many wounded.[31]

After the war, in a syndicated nationwide newspaper series and in his memoirs, General Wainwright, although a confidant of MacArthur, provided invaluable insight to future commanders with three basic observations about what he felt doomed the Bataan-Corregidor campaign: "The Army high command made three major military mistakes in the Philippines. Ranking officers failed to visit troops in the front lines when all we had to offer our people is morale. Second: we shouldn't have had to rely on half-trained Filipinos. More troops should have been sent from the United States before the war. And the last mistake he blamed on MacArthur, 'We should never have discarded the Grunert Plan [WPO-3] of retreating into Bataan for that grandiose scheme of getting the Japs at the beaches with a paper army.'"[32]

From his HQ on Corregidor, Wainwright was unaware of General King's plan to surrender on April 9. Up until the eighth, Wainwright had received direct orders not to surrender but to fight on at all cost. Not contacting Wainwright, a difficult and final decision was made by King, who at the time and in later years said he was prepared to be court-martialed for his actions but felt the decision was made in the best interests of his ragged, diseased, and starving army. Other than the evacuation of a few key personnel, including doctors and nurses and a number of intelligence officers, there were no plans to evacuate the soldiers from Bataan to Corregidor. The Corregidor garrison by early April 1942 was home for some fifteen thousand troops and civilians. Furthermore, there were few boats available, and little or no protection for an evacuation was contemplated. Those on Bataan were trapped and doomed to the fate of death or becoming prisoners of war.[33]

By late in the afternoon on April 9, all communications and hope of recovering stragglers from Bataan was halted. Wainwright and Moore increased the defensive on the Rock, yet there was little they could do to assist those on Bataan. The Japanese moved rapidly to position artillery to bombard the Rock. To avoid hitting the captured troops being marched out of the Bataan Peninsula as well as the two field hospitals with more than two thousand sick and wounded, Wainwright delayed any US artillery response from Corregidor into Bataan to shell the Japanese.

General Moore, who in postwar years was deeply moved by his experiences on Corregidor, recalled that the sight across the bay from Corregidor to Bataan was terrible. As ammunition dumps were being blown by the troops, the Japanese kept up their aerial strafing and bombing as "refugees from Bataan poured into Mariveles looking for boats, rafts, *bancas* (small native boats) and any other means of keeping afloat across the two mile channel." About 2,300 soldiers and civilians managed to survive the bay crossing and reach the Rock. Yet even more disturbing, from the watchtower above Malinta Tunnel, Moore was able to see through his binoculars the long lines of captive troops walking north in columns of fours from Mariveles along the East Coast Road. He was an eyewitness to the beginning of the atrocities of the Bataan Death March.[34]

Almost at once, air raids intensified on tiny Corregidor, following the surrender on Bataan. Deep inside the tunnel, BG Lewis Beebe, Wainwright's chief of staff, recorded in his diary on April 16, "The Japs are gradually taking this place apart." The Japanese were behind their planned schedule to control the region and were eager to mop up the offensive and take the Rock. News reports were still able to reach the island by wireless radio and the occasional submarine that sneaked under the Japanese patrols. There was little or no good news to report to the home front from the Pacific Theater during all of 1942. The only glimmer of good news came from word in late April 1942 that the US Army Air Corps had bombed Tokyo and the Fightin' Texas Aggies had "mustered" on Corregidor.[35]

THIRTY SECONDS OVER TOKYO

As the defenders of the Rock continued to be bombed and cut off from any hope of relief, a joint Army-Navy task force delivered a top secret American calling card by bombing Tokyo on April 18, 1942. The mission of the sixteen twin-engine B-25s, stripped down to nothing except fuel and bombs and launched four hundred miles from Japan off the pitching deck of the *USS Hornet*, was commanded by then Colonel Jimmy Doolittle. Along with his second in command, Texas Aggie Major John A. Hilger '32, were Aggie pilots Lt. Robert M. Gray '41, Lt. William M. Fitzhugh '36, Lt. Glen C. Roloson '40, and Lt. James M. Parker Jr. '41. Corregidor veteran **Lt. William Boyd '38** later recalled his response to the raid, which was considered by scores of Pacific veterans after the conflict as the one item of good news during the early stages of the war: "When we heard the news, I think it was on April 21st, that bombers had bombed Tokyo we couldn't imagine at the time how they got close enough . . . but it was great news."[36]

The Doolittle Tokyo raid was a spectacular one-way mission. So secret was the mission, President Roosevelt was not told about the plan until the planes had taken off from the *USS Hornet*. Upon learning of the success of the raid, the president beamed with excitement, yet avoided reporter questions on details about the mission by only saying the B-25s and their crews came from Shangri-La to carry out their mission. Most on the B-25s were able to make the Chinese mainland and crash-land (except one plane crew, which landed near Vladivostok)—hoping to be aided by friendly troops and citizens that were pro-American. Some crews died on landing, a few were captured and executed by the Japanese occupying China, but most made it to safety, including all the Texas Aggies on the mission. Lt. Parker received the Distinguished Flying Cross (DFC), as well as Lt. Gray, who was later killed in action near Assam, India, on October 18, 1942. Hilger received the DFC for his role in the Tokyo raid. He was later awarded a Silver Star for a high-risk mission along the Yalu River during the Korean War in 1950. He completed a thirty-year career, retiring as a brigadier general with the Distinguished Service Medal and three Legion of Merit awards.[37]

Captured American fliers were in high demand and much hated by the enemy. The Japanese had long portrayed themselves as invincible, and thus the Tokyo raid was a surprise blow to Tojo and his warlords. The captured Doolittle crews were subject to physical and mental torture and execution. For example, they were taken one at a time and forced to march miles blindfolded. Once stopped, the victim would hear orders and the marching of a firing squad; the Japanese would lower their rifles in the act of firing, only to stop. A Japanese officer would then come up to the flier and say, "We are the Knights of the Bushido of the Order of the Rising Sun; we do not execute at sundown; we execute at sunrise." The American public did not learn of the fate of the executed Doolittle Raiders until April 21, 1945.[38]

TEXAS AGGIE MUSTER ON THE ROCK

By mid-April 1942, the conditions on Corregidor had vastly deteriorated after weeks of Japanese aerial bombing and bombardment by long-range guns from Luzon and Cavite. Ordered to hold at all cost, the roster of the wounded increased daily as did the graves of the KIA—their crude burial sites marked only with tent pegs and name tags. Food was in short supply and freshwater scarce. Except for an occasional submarine that ran the Japanese blockade, Moore's command received little or no supplies or news that relief was on the way. Undeterred by the situation, the two dozen Fightin' Texas Aggies on the Rock briefly turned their attention to their alma mater and the fight for Texas independence.[39]

The Texas Aggies defending the Rock made worldwide news with the announcement by the United Press flash report that they had observed one of their alma mater's most sacred traditions—Aggie Muster. Dating from the founding of the Lone Star state in the 1840s, the cadets and former students annually honor the memory of those who had gone before them by an annual April 21 observance on San Jacinto Day. The eighteen-minute battle for the independence of Texas at San Jacinto was a far cry from the Rock. Events had been held for decades on San Jacinto Day, a state holiday, but none had more far-reaching significance than the "reported" observance from Corregidor on April 21, 1942.[40]

The detailed story of the famed 1942 Muster on Corregidor is chronicled in the book *Softly Call the Muster* (1994). The Corregidor events were orchestrated by then-captain Tom Dooley at the direct request of General Moore. Although the UP news report stated that the Aggies had "gathered" in the "Spirit of San Jacinto" in the Malinta Tunnel, the report was not completely accurate. The near around-the-clock shelling of the isle and the emergency nature of events in the tunnel to care for the wounded and sick, as well as the battle being waged against the Japanese, would have precluded such a gathering. Nevertheless, given the tenuous situation in the Pacific in general and on Corregidor in particular, the news of the Texas Aggie Muster was greeted as exciting news on the home front. Clarification of the events on Corregidor that San Jacinto Day on the Rock were provided later by Tom Dooley at the annual campus Muster in 1978:

> General Moore wanted to discuss the thought of the upcoming April 21st. He knew I was an Aggie and said that he wanted to get a list of the Aggies still fighting there. Although the account nowadays says that they gathered on April 21st, it was impossible . . . to congregate because they could not be spared from their [defensive] positions.
>
> So, we had a roll call, and a muster is a roll call. We got all the Aggies listed, and I contacted one of the two (news) correspondents still on the island . . . to get the story back to the states.[41]

According to Dooley, at the time the news flash was sent about the "Aggie Muster" on Corregidor, the report served several purposes: "It gave a good plug for the state of Texas . . . a good plug for Texas A&M," and it notified relatives that they were still alive and "fighting." A secondary yet more critical listing of the names to be wired to Texas was, as Dooley noted, a good way "to establish our [G.I.] insurance policies in the event any of us were lost in battle."[42]

The news from Corregidor about the Aggie Muster captured the imagination of the nation. Front-page headlines in the *Houston Post* on April 22, 1942, proclaimed, "Corregidor Aggies Fete San Jacinto—35 [actually the number was 27] Texans Bear Down on Famed Fight Song," and *TIME* magazine had already referred to the perilous situation at Corregidor as "The Last Stand," followed by a second article, "Lone Star on the Rock." The parallels with the defenders of the Alamo and the victors of San Jacinto were both significant and timely. The story of the Aggie Muster received extensive recognition, as Texas Senator Tom Connally from the floor of the US Senate noted, "It must stir every Texan's heart to know our Texas boys who are wearing the uniform and who are under daily attack by the enemy in Corregidor carry with them the Spirit of San Jacinto in the dark hours of their trial."[43]

On April 21, the news from Bataan was very grim. Twelve days after the surrender, the largest contingent of POWs marching up the East Highway reached Camp O'Donnell. The smell of rotting flesh and human waste covered by millions of blue blowflies greeted the haggard prisoners. Only three small water faucets were to serve thousands of sick men. As one prisoner recalled, "Hundreds entered O'Donnell this April day and hundreds would never leave alive."[44]

Conditions continued to deteriorate on the Rock after April 21, as the water supply was limited, rations cut to thirty ounces per day, and the number of wounded and ill (with many bringing disease during the evacuation from Bataan) was mounting. Aggie **Captain Hervey H. Whitfield '34** had escaped Clark Field and was reassigned to Del Monte Air Field on the southernmost Philippine island of Mindanao to fly a much more dangerous mission bringing in quinine and medical supplies to the island in an unarmed single-engine 1934 Waco UC-72 biplane they called the "crate." A small group of pilots with three secondhand obsolete planes, known as the "Bamboo Fleet," were tasked with resupply of Bataan and Corregidor with the bare essentials. Upon an interview after being awarded the Distinguished Flying Cross, Whitfield recalled, "We were out of quinine then, so I brought in a plane load of whisky and candy, and took out some evacuees." After dozens of flights dodging Japanese Zeros, on May 5, Whitfield flew the last flight out of Kindley Field on the Rock before the Japanese landed. After an additional year of flying in the Pacific, he was awarded the Distinguished Flying Cross with Oak Leaf Cluster for gallantry, promoted, and transferred to Venezuela to train South American pilots for the Allies.[45]

A few submarines that surfaced in the dark of night delivered limited supplies and proved to be the last direct contact with the outside world for the next three and a half years. The *USS Spearfish*

(SS-190) made the last trip into Manila Bay on May 3, picking up the final batch of military records and evacuating twelve nurses and key officers. Winding through minefields and dodging Japanese surface ships, the ship's captain noted in the log upon departure, "Observed moonrise. Heavy shelling of Corregidor continued . . . speed five knots to escone [*sic*] illumination caused by explosion of ammunition dump" on the Rock. The smuggling of official military records out by order of both Wainwright and Moore was crucial, in addition to a complete roster of those still alive, as were promotions and citations that would bear on their pay allotments for their dependents in the case of capture or death. Between the bombings and shellings, Moore deployed the troops along the beach defense and added more than fifteen miles of barbwire, land mines, and traps for the expected Japanese landing.[46]

THE FINAL ASSAULT: "THE NIPS ARE LANDING"

By late April, the landscape of the Rock resembled the surface of the moon. Nearly all the guns and gun emplacements were twisted and destroyed. The water supply was crippled, all electricity cut, defensive positions of barbwire and machine gun emplacements along the beach wiped out. The soldiers and marines along the beach clung to what little shelter they had in the barren rocks. Generals Moore and Wainwright, two seasoned officers, captured the intensity and fierce bombardment:

> It did not seem possible that the tempo of the Jap shelling could possibly be increased. But May 4 it reached its all-time high during a five-hour period from 7 a.m. until noon.
>
> General Moore and I, making a careful check of that overwhelming artillery assault, discovered that the Jap batteries hit Corregidor with five-hundred-pound 240 mm. shells every five seconds during the entire five-hour period. The big shells whined in and struck us amid a shower of men, guns, dirt, rock, and debris with clock-like precision. They fell at the steady rate of twelve every minute, which meant

> thirty-six hundred of the shells for the five-hours, enough shells to fill six hundred trucks.
>
> Moore and I, delving further into the mathematics of the fury, estimated at the end of the five incredible hours that the Japs had hit the Rock with 1,800,000 pounds of shells [estimated to have been 16,000 shells in 24 hours on May 4]. These were statistics which ignored the other beating we took that day, for we also had thirteen air raids.[47]

By early May, the Japanese had concentrated forces for a massive assault on the north side of the island, the area closest to Bataan. Only a three-day supply of water remained. On May 5 Corregidor received its three hundredth bombing attack since mid-December 1941. The Rock was prepped for attack. The narrow tadpole tail area of the Rock, Kindley Field, was low and easy to access and provided the defenders and attackers with little or no cover. The enemy pounded the entrance of the Malinta Tunnel at a rate of three hundred bursts a minute. In the hours before the Japanese landing, General Moore held a meeting in the dust, dim lights, and smells of the command lateral with his section chiefs to review last minute responsibilities:

> Let's review the bidding. The enemy has increased his water lift capacity of Bataan. He's spotted barges along the coast and loaded some of them with tanks and artillery. And he's concentrated his fire on Malinta Hill and north shore roads for the past five days. That spells an invasion attempt. Since he knows we'll fight, he'll probably come at night. Excluding Filipino employees, hospital staff and patients, Navy Communicators and supply people, we have 6,500 men who can shoot. And we have plenty of rifles and ammunition and machineguns, about fifty 75mm guns, and two working 155s. Warn the major commands to be especially watchful for signs of a north shore landing.[48]

At 11:15 on the night of May 5, 1942, General Moore, commanding the Rock's defensive forces, called General Wainwright, calmly stating, "The Nips are landing out near North Point." Within hours, the enemy occupied a stretch of beach between Infantry Point and

North Point down near the end of the island's tail. The first enemy force in mass landed as a rising full moon revealed their silhouettes along the shoreline at the strongest point of the beach defended by the 4th Marines. In the early hours, the Marines slaughtered the first wave of invaders—the Japanese suffering 70 percent casualties while still in the water in what one Japanese observer, Lt. Kazumaro Uno of the Imperial Japanese GHQ Army Press Bureau (who published in 1942 the only English version of the landing), noted was a "sheer massacre." In turn, the Marines also took heavy casualties. Critical to this phase of the fighting was USMC Aggie **Major Paul Armstrong Brown '29**, Company B, First Battalion, 4th Marines. Weeks before, Brown, a native of Galveston, had been wounded by bomb fragments and received a Silver Star for defending a unit of men during a hostile bombing attack; now he and his men had their backs to the wall with the number of wounded mounting and ammo running low. The Japanese brought up additional barges of troops, finally eked out a reinforced small beachhead, and were able to regroup and doggedly gain a foothold. Moore moved more troops into the fight from other areas of the Rock, yet the Americans and Filipino reserves were unable to stem the onslaught.[49]

Back in America, the valiant stand on Corregidor had little impact on military or civilian morale—because the full account of the defense, due to a news blackout, was not known at the time. While viewed with shock across the United States, commentators compared it with the stand at the Alamo. And it did impact the men that defended the Rock. Hundreds of poems were written by American troops about Bataan and the plight of the siege of Corregidor; a PFC of the 59th CA, Leroy Gant, wrote the following:

CORREGIDOR

How many days, how many nights
have we suffered through this war?
Hopes fading fast that we'll be saved at last,
from this hell on Corregidor.
The enemy is near, but there is no fear

of what may lie in store.
For death is a relief from the misery and grief,
that we have seen here on Corregidor.[50]

The final weeks of the battle for Corregidor was costly to both sides. The siege of the Rock had lasted for twenty-seven days. US losses were more than two thousand, and the Japanese lost more than five thousand men from both malaria and the invasion. The famed "Gibraltar of the East" was a landscape of scorched earth and haze; Corregidor was finished. The total punishment inflicted on General Homma's 4th Division far exceeded that of the US defenders—so much so that Homma and the remnants of the 4th were transferred back to Japan and permanently demobilized. The American defenders of Corregidor had interrupted and delayed thousands of tons of supplies, troops, and ships and disrupted the Imperial Army's timetable and German-influenced blitzkrieg-style tempo of operations across the southwest Pacific—quite possibly saving Australia from invasion.[51]

General Moore had predicted the Japanese landing would come the night of a "damn full moon!" He was right: thousands of fresh Japanese troops, as Admiral Ugaki noted in his diary, took full "advantage of the moon" and waited in barges in the moonlit predawn darkness, ready to land. The fanaticism of the invading troops, marked by the corruption of the Bushido-samurai spirit and an undying reverence for the Emperor, infused in ordinary peasant soldiers the theme of the Japanese Imperial national anthem:[52]

I shall die only for the Emperor,
I shall never look back.

And, in fact, they didn't look back as hundreds of troops were killed in their landing barges and on the beach. The first wave of the Japanese landing hit the beach at 11:30 p.m., May 5, 1942, and fighting at close quarters continued through the night with US casualties mounting and no way to evacuate them to the hospital in Malinta Tunnel. During the night, the Japanese added additional snipers and landed more troops. The final blow to the defenders was the landing of tanks that were able to move inland quickly. During the fighting, often hand to hand, **Lt. John L. Lester '29** was wounded and died defending the Rock on May 8. In Malinta Tunnel, the freshwater supply was nearly depleted and the number of wounded was growing. Knowing the end was near, Wainwright and Moore conferred in the tunnel and agreed that surrender in the face of possible annihilation could save lives. Moore at once ordered that the American banner be lowered and burned so it would not fall into enemy hands. It was agreed that a broadcast would be made and surrender announced at twelve noon, May 6, 1942. Wainwright radioed Roosevelt, "There is a limit of human endurance, and that point has long passed." In a carefully prepared dispatch from the War Department to the media, strong concerns were expressed about the "out-numbered, out-gunned, half-starved and short of ammunition" defenders as they made a "heroic last stand." Newspapers across America greeted the nation with morning headlines: "Japs Land on Corregidor." There were few details of the status of the men and their treatment—only the last message from the radio operator, Private Irving Strobling, sent as the power blacked out: "Give 'em Hell for Us. God Bless you and Keep you." Corregidor went silent.[53]

While all mourned the loss and capture of Corregidor, the editor of the Brownwood, Texas, *Yellow Jacket* daily instead voiced indignation that our troops had been seemingly abandoned—singling out the contribution of the Texas Aggies:

> News releases tell us that Corregidor Fortress has fallen to the enemy. Reason: shortage of supplies and re-enforcements. Why is it that a nation like ours must leave those men stranded and at the mercy of the enemy? The United States is the wealthiest nation in the world, possessing greater natural resources and more ingenious population than any other country.
>
> Corregidor Fortress has fallen! And with it have fallen [Texas] Aggies! Too little too late! Our politicians seem to be too busy log rolling and pork barreling to realize that there is a war to be won, not votes to be sought.

> Then let the parents and friends of those Aggies who have laid down their lives that we might keep ours get behind their representatives in government. Let them risk our ships to get war materials to the battle front. Aggies and other American boys are out there risking something that can't be rebuilt or bought with money.
>
> Let us replace the excuse, "too little and too late," with the motto, "enough and on time." Let's start winning this war![54]

Like the surrender of Bataan, the surrender of the Rock proved very complicated, as the commanding Japanese General Homma, who spoke English perfectly, turned to his interpreter and demanded, in Japanese, the surrender not just of Corregidor but of all US and Filipino forces in the Philippines. The uneasy process was not completed until General Wainwright was transferred to Manila and ordered to broadcast a prepared message across the archipelago, particularly to the leader of the largest remaining contingent still fighting, Major General Sharpe, commanding the Visayan-Mindanao troops. As Wainwright walked from the Malinta Tunnel to the dock, he noted,

> [My men] were in very bad shape. They had not been fed or given any water during that terrible time. They were in very bad shape. But as I walked through them they all got to their feet. Some stood at attention and saluted as I passed, and I raised my hand to my old sun helmet. Others just stood, took off their hats, and had them across their chest. I felt the tears welling up to my eyes and could do nothing to stop the emotion. I am a student of the Civil War, but not until then did I know how General Robert E. Lee felt after Appomattox.[55]

Both American and Japanese were confused and bewildered in the hours and days immediately after the surrender on the Rock. General Moore noted in the after-action report that as he, General Wainwright, Colonel Pugh, and Major Dooley, all covered in dust and dirt, walked down to the dock at 1400 hours on May 6 to meet the Japanese commander, "Dead and dying were on every hand, the proportion being about three Japanese to one American." Hundreds of badly mangled dead bodies covered the island and floated in the shoals. The Japanese used American-Filipino work crews to stack the Japanese bodies five high and burn them in front of the entrance of the Malinta Tunnel, the ashes collected and shipped back to Japan for ceremonial burial. The American dead were handled last and with much less care—most placed in shallow unmarked graves, as the Japanese forbade any inventory of the wounded or roster of the dead.[56]

Much like the first hours after the fall of Bataan, General Wainwright and his staff on Corregidor were singled out for intensive interrogation. The Japanese were surprised to learn there was no secret underwater tunnel between Bataan and Corregidor. The interrogators became very frustrated, as they could not get details on the location of the American and Filipino treasury and silver horde that had secretly been packaged and dropped into Manila Bay near Fort Drum. During the Japanese interview process, the Americans stood firm and provided misinformation whenever possible; in one instance, after questioning former Texas Aggie yell leader Major Tom Dooley, the Japanese intelligence officer threw up his hands and said, "I cannot see how you are the general's aide and know so little."[57]

American troops and civilians wandered the island for a couple of days collecting personal items and scavenging for food before being herded into a narrow holding site at the Kindley Field Garage Area on the lower east side of the Rock. More than twelve thousand were POWs, with a thousand sick and wounded in the laterals of the Malinta Tunnel. There were fewer of the mass atrocities that marked the Death March in April, yet many POWs were bayoneted for the smallest offense and there were a number of random executions. The conditions in the confined area were deplorable, with little food, a shortage of water, and no medical care—and more than thirty deaths. Lt. Col. McDavitt '33 recalled the confinement in the crowed area on Corregidor was "the filthiest period of time I've ever seen." The POWs were held in the blistering Pacific sun for nearly two weeks until May 23 and then loaded on small ships, hauled across the bay to the docks at Manila, and marched through the streets of the capital in front of throngs of Filipinos. They were divided by rank among the

POW camps at Bilibid Prison on the outskirts of Manila and Cabanatuan, north of Clark Field. Some two hundred POWs with technical expertise to run the power and water were held on Corregidor to do cleanup and repair work.[58]

The Japs had hoped to shame the Americans, yet their plans backfired as the Filipinos lined along the march through downtown and reached out, many with tears, in attempts to help the beleaguered troops. Of the

TABLE 4.3. Texas Aggie Defenders of Corregidor, 1942

Lt. William Boyd '39**	Maj. John V. King '22**
Maj. Paul Brown '29**	Lt. John L. Lester '29*
Capt. Stockton D. Burns '35	Lt. John McCluskey '36**
Capt. Wilbert A. Calvert '38**	Capt. Jerome A. McDavitt '33
Lt. Clifton Chamberlain '40	Maj. Gen. George F. Moore '08
Lt. Lewis B. Chevaillier '39	Capt. Chester A. Peyton '33**
Capt. William M. Curtis '32**	Lt. Carl Pipkin '39**
Maj. Tom Dooley '35	Capt. Henry A. Schutte Jr. '39**
Lt. Stanley Friedline '40*	Capt. Willis A. Scrivener '37**
Lt. William A. Hamilton '40	Lt. David Snell '37
Capt. Graham M. Hatch '31**	Capt. Roy M. Vick Jr. '35**
Lt. Urban C. Hopmann '40	Capt. Hervey H. Whitfield '34***
Sgt. Hugh Hunt '38	Lt. Charlton Wimer '40
Lt. Andy James '38**	

* Killed in action (2).

** Killed while Japanese POWs (13).

*** Ordered to pilot the last supply plane mission off Corregidor, May 5.

Note: Thirteen of the twenty-four Texas Aggies taken captive died as POWs; eleven returned home.

Sources: Association of Former Students, AFS World War II Files and Records, Cushing Library; Association of Former Students, *Directory of Former Students of the A&M College of Texas 1876–1949*, College Station: 1949, pp. xxvii–xlviii.

twenty-seven Texas Aggie defenders on Corregidor, two were killed in action, and one—Captain Hervey Whitfield '34—was ordered to pilot out one of the last supply missions to the Rock. Of the twenty-four Aggies captured May 7–9, 1942, on the Rock, thirteen died as POWs at the hands of the Japanese during the thirty-nine months prior to the surrender in August 1945—and *only eleven* returned home to Texas. Famed columnist Drew Pearson wrote in his nationwide syndicated newspaper column, "Although General MacArthur gathered all the headlines, praise and honor . . . one unsung hero who has done a great job is Major General George F. Moore '08, in command of the harbor defenses of Corregidor."[59]

With the fall of the Rock, the American and Filipino combatants entered the prisoner phase of the war in the Pacific. Dividing the wounded and sick troops among a dozen POW camps during the balance of 1942, the Japanese allowed no visits by the International Red Cross as well as no outgoing mail. Families, given no location or information about their relatives, were unable to write until mid-1943. The War Department, still worried about giving the enemy details of the devastating events at Pearl Harbor and the full cost of the Bataan-Corregidor defeat, maintained a near news blackout about events in the Pacific.

★ CHAPTER 5 ★

YOU ARE SLAVES OF THE JAPANESE EMPIRE

> We are not concerned about how many die. The only thing we want to know in the morning is how many died the night before—just so we know how many are left in the camp to work.
>
> JAPANESE COMMANDER, CAMP O'DONNELL

> The small amount of food that we had been getting had deteriorated in quality until it was almost impossible to eat. There were so many weevils and worms in the rice that it was half weevils, worms, and rocks. One day at noon, I decided to count the number of weevils and worms in my cup of rice. I counted eighty-two insects in this single cup of rice. I knew if I did not eat insects and all I would have very little rice, so I just put them back in the rice and said to myself, "That's all the protein you will get anyway."
>
> CAPTAIN JOHN COLEMAN '29

Arriving at Camp O'Donnell near Capas covered in sweat, dirt, blood, and filth after the nauseating train ride from San Fernando, the prisoners from the Bataan Death March were herded through the stockade gates. The camp was the remnants of the unfinished Filipino Army training base under construction prior to the outbreak of the war. Japanese guards moved the POWs at bayonet point into an open field to stand in the sun for hours. For the first time since the surrender, the Japanese attempted a count of all prisoners. After hours of counting and recounting, most of the new arrivals received a small bowl of dirty, maggot-laced rice—about two handfuls.[1]

Each new arriving group of prisoners would stand for a harangue from the camp commander, Captain Tsuneyoshi Yoshio. Standing on a small box, the captain yelled more than he spoke. In a long rambling speech, the POWs were told that they were an inferior race and, in fact, worthless slaves of the Japanese Empire. Dressed in oversized tall riding boots and spurs, baggy shorts, a white shirt draped with medals, and a ceremonial sword that hung to his ankles, the captain stressed they would be treated as such and owed their lives to the goodwill of the Emperor. There would be no rank in the camp and all prisoners must salute and bow to every Japanese soldier. He made it clear that he detested the POWs and any violations would result in instant execution. He told the POWs "that Americans were dogs, that they'd always been dogs, and that they were going to be treated like dogs" and concluded his rant by saying, "Your children and my children shall be enemies to the end of time. You will die from old age under our command." It soon became apparent that conditions at O'Donnell were comparable to the harsh treatment of the Death March.[2]

General Edward King, transported to the camp in advance of the arrival of his troops, was at the main camp gate when the battered soldiers slowly marched in. He was much distressed at the brutal conditions and blatant Japanese disregard for the POWs under what the Japanese addressed as the "so-called Geneva Conventions," declaring they were not prisoners of war but only captives of the Imperial Army; the Japanese Army made and enforced their own rules. General King—slapped so many times by the Japanese that the general's eyes were black and swollen—greeted and spoke to as many of the arriving groups of Americans as possible. Clearly believing that if he made it home, he would be held accountable for the surrender on Bataan, he reminded each group he spoke to, "You men remember this. I surrendered you; you did not surrender. I'm the one responsible for that, and the blame and disgrace are mine, not yours, so let me carry them.

You've suffered far too much as it is. All I ask that you obey the orders of the Japanese so that you don't bring further pain on yourselves."[3]

Guards once again conducted a shakedown of the prisoners to take away any remaining personal items hidden during the march to the camp. Japanese coins or documents were grounds for immediate execution. It was very obvious the enemy had no intentions of either honoring the Geneva War Convention or working with the International Red Cross. The result was a total blackout concerning the outside world. Neither the authorities in Washington nor families of the prisoners had any word of their status—dead or alive. The Texas A&M's *Texas Aggie* publication received hundreds of calls and telegrams on the status of the Aggies from family and friends, with the editor reassuring them, "No news has been received as to the fate of the A. & M. men in the Philippines since the fall of Bataan and Corregidor—it is considered likely the great majority of them are prisoners." Washington was more preoccupied with the planning for a "cross-channel" operation in Europe, with General Marshall building up expectations in his May 1942 West Point graduation speech, saying that "American troops are landing in England and will soon land in France." There was no mention of the fate of the defenders of Bataan and Corregidor![4]

Once Captain Yoshio finished his boisterous "welcome," the POWs were divided among old bamboo-framed *bahai* huts with *nipa* roofs—no doors, no bunks, and no running water or latrines. The camp was surrounded by a barbwire fence and guard shacks on stilts. Camp O'Donnell was divided into sections, one for the Americans and a second for Filipino soldiers. Designed to hold about 18,000 men, the camp, designed in early 1941, ballooned to more than 55,000 soldiers (9,300 Americans and more than 47,000 Filipinos) packed into the one-square-mile camp, some 617 acres. Three small, low-pressure water taps resulted in a twenty-four hour per day vigil and a long slow moving line of men to fill only one canteen per soldier. Some in line fell asleep while waiting and some died while waiting. The Americans placed their own guards to control crazed men who demanded more water than allowed. There was no bathing by order of the camp commander, as it was viewed as a waste of water. The contaminated water only helped to spread dysentery.[5] Here is a detailed list of rules laid down by the Japanese Commandant at Camp O'Donnell:

- The Japanese Army does not recognize rank of the prisoners of war.
- Prisoners will salute all Japanese officers and soldiers while wearing headgear and bow appropriately when not.
- Daily roll calls will be made.
- Men will not leave the barracks between the hours of 7:00 p.m. and 6:40 a.m.
- Stay more than three meters away from the fence surrounding the camp at all times.
- Water will be economized. Only sponge baths are permitted.
- No smoking within twenty feet of a building.
- All borrowed articles from the Japanese will be carefully accounted for.
- Anyone disobeying orders or trying to escape will be shot to death.
- All requests should be sent through proper channels.[6]

THE RISING SUN

As the Japanese spread their Greater East Asia Co-Prosperity Sphere of influence and military confrontation across Asia, the Japanese Imperial Army was forced to create an extensive network of more than 150 internment camps in ten different countries.[7] These prisoner of war camps were a low priority to Tokyo, and the Japanese had little concern for the welfare and death rate or what others thought of their prison camp conditions. In the aftermath of the surrender of American and Allied troops in the Philippines and across Asia, more than 290,000 prisoners of war were held in camps in the Philippine Islands, Japan, Korea, China, Thailand, French Indochina, Singapore, Java, the Dutch East Indies, Burma, and Manchuria. The primary prisoner of war camps on Luzon included O'Donnell, Cabanatuan, Nichols Field, Bilibid Prison, Tarlac, Las Pinas, Pasay, Corregidor, Fort Santiago, and Fort McKinley. By May 1942, the Japanese Imperial Army extended military control across the western Pacific to an area that covered nearly two million square miles in size, spanned five time zones, and comprised a native population of some one billion five hundred million people.[8]

All the POW camps were notorious and brutal to those interned, yet Camp O'Donnell, the first camp stop for most American POWs, quickly set the benchmark for starvation, disease, brutal treatment, and death at the hands of captors. There was not enough housing and many slept on the open ground. The Japanese demanded work gangs, but only about 30 percent were healthy enough for working all day in the hot sun. Hundreds of sick, wounded, and starved prisoners were laid like cord wood end to end on the floor of huts—saturated in vomit, blood, and feces and covered with flies and maggots. American medical personnel attempted to comfort the sick, but without medicine and clean conditions, their efforts were generally useless. In this grim environment, a "Zero Ward"—or as one chaplain soon called it, "The Pearly Gates," or "St. Peter's Ward"—was set up for those near death. The crude and primitive hospital was more the camp's de facto morgue than clinic. As the days passed, a prime concern was where to stack all the bodies. The overwhelming cause of death in the camp was complications caused by acute dysentery. Soon the death rate in the camp soared to one death every fourteen minutes—more than forty Americans per day—and some reports, given the fact there are no clear records, place the deaths during the first six weeks at more than two hundred per day, with Filipino deaths exceeding three hundred per day. One out of every six Americans who entered Camp O'Donnell died.[9]

Among those completing the forced march to Camp O'Donnell were Texas Aggies from across the state of Texas: **Captain Adolph H. Giesecke '26**, an Infantry officer from San Antonio; **Lt. Col. Rufus H. Rogers '26**, staff officer in the 81st Division from Hillsboro; **Captain Jack W. Kelley '29**, a pilot in the 19th Bomb Group from Texarkana; **Lt. William Culp '38**; **Lt. James M. Henry '39**, a pilot in the 24th Pursuit Group from Kingsville; and **Captain Ross I. Miller '39** from Bryan, a combat engineer in the 101st Engineers. Except for

Lt. Culp, who returned home in August 1945, all would die within two years of captivity.[10]

During the first weeks of Camp O'Donnell operations—"Camp O'Death" to the men—from April 10 to May 16, more than 1,500 Americans and an estimated 20,000 or more Filipinos died. Lack of clean water; poor, bug-infested food; no medical treatment; harsh work conditions; and frequent floggings increased the death rate weekly. The cruelty of the camp was confirmed at the postwar War Crimes Tribunal held in Tokyo and Manila, which chronicled the brutality, including, for example, extensive torture; burning prisoners with cigarettes, candles, and hot irons; and the "water treatment." The first few weeks at Camp O'Donnell were a harsh extension of the brutality on the Bataan Death March. The guards routinely singled out the weakest POWs, some little more than walking skeletons, for beatings. While some postwar apologists have tried to downplay the hideous conditions and brutality, the plight of the POWs was well known by high-ranking Japanese military and civil authorities, who made frequent camp visits. After a hasty camp visit, one Japanese general snapped after seeing the poor conditions: "Your men are not starving. They need more exercise." To cover up the conditions in the camps, the International Red Cross was routinely forbidden to inspect and visit the POW camps. If Red Cross supplies arrived, they were stored for use by the Japanese. Furthermore, there were abundant food supplies available in the countryside surrounding the internment camps. Camp Cabanatuan, for example, was located in the heart of a highly productive rice region. As a detailed postwar report and investigation by the Office of the US Provost Marshall General bluntly noted, "The Japs deliberately held the prisoners on a starvation diet."[11]

Piles of rotting corpses in the camp created a near unbearable stench. Following a heated confrontation with the camp commander and staff, the American chaplains in the camp prevailed to prevent the Japanese from burning the bodies of the dead in an open fire pit. Burial crews put the dead soldiers on litters fashioned from shutters, old doors, and blankets swung between two bamboo poles. The corpses were moved outside the camp and placed in shallow unmarked mass graves, many without dog tags or identification. American officers attempted to record the name, rank, and date of death, but still many unidentified prisoners were abruptly buried. During the early burials, the Japanese did not allow prisoners to put up grave markers. Packs of wild dogs roamed the camp perimeter, often unearthing the dead. And during the rainy season, if not weighted down by rocks, bodies would literally float out of the graves.[12]

Conditions at O'Donnell became so deplorable by late May that the Japanese realized they had to move the POWs or face losing hundreds more prisoners each day. Furthermore, camp commanders were being contacted from Tokyo on the status of able-bodied men to work local projects and also those fit to be shipped to Japan and Korea to work in the mines and factories. The Japanese authorities were also concerned about the rising death rate among the Filipinos. Beginning in June, they released more than twenty thousand sick and wounded Filipino POWs from Camp O'Donnell with little or no accounting. There was no such concern for the release of the American POWs, as more than nine thousand Americans were transported some fifty miles eastward over a four-day period to the new camp at Cabanatuan. Senior officers above the rank of colonel were relocated to the holding camp at Tarlac. One survivor recalled of the transfer, "Only the dying seemed to be kept in O'Donnell." Unlike the death squads along the Death March route on Bataan who bayonetted the stragglers, many of the walking wounded and sick were transferred by truck.[13]

During the last week of May 1942, American prisoners were being moved from camp to camp. In addition to moving those from Camp O'Donnell, the nine thousand POWs on Corregidor, after spending nearly three weeks on the open 500-foot wide and 1,500-foot long concrete slab at the 92nd Garage Area on the Rock, were loaded on three Japanese freighters. Transported across Manila Bay, they were marched—or paraded in columns of four through Manila down Dewey Boulevard flanked by thousands of Filipino onlookers—six miles to the old Spanish-built prison of Bilibid. To make room for the Americans, the Japanese had released nearly a thousand hardened criminals, including dozens of convicted murderers. Bilibid would be used for various groups during the war as the Japanese worked to manage their overwhelming number of POWs. Held only for four days in Manila, the Corregidor prisoners were marched to the railway and loaded on cattle cars for the trip to Cabanatuan, located about sixty-five miles north of Manila in Nuevo Ecija Province.[14]

CABANATUAN

The prisoners from Corregidor arrived three days before the mass transfer of American POWs from Camp O'Donnell arrived. As the Bataan Death March survivors entered the camp at Cabanatuan, the Corregidor soldiers were shocked at their condition, ragged attire, and general poor health. While those on the Rock had been held in outside detainment after their surrender, nonetheless they had had a better diet and had not been exposed to the horrific Death March.[15] One soldier remembered, "The shock of seeing the guys from O'Donnell coming in was like something sticking in my throat. It was like watching a horror movie. These guys were like walking zombies. Skeletons walking toward you with skin hanging on the bones. Heads look like skulls. Then there was that color—yellow, white, grey. Their eyes were just yellow."[16]

In spite of the brutality and death at O'Donnell, Cabanatuan is often remembered over all the camps in which the Americans were held during the war in the Pacific. One reason is that nearly all the American POWs at one time or another were processed through one of the three camps at Cabanatuan, and second, it became well known for the dramatic US Army Ranger raid that liberated the camp in January 1945. In fact, the camp was very similar to O'Donnell, covering about four hundred acres on a treeless plain, surrounded by eight-foot barbwire fences and guard towers with spotlights and machine guns. The huts, or *bahag* (Tagalog for "house"), and crude water supplies were as bad as at O'Donnell, and with the rapid influx of prisoners, the camp was soon overwhelmed with sewage problems, poor food, and little or no medical care; the odors of death and human waste pervaded the air. Due to the rationing of water, each prisoner was allowed a maximum of only one canteen per day, and the POWs were unable to take a bath for more than forty-five days after arrival. The average daily diet rarely reached one thousand calories. While scurvy and pellagra, due to vitamin deficiency, tormented the men with bleeding gums and scaly sores, they dealt with yellow jaundice and severe fungus infections, and soon a new wave of sickness spread through the camp—encephalitis, elephantiasis, and tuberculosis. Mosquitos continued to spread both dengue fever and malaria. The number of deaths during the first weeks in the new camp soon equaled that of Camp O'Donnell.[17]

Conditions had not improved at Cabanatuan. The following chilling sadistic and inhuman account of those collected into the "near death ward" is taken from *Bataan and Beyond (1978)*, written by Texas Aggie Captain John Coleman:

> The Air Group Commander Colonel Bill Maverick asked if I would take charge of a barracks, the sick bay, and told me to take as many men as I needed to help this detail. I did not know what to expect, nor could I have imagined it. I appointed eight men to go with me.
>
> I was stunned beyond description when we got to this sick bay and looked in. There were about ninety men lying on the ground in the dirt, naked and unconscious. They were skin and bones. These were the last of the men moved from Camp O'Donnell. Most were lying on their backs, some were on their sides. Their hair and beards were a tangled mess, soiled by their own excretion. Their mouths hung open and their eyes were half closed. They all looked like dead men.
>
> Most of the men who had dysentery had defecated just as they lay. The only thing we could do was to remove the soiled dirt and replace it with fresh soil. We tried to drop water on their lips and into their mouths so they could swallow it, but if we tried to drop it down their throats they would strangle—none of them uttered a word.
>
> They could not even wash the filth from their bodies or cloths, matted hair, beards. They were mentally repressed, had swollen limbs from beriberi, unhealed, festering wounds that were never treated. No attempt was made by the Imperial Japanese Army to furnish any kind of medication to alleviate the suffering. The International Red Cross

> tried to give them medicine, but the Japanese government refused to let it help in any way.
>
> They were far away from family, friends and the nation they loved. They had given their all. It was hard to realize and harder to accept that it should end like this. This was the worst detail I was ever to serve on. All these ninety men were dead within four days.[18]

The brutality by guards at Cabanatuan continued unchecked. The Japanese were brutal in the punishment of those who attempted to escape. Four men tried to escape and were captured and tied to posts to be beaten for hours by the guards in front of all the assembled prisoners. The four were then made to dig their own graves and, as the camp watched, were then shot in the head point blank standing in the dug holes. Coleman recalled, "A lieutenant colonel and Navy lieutenant, that tried to escape were brought back to the camp, after the beating the lieutenant had his left eye ball dangling from its socket down to his cheek. The two men were then tied to a truck and dragged through camp. When the lieutenant colonel could not stand [upright] any longer they stopped, a Japanese officer drew his sword and beheaded him. They threw his head and body into the back of the truck and drove out of sight." The Japanese looked for cold-blooded opportunities to decapitate POWs. They believed decapitation was the ultimate insult, inasmuch as any man who was decapitated would never be reunited with his soul and thus never enter heaven. Many of the stubborn Americans prisoners denied their captors satisfaction by laughing during beatings. As a consequence, more escapes were attempted, as the POWs felt it a better option than being tortured and dying in camp. On occasion as many as ten escapees were captured and executed at one time.[19]

Texas Aggies transferred from Camp O'Donnell to Cabanatuan included tank **M.Sgt. William Boyd '27**; **Lt. Hugh A. Derrick '39** of the 71st Engineer Battalion from San Antonio; pursuit pilot **Lt. Howard P. Hardegee '39** from Ben Wheeler; **Lt. Orman L. Fitzhugh '40** from Ft. Worth; **Lt. Melvin R. Millard '40** from Abilene, a member of the 200th Coastal Artillery unit on Corregidor; as well as pilots

Lt. John W. Muse '40 from Dallas, **Lt. John R. Noles '39**, and **Lt. James R. Davis '42**, all three being members of the 27th Bomb Group. Of this entire group of nine soldiers and airmen, eight died as prisoners of war at the hands of Japanese; only **T.Sgt. John J. Moseley '40** from Quanah, Texas, survived to return home.[20]

The harsh conditions and brutality in the camps took a terrible toll on the prisoners. The losses far exceeded those on the battlefield. Most of the men who died at Cabanatuan were troops captured on Bataan. From June through August 1942, more than 1,500 Bataan survivors died of complications from illness due to malnutrition and lack of medical care. By year end, more than 3,500 of the 7,300 men at Cabanatuan had perished. Almost all these deaths could have been prevented had the Japanese provided the basics of food, shelter, medicine, and water. One colonel recounted that in his regiment of more than 1,000 men, 25 had been killed and 75 were missing in action at the fall of Bataan. After arrival at Camp Cabanatuan, 453 additional men of the unit died in camp at the hands of the Japanese. Living and sanitary conditions further deteriorated as the camp was hit by a diphtheria epidemic. **Captain Rudyard Kipling Grimes '38** of Abilene, commander of Company A, 57th Infantry (PS), died during a diphtheria epidemic that struck the camp in the fall of 1942. The Grimes family was posthumously presented the Distinguished Service Cross by General Wainwright on January 18, 1947, at Fort Sam Houston, San Antonio, for his heroism in action on Bataan on January 12, 1942.[21]

During the imprisonment, the Americans were interrogated or "quizzed" by Japanese intelligence officers about the operations on Bataan and systems operations on Corregidor, such as the communications and water supply, and they were questioned about planned Allied operations, of which, for the most part, they had no operational knowledge. The Japanese were very interested in American tank operations and tactics. Captain Tom Dooley concluded from these interrogations that the Japanese feared American artillery and tanks the most. The long-range intensive bombardment of the Points sector at the tip of the Bataan Peninsula in January from the big guns on Corregidor amazed the Japanese. American tanks, which were overestimated in numbers, were the reason the Japanese landed in south Luzon and not in Manila Bay as planned. Dooley estimates from field reports that the Japanese overestimated the US tank strength anywhere from 33 to 900 percent (158 to 1,080 tanks). The most the American tanks defenders had at any one time was about 30 operational tanks. Timely supply of fuel and repair in the field of battle was a major obstacle to US tank operations, and furthermore, they were used to primarily cover the retreat into Bataan and were never fully employed in offensive operations. The Japanese eventually landed about 200 tanks on Luzon, inferior in armor but better adapted to the tropical terrain and better armed with a very effective 47mm gun (US M3 tanks were armed with a 37mm gun). Japanese tank doctrine viewed armor as only support for the infantry, and thus, during the balance of the war, the Japanese never developed an adequate offensive deterrent to the American tank.[22]

ESCAPE AND DIE

In an effort to prevent escape attempts, the camp commander organized the prisoners into groups of ten, often referred to as "shooting squads," for roll call and accountability. If one or more of the ten tried to escape, *all the men in the squad* would be tortured and executed. In one case, a group of nine was on the verge of execution when it was believed a member of the ten-man squad had escaped. Escape and recapture was greeted by a sentence of sure death. However, there had been no escape, as the tenth man's body was discovered in the dust and grime underneath one of buildings where he had crawled to die—he was clutching the uneaten portion of a dead rat. As one American lamented, "Dying was easy for the prisoners, but living was hell."[23]

Work details were soon demanded for light duty as well as heavy work gangs. Prisoners worked on airport runways and ramps, rebuilding bridges, road projects, and building construction as well as clearing battle-damaged equipment. Some three thousand worked in farming projects on about five hundred acres, growing food for the Japanese, little being given to the POWs. Planting, hoeing, and hauling water were endless tasks. They were marched to the fields barefooted as a precaution against escape and worked all day in the burning sun, which also took a toll on the men. If a prisoner was found smuggling hidden vegetables in his ragged clothes, he was beaten and in some cases beheaded. There was no mercy and very low morale. The Japanese circulated rumors that the farming was based on a five-year plan. There seemed to be no end in sight. One observer noted, "What threw the POWs off most was not simply the viciousness of the Japanese but their unpredictability—the accusations, outburst, and ensuing repercussions. They had rules, which they made, re-made, and disobeyed. Violence against the POWs was triggered by language problems, cultural differences, racial animosity, and the cold blooded desire for revenge. Seemingly random, it collectively amounted to a systematic abuse of thousands of Allied prisoners of war. The violence against the POWs on Bataan was not unusual but became the norm."[24]

The Japanese continued segregating the POWs with the transfer of all the general officers and 106 colonels to Tarlag Province on June 9, 1942. Generals Wainwright, King, Moore, and Beebe were the ranking members. Each general was allowed to bring a limited number of staff aides with them. The camp conditions remained harsh and the treatment strict, yet there was additional food provided and no work details. The official postwar US Army Provost Marshall Report noted, "The Japanese delighted in humiliating high ranking officers." On the morning of August 11, 179 officers, senior noncommissioned officers, and orderlies were among the first American prisoners to be placed on prison ships and transported to Japan, Korea, and Formosa to camps.[25]

The American POWs were loaded on the *Nagara Maru* with the general officers billeted on the main deck adjacent to a group of Japanese officers and provided the same food as served to their Imperial captors. The remainder of the prisoners were herded into the forward below deck hold and held in typical troop berth of rough wooden shelves for beds, poor ventilation, and no access to the upper deck. The food was not as good as that provided for the generals but much better than the food in the Philippine camps. Three Texas Aggies—General Moore, Major Dooley, and Colonel Edwin Aldridge—were on the *Nagara* for the four-day voyage to Takoa, Formosa. Before transfer

The only known picture of the top-ranking American general held prisoner at the Tarlac camp on Luzon taken in April 1942. In this captured Japanese photo, Maj. Gen. George Moore '08 is seated on the far left, front row, followed by Lt. Gen. King; Lt. Gen. Wainwright; Colonel Ito and Lt. Omura, Japanese Army; Maj. Gen. Parker; and Maj. Gen. Jones. Standing left to right, Japanese guard; Brig. Gens. Lough, Funk, Weaver, Brougher, Beebe, Bluemel, Drake, McBride, and Pierce; Colonel Hoffman; and two Japanese guards. Five additional American general officers not pictured were held in the southern islands. (Courtesy of the author's collection.)

to the *Suzuya Maru* for the final leg of the trip to the work camp at Karenko, the POWs were lined up on deck, stripped naked, and given a full body cavity examination, which General Wainwright noted, "centered around the rectum." They arrived on August 14, 1942. The harsh treatment for those left behind did not improve.[26]

In mid-August, the generals and colonels from Camp Casising near Malabalay, Mindanao, were assembled and shipped on the *Lima Maru* to Formosa. Joining the group from Tarlac headed by Wainwright were Brig. Gens. William Sharp, Guy Fort, Joseph Vachon, and Filipino general Manuel A. Roxas—who would survive and become the first postwar president of the Philippines. By September, the camp at Karenko became home to a dozen Allied generals from Singapore and included Sir Arthur Percival and General Ian McRae. Conditions for the general officers proved slightly better than those for the junior officers and enlisted troops. The guards routinely practiced cruel acts to torture and demean the weak prisoners. The Japanese often made up new rules on the spur of the moment, followed by beatings that never stopped. However, as the weeks and months passed, it was the hunger from malnutrition that caused much pain and illness. General Wainwright recalled, "Our months of half-rations on Bataan and Corregidor and then the starvation diets of our imprisonment were beginning to catch up with us . . . we were haunted by hunger." Starvation was so acute at Karenko, the prisoners grimly joked about counting the two or three beans in the bottom of their watery soup. Dividing up the food rations became more difficult each day. Many of the men were desperate. "We voted for Major General George Moore to divide the food," recalled Wainwright. "He accepted on the grounds he could split the rice and soup behind a closed door, so there could be no supervision. We would wait outside, bereft of anything on our minds except our never-ending excruciating hunger."[27]

DAVAO PENAL COLONY

In the fall of 1942, death at Cabanatuan was still a daily occurrence. Rumor spread in the camp that the Japanese were planning to transfer up to a thousand so-called healthy POWs with technical skills to a new camp. Speculation was that the transfer would be to either Japan or China as part of an industrial work detail. While many were wary of being shipped to Japan, the Japanese soon assembled the prisoners for shipment not to the homeland but to the southernmost island in the Philippine Archipelago, Mindanao. Many who gathered to be shipped out reasoned the new location could not be worse than Cabanatuan and, more important, possibly offered more food and a better location to escape. Yet in fact the constant moving and relocation proved a very distressing feature adding to the uncertainty and stress of the indefinite period of incarceration. One debriefing noted, "The future offered only visions of continued hunger, cold, disease, forced labor, and continued subservience in the face of shouting, slapping, and beatings."[28]

In a tropical rainstorm, more than a thousand prisoners were marched from the camp to Cabanatuan City, loaded on railcars for transport to Manila, and housed overnight in the Bilibid Prison. The next morning, October 28, 1942, they were marched, this time with no crowds or onlookers, to Pier 7—known in its heyday as the "million-dollar pier"—and loaded onto an old coal-burning cargo trawler, the *Erie Maru.* Some seventeen Texas Aggie officers being transferred to Davao included **Captain George H. Peets '30**, 31st Infantry; **Captain Gus H. Froebel '35** from San Antonio, a staff officer in the 86th Field Artillery; **Captain Travis E. Perrenot '36**, 24th Field Artillery also from San Antonio; and **Lt. Donald W. Petersen '40,** a pilot in the 27th Bomb Group from Ft. Worth.[29]

As the prisoners boarded, they were immediately concerned because the balance of the cargo included hundreds of drums of highly explosive aviation fuel. In usual official fashion, the Japanese neglected marking the ship as a prisoner of war transport, which made it highly vulnerable to US submarine patrols. Unable to complain, the POWs were crammed into two below deck, poorly ventilated holds. Commanded and staffed by Japanese Navy personnel, the prisoners did seem to receive better care, water, and food—as was very evident by the fact that there were only two deaths in transit.[30] The eleven-day journey by sea ended at the dock of an old Lasang Lumber Company on the south side of Mindanao. Unloaded at dark, the prisoners were marched seventeen miles through the jungle in a rainstorm to an old remote Filipino prison camp, "sort of a hell hole," in the middle of a swamp—the Davao Penal Colony, or "Dapecol."[31]

Arriving at the remote location, the POWs were greeted by about nine hundred American and Filipino prisoners who had been captured on Mindanao by the Japanese on January 20, 1942. Among those welcoming the Texas Aggies were **Captain Sidney R. Greer '35**, a former Texas Highway Department engineer, and **Lt. Col. Rufus H. Rogers '26**, formerly a husky animal husbandry teacher at Del Rio High School in south Texas, both of whom had been in charge of construction at Del Monte airfield on Mindanao. Rogers, one of the last American commanders to officially capitulate, surrendered on May 17, 1942, as commander of the 33rd Infantry Regiment located in the mountains of northeast Cebu Island. Two of the longest interned

US naval reconnaissance photo of the damaged and sinking POW ship, the *Oryoku Maru*, at Olongapa, Luzon, December 15, 1944. The white dots between the ship and shore are splashes in the water where POWs swim to evacuate the doomed ship; among the survivors were eleven Texas Aggie officers. (Photo taken by an F6F-3 aircraft from VF-11 Squadron off the USS Hornet. Courtesy of NARA.)

POWs at Dapecol, they were sent to Japan aboard the *Oryoku Maru* on December 13, 1944, which sank on December 15 (see chapter 6 for more on the *Oryoku Maru* and other Hell Ships).[32]

While it was a change of scenery from Cabanatuan, the conditions and guards were no better. The guards, led by camp commander Major Maida, were not regular army troops but instead what the prisoners called a bunch of nonmilitary "Taiwanese yard birds," mostly very young, untrained guards who were passed over for regular service in the Imperial Army. Nonetheless, they continued a near nonstop reign of torture and cruelty. Holding the power of life and death, the brutality soon began. Dapecol soon grew to more than 2,400 POWs, with the addition of troops captured in the Visayan Islands, more than half of whom were sick and unable to work. Prisoners were reduced to wearing only a loin cloth or G-string and had no shoes. It was assumed the near naked dress would dissuade the POWs from attempting escape through the surrounding harsh jungle and swamp. Those who did not comply with camp rules were hung by the thumbs, with some having their thumbs pulled off by the wire. One disabling action practiced by the guards was to hit a POW on the top of the bare foot with his rifle butt, usually breaking the foot and permanently crippling the soldier with one blunt strike.[33]

Colonel William Dyess of Abilene, who would make a daring escape from camp in 1943, wrote one of the most compelling accounts of the Bataan Death March and POW camp conditions. Dyess noted that there was a great deal of forced labor at Davao, and a mixed grouping of airmen, sailors, and marines, mostly "city boys," were assigned to permanent plowing detail at the jungle farm. The plows were one handled, with one wooden blade, and "belonged in a medieval museum." The beasts of burden were humped cattle with rings on their noses. The cattle were uncontrollable, doing more damage to already planted patches of growing crops. Dyess noted the following:

> I am a country boy from Texas and have chopped and picked cotton, hoed corn, and tended truck patches, but I never learned to plow. The only man there who ever had was a graduate [unnamed] of Texas

A. &. M. College. He [the Aggie] commented: "Man and boy, I plowed with stubborn Texas mules, but all my experience with them is no help with these misborn dromedaries [camels]!" After a day's plowing, as the Japanese guards yelled and cussed the prisoners to gain control, Dyess recalled the field looked as if it had been dive-bombed, strafed, and fought over by tanks.[34]

By mid-1943, accounts of the harsh battles on Bataan had gradually begun to leak into the news media across America. Up until this period, most Americans had no knowledge of the scope of the war being waged in the Pacific. In addition to the descriptive and gruesome reports from Captain Dyess and his fellow escapees, Army nurse Captain Juanita Redmond Hipps chronicled a blunt account of conditions on Bataan and Corregidor prior to her evacuation to Australia in April 1942. In June 1943, two Hollywood movies were released: first, *So Proudly We Hail!*, based on Hipps's bestseller memoir, *I Served on Bataan* (the first of some five movies between 1943 to 1945 on Bataan and Corregidor), and second, the feature-length film titled *Bataan*, starring Robert Taylor. These movies were box-office hits but did nothing to improve the conditions in the prison camps or allow the International Red Cross access to assist the medical needs of the POWs.[35]

As the cruel conditions, bad food, poor medical care, daylong work, and morale took many swings, time continued to drag on. Unheard of medical conditions in civilized society crippled many of the men. Captain Robley Evans, taken prisoner on Bataan, survived the march and O'Donnell only to become blind due to vitamin deficiency. Thus POW camp life for most of the Americans in the Philippines was a living hell. In time, the Japanese began allowing a rare Red Cross package from home, limited church services, and some gatherings to include "variety shows" hosted by the POWs. A Christmas Eve service was allowed in 1943. Intended to be a prayer service, the Japanese at Dapecol instead showed the despondent POWs motion pictures of the US battleships being bombed and sunk during the attack on Pearl Harbor—two years earlier! None of the prisoners had ever seen the film and up until the showing had only heard rumors of the extensive blow to the US fleet. In a brief moment of triumph, a small group stood to sing "God Bless America" and were ordered to sit or be punished. Within minutes, thousands were on their feet singing at the top of their lungs, drowning out the guards' commands and echoing the tune through the nearby jungle. One soldier remembers, "When we got through singing, there wasn't a dry eye in the whole crowd." The guards did not like it, yet they could not stop the singing as the POWs wandered slowly in the dampness and darkness back to their dirt floor huts.[36]

The occasional Red Cross package distribution aside, when the camps were finally recaptured, there were large stockpiles of packages, food, clothing, and bags of months of old mail found that were never distributed. As late as January 1943, the US Office of War Information had no confirmed list of Americans held prisoner in the Philippines, which proved very convenient for the Japanese captors ignoring both mail and requests from the International Red Cross. Some camps allowed church services and provided reading material but little or no outside contact. Work details were increased and Prime Minister General Hideki Tojo ordered all POWs, including officers, to be evaluated; those deemed healthy enough to travel marched to Manila to board ships for work camps primarily in Japan, Korea, and Manchuria. Shipments of prisoners began in late 1942 and gradually increased in number by late 1944. Diseases and brutality continued, as did the death toll, which exceeded 2,600 at Cabanatuan alone.[37]

MUKDEN

One of the most remote prisoner of war camps was in Mukden (Hoten), Manchuria, at the Mitsubishi Machine Tool Plant. The earliest American POWs from the Philippines arrived at the remote industrial complex in the fall of 1942, transported on the freighter *Tottori Maru*, a ship owned and operated by Mitsubishi in order to rush the POW workers to the factory to manufacture replacement parts for the Zero fighter planes. The poor condition of the arriving POWs shocked the factory managers, who needed healthy workers. This cold, desolate location was the holding area for 1,485 Americans as well as more than a hundred Australian and British flag officers and members of their staffs (captured from Singapore in February 1942). The brutality of the guards continued unchecked. Work details walked some five miles in the bitter cold conditions, ranging to forty degrees below zero, and work was expected of all interned, regardless of rank. Within weeks, more than 175 frozen POW bodies were stacked in a makeshift morgue, awaiting burial. That the Texas Aggies held at Mukden and survived to return home is an indication of their courage: General George Moore '08, Major Tom Dooley '35, Tech Sergeant John Moseley '39, Col. Edwin Aldridge '16, Captain Stockton Burns '35, Lt. Bill Hamilton '40, Lt. Urban Hopmann '39, and Captain Jack Walker '36. An interesting Aggie POW was T.Sgt. Moseley, who was the first to arrive at Mukden in late 1942, swept up in the wartime draft by the New Mexico National Guard in 1941. As an aspiring park ranger with the National Park Service, Moseley, who majored in landscape architecture, became an intern at Carlsbad Caverns in New Mexico. He and six of his friends at the park were inducted into the 515th Coast Artillery Regiment (AA), hastily trained, and sent to the Philippines. An accomplished artist as a cadet at Texas A&M in the late 1930s, he continued his avocation in prison camp, designing the annual Christmas program and laying out the military cemetery at Mukden. T.Sgt. John Moseley published the POW camp newspaper, *Nor Iron Bars*. In all, by early 1945, 405 senior officers and civilian administrators from across the Pacific Theater were interned at Mukden, China, along with about 1,400 additional Allied Army captives.[38]

A number of American prisoners were able to keep diaries hidden on scraps of paper and small notebooks. Many documents were confiscated, some water damaged, some buried and never found, but a few such as General Wainwright, General Beebe, Tom Dooley '35, Carl Abney '34, and Edwin Aldridge '16 compiled notebooks and diaries that survived. Given all the confusion on Bataan before and after the surrender as well as the multiple transfers of POWs among camps and Hell Ships, these surviving chronicles, while few, recorded a detailed firsthand look at camp conditions, torture, medical treatment,

position Babcocks B.P. Art and some Tanks
The Two opposing Tank groups had a battle
here and 3 Jap Tanks knocked out. That
stopped the Japs for the day. Once they
get put off their schedule it takes them
some time to get started again. Just be
fore dark the Art put down a barage on
the Town which again threw them off
schedule. Gen. Stevens and Gen Selles
both came by our C.P. Selleck was through
and said so and left the area. Stevens
was much disgusted and in low spirits.
He wanted to stay so Gen Jones placed him
in charge and let him have the 51 Inf
to help out. The Japs made it easy
by not advancing. Another blunder for
them as there was very little in their front
at the time however they may not have
known it. Most of us think they must have
had a prearranged schedule that was not
clicking and it took too much time
to make the necessary changes. During
the day Soriano joined us. Did not recognize
him at first, neither did he recognize me.
I made him acquainted with the others in
the C.P. Late that afternoon we got out the
order for withdrawal north of the San
Fernando River. Mack and I had been all
over the area looking for a CP but could
not find one that connected by wire with
Plaridel except the wires to Manila and all were
out so we stayed in Plaridel. JAP Planes
were flying around all day and let
loose occassional bursts of MG fire on
the Town. Natives were moving in every
direction. No one seemed to know just
where he was going. After lunch Gen J.
told me to see if I could find out just where
we were going to go. So I went to North
Luzon Hq at [illegible] and then went to look
for Gen Parkers C.P. Got as far as Guagua
where I ran into a Traffic Jam that
was impassable. JAPs had bombed the
area and had fires going on everywhere
including lots of cars of ammunition
cars so had to return without getting to
Bataan. Well we had some new years eve
that night waiting for our time to pull out.
We had a couple of light drinks to bring in
the new year. At 3:00 AM Shrieve and I pulled
out for Bataan with no idea where we
or any one knew where. Traffic was a
solid stream, no passing as all were
driving without lights, many narrow
calls but no collissions. I stopped at
Guagua to find out where we were to go
Shrieve went on to Gen Parkers C.P. to
find out the same information. I ran into
Fisher Class 27 He was looking for some
prime movers to take some NAVY 8"
guns to Bataan He found some but could
not move them all. Not a civilian around.
place deserted and a mess. Had been
heavily Bombed and most of the Town
gone. Lots of Ammunition had been
collected there and it had gone up
in smoke. About 5 AM I ran into an
officer who gave me the information

Many prisoners secretly kept "notebooks" before and during captivity. This is a page from the notes of Colonel Edwin E. Aldridge '16, 61st Infantry Division. (Courtesy of the Aldridge Papers, Cushing Library.)

and most importantly rosters of Americans and their disposition. For example, for those on Bataan, any accurate unit records of personnel, their combat status, and their location were lost after February 1942. In an effort to confirm those held captive, Major Dooley and Colonel Aldridge at the Mukden camp each separately created an underground "sign-in" logbook with full name, home address, and signature of all officers in holding. In another set of notebooks, Abney recorded detained data on all officers he came in contact with, including data on some twenty Texas Aggies from camps at O'Donnell, Cabanatuan, and Bilibid. Before he was removed from Bilibid and in advance of his death (of wounds incurred on the *Enoura Maru*), on the *Brazil Maru* en route from Formosa to Japan on January 28, 1945, Abney entrusted his notebooks to a friend who after the war mailed them to his family in Marshall, Texas. Many of the diaries or notebooks contain entries detailing their favorite "fantasy" home cooked recipes. The obsessive preoccupation with food and the ongoing starvation condition in the camps over time was followed with daydreams about the ingredients for the ultimate meal upon freedom.[39]

Unlike the jungles of Bataan, the weather was very cold, windy, and damp. Work was limited to the factory, where oftentimes the Japanese marveled at the technical skills of the American POWs. Little did they know that, when asked to design a new part or fix a machine, the prisoners built in systems and aviation parts that soon failed and often crippled the expensive tooling machines. Knowing they were making parts for aircraft, the POWs adopted the motto, "No part will leave this factory in working order!"[40] Given the higher rank of internees at Mukden, there was an even greater effort in mid-1945 to push back at the Japanese and their means of treatment. Major Tom Dooley captured in his diary an effort to put the Japanese camp commander on notice that there was a complete disregard for the rules codified in the Hague as well as Geneva Conventions in the Japanese much touted "Code of Bushido" regarding the treatment of POWs. Submitted under the signatures of three general officers representing the American, Dutch, and British prisoners, it was a point-by-point review of the violations of international standards. An excerpt from this document drafted in

Formosa in May 1944, which included treatment, living conditions, meals, mail service, clergy visits, and medical care detailed the violations as follows:

STATUS OF OFFICERS

a. **Rank**: No POW may be deprived of his rank and all are entitled to respect: The Japanese do not recognize rank for the POWs. It is not normally used in addressing POWs who have been informed that they are all of one rank level with the enlisted men.
b. **Seniority**: Officer POWs salute only officers of equal or higher rank: The Japanese demanded all POWs, including those of the highest rank, to salute all Nippon army personnel, including the most junior privates.
c. **Humane Treatment**: POWs should at all times be treated with humanity, protected against acts of violence, insult, and public curiosity: POWs, including officers of the highest rank, have been repeatedly struck with the fist, boot, and rifle butt for offenses often most trivial, in many cases they have not understood for what offense.[41]

The written protest by the general officers did no good. In addition to the bitter cold, starvation diet, and brutality of Mukden POW camp, there was, unknown to most prisoners and Allied officials until the war crimes trials of 1946–47, a very dark side of top secret biological experimentation by Japanese doctors and technicians on POWs at Mukden. Various inhuman "medical" experiments, performed on both Chinese and Russian POWs, began as a ruse to improve health conditions at the prison and a promise to lower the death rate, which had already declined by early 1945. In fact, the "medical treatments" performed by a special organization known as the Kwantung Army's Anti-Infection "Unit 731" did not provide vitamin additives or protein or health enhancements but instead were experiments to test forms of botulisms and toxic illnesses suited for Western "Caucasians" in hopes of developing a deadly strain of bacterial microbes to infect the US Army if and when they landed on the homeland of Japan. Some reports do exist of American and Allied POWs being held in small holding containers for weeks and subjected to various toxins and biological agents—and not allowed to bathe, talk,

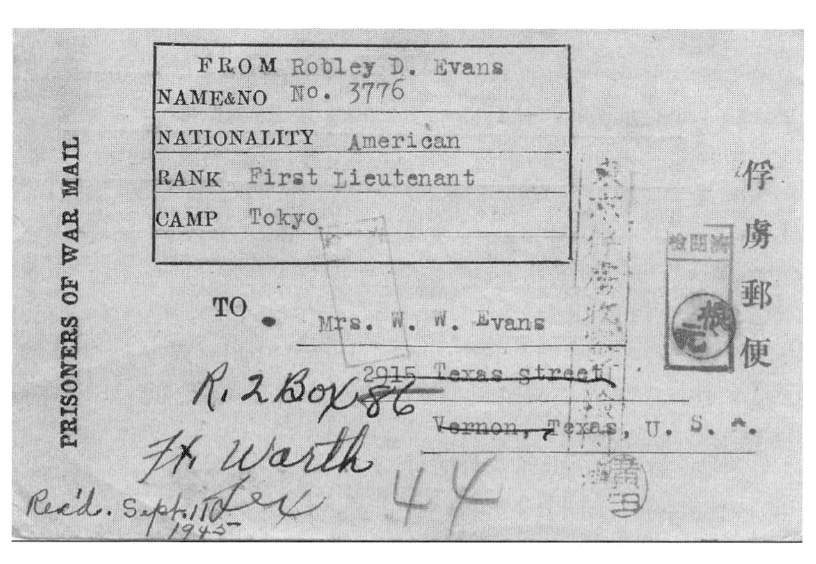

PRISONERS OF WAR MAIL

FROM Robley D. Evans
NAME&NO No. 3776
NATIONALITY American
RANK First Lieutenant
CAMP Tokyo

俘虜郵便

TO Mrs. W. W. Evans
~~2915 Texas street~~
R. 2 Box ~~86~~
~~Vernon, Texas~~, U. S. A.
Ft. Worth

Rec'd. Sept. 11 1945

44

DATE July 31, 1944

Radiogram received. Take care of yourself. Make plans for us living together. Physically well. Mentally improved. Morale is high. Best regards to Mr. Williamson, Dr. Walton, Mr. Hotard. Love and pray for an early reunion. Your letters source of great enjoyment. Send pictures of family.

Robley D. Evans

東京俘虜収容所

Brief letters on three-by-five postcards were the only correspondence allowed by prisoners. This note from Robley D. Evans '40, imprisoned in Japan, sends greetings to his family as well as Dr. T. O. Walton, president of Texas A&M. (Courtesy of the Robley Evans family collection.)

or walk. In other cases, entire barracks were divided into two groups to unwittingly test their reactions to infectious germs given to them sprayed on orange halves—seemingly given to increase vitamin C intake but in fact tainted to infect the body. The extent of such wartime medical experimentation has yet to be determined.[42]

The maltreatment and brutality was further enhanced by the continued mental anguish of not knowing what was going to happen and more important not having any outside contact with family. Some men were never able to make contact with relatives, yet many after more than eighteen months of imprisonment were able to receive mail via the International Red Cross. The process was badly managed by the Red Cross and further hampered by the Japanese who held mail and played mind games with the POWs. An example of how information was manipulated to produce mental anguish by both the Japanese soldiers and their civilian employees is provided in Captain Robley Evans's '40 postwar debriefing, drafted for US Army intelligence gathering evidence for war crimes trials in Tokyo, concerning his treatment during camp internment in Japan:

> In the instance of mental mistreatment by civilian interpreter Frank Quini. Mr. Quini was the son of an American Army Captain and a Japanese women, and was employed as a clerk of the United States Embassy [in Tokyo] prior to the war. After the outbreak of the war Quini renounced his American citizenship and swore allegiance to the Japanese government. These were Mr. Quini's own statements. On or about 16th May, 1944 Quini informed me that camp officials had received a radiogram for me. Quini's words were, "We have received a radiogram about your father [W.W. Evans]." It was known that my father was in poor health. Continuous reference was made to this radiogram for the next six weeks. The camp officials refused to give me the message, or the contents of the message. On or about 1st of July, 1944 the Superintendent of the Hitachi Daide Mine visited our camp and I asked him for the message and he instructed Quini that it be given me. The text of the message was, "FATHER W.W. Evans DIED February 4. Signed MOTHER."[43]

CHRISTMAS II IN HOTEN

'TWAS THE NIGHT BEFORE XMAS
AND ALL THROUGH THE HOUSE
LITTLE CREATURES WERE STIRRING,
EACH ONE WAS A LOUSE.
ALL THE MEN WERE A SLEEPING
OR WE MIGHT SAY "ALMOST",
EXCEPT FOR THE NIGHT GUARDS
WHO LEANED ON THEIR POSTS.

NO STOCKINGS WERE HUNG
BY THE PETCHKAS WITH CARE
IN THE HOPE THAT ST. NICHOLAS
SOON WOULD BE THERE,
FOR OLD SANTA WAS BUSY,
SO FAR, FAR AWAY,
THEY WERE SURE THAT HE
WOULDN'T BE WITH THEM
THAT DAY.

BUT THE GRIPES AND THE HOLLERS
WERE CERTAINLY FEW,
FOR TOMORROW'S A DINNER
WITH `TAKUSAN NIKKU';
AND DOWN AT THE `KAISHA'
THERE'S A SPECIAL TREAT,
A PROGRAM AND SINGING
AND GOODIES TO EAT.

NOW WE'VE COME FAR TOGETHER
THERE'S FAR TO GO YET.
AND WHEN WE GET HOME AGAIN
THERE'S LOTS TO FORGET.
SO `KYOTSKI' AND `BANGO'
AND KEEP IN THE RACE,
FOR THE CHANCES ARE
NEXT YEAR
WE'LL BE GONE FROM THIS PLACE.

SECOND ISSUE OF HOTEN WAR PRISONER'S PAPER. PUBLISHED DEC. 24, 1943 — SUBSCRIPTION RATES — 1 COPY PER YEAR, 1 BUN AND 2 FAGS LT. W.D. THOMPSON EDITOR, STAFF ARTISTS { MOSELEY PHILLIPS PINSON

A page from one of the only known newspaper flyers to be printed inside a Japanese POW camp. This was developed by T.Sgt. John J. Moseley '39 for the December 1943 Christmas issue, Hoten Camp, Mukden, China. (Courtesy of John J. Moseley '39.)

I SHALL RETURN

The years and months took a toll on the thousands of Allied prisoners of war held in camps across Asia. By late 1944, there was a measured and increasingly brutal shift in official policy in Tokyo toward POWs as more and more prisoners were shipped to work camps in Japan and on the mainland, leaving behind the sick, wounded, and decimated men deemed unable to work. The rapidly approaching American forces across the Pacific also prompted a ruthless policy to eliminate all evidence of the treatment and conditions of the POWs. This policy was soon confirmed by the direct orders to the Imperial Army camp commander at Puerto Princesa Prison Camp, at Palawan, Philippines. Lt. Sato, known to the POWs as "The Buzzard," was instructed to kill all prisoners and disguise the deaths as the result of an American bombing raid on the camp. In an act of blatant premeditated mass murder, on December 14, 1944, 150 American military prisoners, many from the 59th US Army Coast Artillery and the 4th Marines on Corregidor, were herded into a primitive underground air-raid shelter on the premise that the camp was expecting an attack. The ends of the hut were sealed, and then the defenseless POWs were covered in gasoline and set on fire. Those who did not die in the initial execution were bayoneted or shot. The panic that followed allowed a few Americans to escape into the jungle and onto the coast. With the assistance of friendly natives, some were guided to American forces. The preplanned elimination of American POWs had begun.[44]

The massacre of the prisoners was the beginning of the final stage of the Japanese increasingly frenzied acts of murder, rage, and ruthlessness. As American forces closed in on the Japanese in the Pacific, the Imperial soldiers would become more unpredictable as well as prone to honor the Emperor by dying an honorable Bushido death. From the War Ministry in Tokyo came direct orders to all camps outlining plans and means to address the "final disposition" of the POWs and "to dispose of them as the situation dictates"—soon to known (and formerly detailed and presented at the Japanese War Trials in 1946–47) as the Imperial August 1 "Kill All Order."[45] The murderous events at Palawan reported by a few that escaped soon invoked concern for

American POWs at Cabanatuan and the other camps across the Philippines. The cold-blooded orders from the highest command level in Tokyo were very clear:

> When the battle situation becomes urgent the POWs will be concentrated and confined in their location and kept under heavy guard until preparations for the final disposition will be made. Although the basic aim is to act under superior orders, individual disposition may be made in circumstances. Whether they are destroyed individually or in groups, and whether it is accomplished by means of mass bombing, poisonous smoke, poisons, drowning or decapitation, dispose of them as the situation dictates. It is the aim not to allow the escape of a single one, to annihilate them all, and not to leave any traces.[46]

The POW cemetery of Mukden, China, designed by T.Sgt. John Moseley '39 and the dedication ceremony shortly after the Japanese surrender. (Courtesy of John J. Moseley '39.)

General MacArthur's return to the Philippines came with the landing of more than 280,000 American troops, the largest landing of the war after Normandy. The landing at northern Luzon on the Lingayen Gulf on January 9, 1945, took place exactly three years after the first Japanese Army recon forces landed on Luzon. The landing was unopposed by the Japanese, who chose to withdraw toward the higher elevations to fight. MacArthur's orders, just like the orders given to General Homma, were to move at once to capture Manila. In the direct path of the American overland advance southward across Luzon was Camp Cabanatuan. Thus what triggered the "urgent battle situation" was left to each camp commander but was primarily driven by how close the approaching American troops were to camps as they swept across the islands.[47]

Aerial photo above Corregidor during the counterattack by the 503rd Parachute Infantry Group on February 12, 1944. The C-47 "gooney bird" shown dropping troops and supplies at the center of the Rock, with the "mile-long barracks" shown in the lower left. Two Texas Aggies, William D. Walker '44 and Charles L. Slover '44, were members of this low-level jump. (Courtesy of the author's collection.)

The few Americans who had escaped the mass execution at Palawan were debriefed in detail by US Army intelligence. Their horrific stories caused an immediate reaction at the highest level of the army to save the POWs. It became apparent that in advance of the army moving into the Cabanatuan area, a rescue of the estimated five hundred prisoners in various stages of poor health at the camp was to be carried out in an attempt to prevent their summary execution by panicked Japanese soldiers. The job of saving the American POWs was assigned to the elite 6th Army Rangers, who with skill, luck, and assistance from local Filipino guerrillas were able to carry out a daring plan in late January 1945 and reach Cabanatuan in time to save the Americans. The entire Japanese camp garrison guards of 523 soldiers were wiped out and the camp burned to the ground, with the loss of two Army Rangers and two prisoners who died from heart attacks during the rescue. The dazed prisoners referred to themselves collectively as the "Ghosts of Bataan," and nearly all these sick, starved, maimed, and ragged POWs were the last survivors of Bataan and Corregidor—left behind to die. The lone Texas Aggie, and former artillery officer at Fort Drum in Manila Bay, in this dramatic rescue was **Lt. Cliff Chamberlain '40** from Marlin, Texas. Held for 999 days, he returned to Guion Hall in College Station to address the Corps of Cadets on April 21, 1945, as campus Muster speaker.[48]

In rapid succession, the US Army and Filipino allies liberated prisoner of war camps at Tarlac, Santo Tomas, the old Bilibid prison, and Los Banos. Most of the camp guards followed Tokyo's advice to blend into the army and change identity to deny any association with the POW camps. Those American prisoners liberated faced a long road of recovery, some requiring hospital care for years. The physical and mental scars would last the balance of each one's life. However, while being left for dead in the deteriorating camp, most felt lucky that they had been spared the torture of the "Hell Ships" and transfer to work camps in Japan and across Asia. After months of brutal treatment, the Hell Ship saga further aggravated the harsh conditions and lowered POWs' abilities to survive, resulting in death for thousands of American prisoners on the high seas.[49]

★ CHAPTER 6 ★

HELL ON THE HIGH SEAS

The prisoners had been so crowded in the holds that they couldn't even get air to breathe. They went crazy, cut and bit each other through the arms and legs and sucked their blood. In order to keep from being murdered, many had to climb the ladders and were promptly shot by guards. Between twenty and thirty had died of suffocation.

JOHN M. JACOBS
ORYOKU MARU, DECEMBER 1944

Information indicates that your son, Captain Cary M. Abney '34, FA, of Marshall, Texas survived the bombing and sinking of the "Oryoku Maru" on 15 December 1944 and was transferred to the "Enoura Maru" which was bombed on 9 January 1945 in Takao Harbor, Formosa. He was then placed on board the "Brazil Maru" and died 28 January 1945 at sea between Formosa and Japan of wounds incurred in the bombing of the "Enoura Maru."

MAJ. GEN. EDWARD F. WITSELL
JANUARY 12, 1948

The final brutal chapter for many of those captured on Bataan and Corregidor ended on the high seas of the Pacific Ocean as the Japanese began a transfer of prisoners of war to work camps across Japan, Korea, and mainland China. After over two terrible years of starvation, beatings, and pain, the Imperial government in Tokyo devised a plan to move the POWs away from the advancing American forces slowly taking control of the Pacific region and use POWs as slave labor in the depleted Japanese factories, dock facilities, and mines across Asia. This massive transfer by sea of Allied troops was estimated to involve more than 126,000 prisoners, who were transported in 156 voyages aboard 134 different Japanese merchant ships. These "Hell Ships," as they were known, accounted for the death and injury of thousands of Americans. The majority of Texas Aggie officers stationed in the Philippines were not killed in combat, with only six killed in action (prior to May 9, 1942). Instead, a total of fifty died as prisoners of war at the hands of the Japanese in POWs camps and aboard the Hell Ships.[1]

A chronicle of the fight for Bataan and Corregidor, followed by the Death March, camp internment, and Hell Ship was vividly provided

San Jose Beach sign at "Bottomside," marking the return of US troops to Corregidor. (Courtesy of the author's collection.)

by **Captain Robert C. Robbins '41** in response to a request from the Association of Former Students at Texas A&M on the status of **1st Lt. Burt Griffin '41**:

August 15, 1946

Dear Mr. McQuillan:

1st Lt. Burt O. Griffin was my roommate for four years at A&M. We went to US Army Engineering School together in June 1941; we went to Philippines together in August 1941. Lt. Griffin and I were assigned to 14th Engineers at Ft. McKinley, P.I. but he was shortly transferred to Canlubang, P.I. near Manila, as instructor in the Engineering School for training Philippine Army Officers under Captain Charles Dempwolf, A&M class of about 1935 in C.E. Dec 7th found him there. He [Griffin] was placed with the 31st Engineer Bn (P.A.) as advisor (for all practical purposes he was Bn CO as a 2nd Lt) and moved with his command to Bataan immediately. During the war on Bataan (nearly five months) he fought on the front lines.

Following the capitulation of Bataan, he and I made the "Death March" together arriving at POW Camp O'Donnell, P.I. after 21 days of "hell". Grif was very sick with dysentery and malaria. I actually saved his life then by smuggling some quinine past Jap guards that I secured on the Black Market at the risk of my neck; also concocting some medicine for his dysentery. In about two months we were moved to POW camp at Cabanatuan, P.I. In November 1942 the Japanese moved 1500 POWs to Japan on the slave ship, Nagato Maru. So terrible were the conditions, the POWs underwent that about 50 American died en route to Japan.

Lt. Griffin was a stretcher case upon arrival at Moji, Japan and I gave him my blanket, but was forced to leave him behind. They promised that he would be taken care of and sent to a hospital. My group was sent to POW camp at Osaka. From confirmed reports I learned that Griffin died at Moji, Japan on 26 Dec 42. His body was probably cremated there.

Robert C. Robbins '41
Captain, C.E.[2]

The story of the brutality on the Hell Ships is as bloody and hideous as the horrible treatment in the POW camps that the prisoners had survived during the early years of their captivity. The transfer was marked by the same problems that had faced the POWs since their capture: poor planning, meager food or medical care, and little concern for their safety or well-being. For those weakened by the harsh captivity, the voyage into the unknown on converted freighters and passenger liners exacted a tremendous toll. In addition to the harsh conditions and treatment, the POWs at sea were caught in the cross fire of Allied forces expanding efforts to interdict and sink Japanese shipping. For some unknown reason, the Japanese Hell Ships, even when shipping their own troops and civilians on the upper decks above the POWs below, did not clearly mark the ships as "POW" transports. The chilling loss of American prisoners and unsuspecting Japanese civilian noncombatants on the ships to friendly fire is hard to fathom, even today. Thousands of POWs had endured the POW camps only to lose their lives at sea when the unmarked Japanese transport ships were either bombed from the air or torpedoed by Allied submarines. More American soldiers died in the sinking of the Japanese transport *Arisan Maru* than on the Bataan Death March or during the hideous first few months at Camp O'Donnell. Of the estimated fourteen thousand prisoner deaths at sea, about thirteen thousand were attributed to friendly fire. Of the over 150 POW Hell Ships, this narrative focuses on those that carried the men of Texas A&M to the work camps in Japan, China, and Korea.[3]

The many shipments of American POWs that took place from February 1942 up until the summer of 1945 included the transport of Texas Aggie officers from the Tarlac camp north of Manila, composed of senior ranking officers and their staff aides. Shipped via Manila, General Moore '08, Colonel Aldridge '16, and Major Tom Dooley '35 were loaded on the *Nagara Maru* in early August 1942 and transferred to Formosa. This four-day zigzagging passage to Takao Harbor, Formosa, during the early stage of the war when the Japanese had control of western Pacific shipping lanes, was without incident and faced no Allied attacks; thus this early voyage stands in stark contrast to the

The brutal death of more than a thousand Americans and Filipinos was constantly remembered by troops that recaptured the Philippines. The sign, honoring the "Knights Serving the Queen of Battles," hung over the route of the Bataan Death March for over a decade until permanent markers were placed every kilometer of the march. (Courtesy of the author's collection.)

In order to place a permanent memorial to those on the Bataan Death March, five-foot-tall obelisks were placed at each kilometer of the Death March between Bataan at Mariveles to the front gate of Camp O'Donnell. These markers are maintained by FAME—the Filipino-American Memorial Endowment. (Courtesy of the author's collection.)

Hell Ship events that would follow in 1943–45. The American officers and men on the *Nagara* slept on mats and were given limited access to the deck. From the *Nagara Maru*, they were transferred to the smaller coastal steamer *Suzuya Maru* (also referred to as the *Otaru Maru*) for transfer to Karenko on the morning of August 17, 1942. Once on the dock, all the POWs were lined up for what the Japanese thought was a humiliating photograph of the Americans "cow-towing" (bowing) in the direction of the Emperor's palace.[4]

The brutal Hell Ship conditions in the fall of 1944 were described in testimony by the Japanese in postwar trials as "normal and [the harsh treatment] cast upon the POWs became circumstances forced upon them in overload the ships." But as one observer noted, the Japanese at the time viewed the American POWs as "foreign, they were white, they were prisoners of war, *disgraced individuals* [predicated on Japanese standards and culture, not Western norms], and miserable objects." Dehumanization and "institutionalized" brutality of the prisoners, consistent with Japanese POW policy at the highest level of the government in Tokyo, contributed immensely to the psychological distancing that facilitated and encouraged the starvation, torture, and killing of allied prisoners. The POWs were little more than cargo or contraband and were considered to have no value or priority.[5]

The chronicle of the Texas Aggies' experience with the Hell Ships is best captured in the voyages and loss of five of the scores of Hell Ships during a six-month period from early July 1944 until late January 1945. By late 1942, American and British intelligence had begun to intercept and decode Japanese naval messages and to track shipments in the East China Sea and western Pacific. Such was the case of a message regarding the cargo and route of the *Shinyo Maru*. The ship's captain was ordered to finish his current job of moving rice and cement and then load POWs aboard on August 19; the ship was held at anchor at Zamboarga for ten more days before proceeding to Manila on September 6. American intelligence failed to decode the message of the "cargo" of the *Shinyo* properly: this was not Japanese troops and supplies but American POWs (totaling about eight hundred) from Camp No. 2 at Davao, Mindanao, who had spent the past twenty-four months building the Japanese airfield at Lasang. The US submarine *USS Paddle* had been assigned to track and intercept what was believed to be an unmarked Japanese troop ship. The crew of the *Paddle* was unaware until after the war that the *Shinyo* was carrying American and Allied POWs.[6]

The unmarked *Shinyo Maru* sailed from Zambanga Bay as the lead ship in a convoy of seven vessels as the *Paddle* stalked the ships and positioned itself to fire at the convoy. Two torpedoes hit the *Shinyo*. Chaos reigned as guards dropped hand grenades down the hatch into the hold and POWs fought and died in hand-to-hand combat while trying to overpower the deck guards. The wounded and dead covered the deck as both the Japanese and POWs scrambled to go overboard. Many POWs were shot swimming away as they struggled from the smoking pitch-black holds and fell into the water. Some twenty prisoners were picked up by a Japanese tanker, the *Eiyo Maru No. 2*, and lined up on the deck and executed. Only three members of the *Shinyo* crew of 50 survived, and 667 of the 750 Allied prisoners were killed. Among those killed in action and lost at sea were five Texas Aggie officers: **Lt. Colonel Rufus Hayden "Bill" Rogers '26**, formerly a vocational agricultural instructor in Del Rio, Texas, who was a camp commander at Davao; **Captain Ross Ivan Miller '39** of Bryan, Texas, stationed on Mindanao with the 14th Engineers, 101st Division, prior to the surrender; **Captain Gus H. Froebel '35** from San Antonio, who was captured on Bataan where he commanded a field artillery unit; **Lt. Donald Peterson '40**, a pilot with the 27th Bomb Group and imprisoned at Dapecol; and **Lt. Maxey C. Chenault '37**, an Army Air Corps pilot assigned the 19th Bomb Group.[7]

An estimated eighty-three POWs swam more than three miles to shore at Sindangan Bay and were rescued and aided by friendly Filipino guerrillas. The Americans crawled ashore naked, most with just a G-string. After giving them medical care and food, the Filipinos helped arrange safe passage for the prisoners back to friendly forces, and commanders radioed Australia for help in the evacuation. On September 29, concerned if there would be enough room on the US submarine for prisoners, a signal was flashed across the bay indicating that there were eighty-one POW passengers (one died of wounds and a second stayed ashore as a radio operator). The sub's captain responded, "We will take every damn one of you!" as native dugout canoes helped load the former POWs on the submarine, *USS Narwhal*, for transfer via New Guinea to the US Army Hospital in Brisbane. For most of the men, this marked the first time they wore shoes and socks again since June 1942. Within weeks, they were sent home, arriving at Pier 7 in San Francisco the day President Roosevelt won his fourth term in office, and they were transferred eastward by train for debriefings by Army intelligence in Washington—followed by a ninety-day furlough. Survivors and evacuees of the *Shinyo Maru* on the

USS Narwhal included Texas Aggie officers **Lt. Harry O. Fischer '29** of San Antonio, member of the 803rd Engineers, and pilot **Lt. Roy B. Russell '42** of the 28th Bomb Squadron.[8]

ARISAN MARU

The Japanese became increasingly nervous at the news that American forces were swiftly moving across the Pacific toward the Philippines. Their disingenuous efforts to load hundreds of prisoners in the existing hostile environment accented their hubris and fanatic efforts to transfer POWs to work in the slave labor camps of Japan. Between July and Christmas 1944, as American forces expanded operations in the Pacific and at the same time in the European Theater, with the Allies pushing from Normandy to Bastogne, an estimated 7,950 American POWs from internment camps across the Philippines were transferred to Manila to board ships bound for Japan. In July 1944, the unmarked freighter *Canadian Inventor* carried 1,100 POWs, including Captain Jerome McDavitt '35, completing a sixty-two-day voyage buffeted by a typhoon in the China Sea prior to docking at Moji, Japan. US Naval Intelligence continually improved its detection of enemy shipping between the Philippines and Japan and by mid-October 1944 was tracking an increased level of intercepts and intelligence summaries on the eve of what would become the Battle of Leyte Gulf. A decoded message mentioned two unidentified convoys in the Luzon Straits. In the lead convoy was the *Arisan Maru*, which was packed with POWs on October 11 yet whose departure was delayed until October 20, 1944, only a few miles from Manila, to wait in safe waters for fear of Allied air attacks. It returned briefly to the dock in Manila, took on fresh supplies, and was bound for Formosa with a cargo of 1,781 sick and weakened American as well as a few British and Dutch POWs—all of whom had spent over a week in sweltering temperatures that soared to over 120 degrees, with access to no latrines, limited water, and only a handful of putrid rice once a day.[9]

The *Arisan Maru* joined a group, known as Convoy MATA-30, consisting of a dozen transports, a supply ship, and three heavily armed destroyers. The cramped holds filled with POWs were partially filled with coal and became a death trap as a few died of dysentery and heat exhaustion. Bloated bodies were piled like cord wood in the hold. The POWs saw no end to the maddening ordeal of the tortured struggle to live, and few were aware of the increased US naval attacks. At midnight on October 23, a pack of US Navy submarines began to attack the convoy and within an hour sunk eight of the twelve ships. Escaping the first attack, the slow moving *Arisan* zigzagged at about seven knots toward the eastern coast of China near Shoonan for shelter. At sundown on October 24, one POW working on deck to prepare the evening meal of rice for the men below reported he felt a jar caused by the hits of two torpedoes. At once, the ship went dead in the water. Tremendous explosions and thick, black smoke erupted from below.[10]

Chaos ensued at once as the Japanese guards cut the rope ladders into the holds, slammed the hatches down, and rapidly abandoned the disabled ship. The initial explosions hit the starboard side near the number three hold and killed hundreds of prisoners below deck. Down below, the POWs attempted to build a human pyramid of corpses and debris to climb out of the burning structure. Japanese guards who had not jumped overboard fought hand to hand with the unarmed Americans, who killed all the cruel captors and tormentors they encountered on deck. Weak and disoriented, a few hundred POWs were able to cling to splintered hatch boards and debris in the rough waters of the Pacific. The ship soon spilt in half and continued to float like a cork in the rough seas. Japanese escort destroyers crisscrossed the choppy water, plowing over the naked and starved prisoners struggling to reach for help and then pulled away into the night, leaving the balance to drown. Amid the prisoners floating in the cold, icy waters and fifteen-foot waves, Japanese destroyers began a massive hunt and counterattack, dropping dozens of depth charges over the American submarines—which took a great toll among prisoners struggling in the water and the submarines. That night, the American submarine force suffered the largest loss of submarines in the war—including the sinking of the *USS Shark* (which fired the torpedoes that sunk the *Arisan*), *USS Tang*, and *USS Darter* and their combined crews of more than 220 sailors. Of the estimated 1,781 POWs on board the *Arisan*, only eight survived. Among the 1,772 Americans who died were *twelve* Texas Aggie soldiers killed in action at sea—Aggies who had survived the bombing at Clark Field, the battles on Bataan and Corregidor, the Bataan Death March, and the brutality of numerous prison camps. On this day, more Texas Aggie officers died than on any other single day in our nation's history.[11]

TABLE 6.1. Texas Aggie Deaths on the *Arisan Maru*, South China Sea, October 24, 1944

M.Sgt. William Giles Boyd '27	20900641	194th Tank Bn.	College Station, TX
Lt. Edger B. Burgess '38	O-365275	HQ Sqdn 19th Bomb Gp.	Ft. Worth, TX
Capt. William M. Curtis '32	O-295071	Harbor Defense Manila	Covington, OK
Lt. Charles E. Gaskell '41	O-421072	34th Pur. Sqdn., 24th Pur. Gp.	Dallas, TX
Lt. James M. Henry '39	O-421084	34th Pur. Sqdn., 24th Pur. Gp.	Kingsville, TX
Capt. James R. Holmes '36	O-021195	60th CA	San Antonio, TX
Lt. Andy M. James Jr. '41	O-409560	HQ USAFFE	Dalhart, TX
Lt. John B. McCluskey '36	O-342105	91st CAC Reg. PS	Anderson, TX
Lt. Melvin R. Millard '40	O-015670	B Btry. 515 CA (AA)	Abilene, TX
Capt. Henry John Schutte Jr. '39	O-024501	HQ Btry. 59th CA	Houston, TX
Lt. John D. Stukenburg '40	O-389605	81st Combat Bn., 81st PA	Ardmore, OK
Capt. Roy M. Vick Jr. '35	O-328575	91st CA Reg. PS	Bryan, TX

Late on October 25, US Navy intelligence intercepted a Japanese message, decoded to state that the unmarked *Arisan Maru* had been loaded with 1,791 men—"presumably prisoners." The failed American intelligence, especially during the disastrous sinking of the POW ships during November and December 1944, continued to prove very costly to successive shipments of American prisoners. To this day, the sinking of the *Arisan Maru* remains the largest loss of American lives in a single maritime disaster—surpassing the loss of the *Titanic* (1912) and *Lusitania* (1914). Families of those lost in the sinking of the *Arisan Maru* did not know of their fate until nearly a year after the sinking, and even then, it took years to reconstruct and verify the roster of those on board the *Arisan.*[12]

Concerns of the families in Texas were reflected in the outreach conducted by E. E. McQuillen '22, Executive Director of the Texas A&M Association of Former Students. McQuillen, known to all as "Mac," and his small staff were in active contact with both the families of the Aggie prisoners in the Pacific as well as friends and other Aggies on active duty around the world. Letters and telegrams poured into College Station requesting information on the status of the prisoners as a direct result of the association's call for information on survivors and families "of our A. & M. casualties" during the updating of records and planning for construction of the Memorial Student Center. In late 1945, when the story of the nine American survivors (five made it to freedom and four were recaptured and imprisoned in Japan) of the *Arisan* reached Texas, many held out hope that more men would be found. Shortly after receiving a personal letter of "deepest sympathy" on the death of her son from General MacArthur, the mother of Lt. Andy M. "AM" James '41 wrote to McQuillen, concerned she had heard "that Andy's name was on a camp's prison list in Mukden [a prison camp in China]," implying that he might still be alive. The list was said to have been stolen from the Japanese by a Chinese guerrilla. The Mukden rumor on Andy and many other rumors proved false. The association received a similar letter from the father of **Captain Henry Schutte '39**, who wrote, "We still cling to our faith in our Lord that through his goodness and mercy he might perform a miracle and bring our boy and a good many of the others back."[13]

Texas A&M University President General James E. Rudder '32, center, is presented a memorial plaque in 1969 for display in the Memorial Student Center, recognizing the Texas Aggies who fought on Bataan and Corregidor. On the left is the American Defenders of Bataan and Corregidor Association President John H. LeClair, and on the right is former Aggie POW Lt. Col. Jerome McDavitt '33. (Courtesy of the author's collection.)

The roommate of **E. Beaumont Burgess '38**, known only as "DE," also wrote McQuillen: "You can imagine my feelings, we all hope to be able to get to all those boys real soon. I am enclosing the only bill I have [$5] at hand and I'd appreciate it if you would credit part of it to Beaumont, I know he'd want a part in the Development Fund for the MSC." Gertrude Curtis, the widow of **Captain William M. Curtis '32**, responded to Mac with a confirmation of the status of her husband's loss on the *Arisan*, recalling, "He was always in high spirits." She concluded, "I feel that these men lived up to the highest American tradition of courage and ingenuity; they never quit, and never lost their sense of humor. They have left a wonderful heritage for our children, and it is up to us to try to live up to their example and make their efforts worthwhile."[14]

TABLE 6.2. Hell Ships, August 1944 to January 1945

Name	*Depart date*	*Voyage*	*POWs*	*Deaths*	*A&M men***
Noto Maru	August 27, 1944	Manila to Japan	1,035	0	2/0
Shinyo Maru	September 7, 1944	Davao to Manila	750	667	7/5
Hofuku Maru	September 21, 1944	Manila to Japan	1,287	1,047	0
Hokusen Maru	October 3, 1944	Manila to Formosa	1,100	36	0
Arisan Maru	October 10, 19 44	Manila to Japan	1,781	1,792	12/12
Oryoku Maru	December 14, 1944	Manila to Japan	1,621	300	11/5
Brazil Maru	December 27, 1944	Luzon to Formosa	250	5	0
Enoura Maru	December 27, 1944	Luzon to Formosa	1,070	390	5/5
Brazil Maru	January 14, 1945	Formosa to Japan	925	375	5/5
Total			9,819	4,612	42/32

* 47 percent POW death rate.

** Aggies on ship (42) and number lost in sinking (32). Two Texas Aggie officers escaped on the *USS Narwhal* submarine.

Note: A partial list of the 154 Japanese voyages by 134 ships to move prisoners of war from mid-1942 to early 1945 estimates a total of 126,064 POWs transported and 14,000 deaths on the high seas and/or deaths due to wounds at sea; see also Gregory F. Michno, *Death on the Hellships: Prisoners at Sea in the Pacific War*. Annapolis: Naval Institute Press, 2001, pp. 309–17.

"LET THEM DIE"

With MacArthur landing in the Leyte Gulf in late October 1944, as promised, Japanese soldiers rushed to gather and evacuate as many healthy prisoners as possible to Japan from the main pier in Manila. Those POWs able to walk were transported from camps at Cabanatuan, Tarlac, and Bilibid and gathered on December 13, 1944, to board the converted passenger-cargo ship *Oryoku Maru*. Of the half-naked men gathered, all but 50 of the 1,621 were Americans (with the rest being British), and of that number, there were more than 1,100 officers. There was a mixture of anticipation and angst as the prisoners stood for hours on the hot pier as the military guards preboarded 1,500 Japanese troops, 1,127 stranded sailors and passengers from previously shipwrecked Japanese ships, as well as more than 500 Japanese civilian men, women, and children. One American officer recalled the scene: "The exodus of so many important Japanese people meant that Japan was losing the war." The Americans waiting on the pier were ordered to turn their backs as 728 urns of ashes of Japanese soldiers were placed on board for return home. Surely spies watched—as the Japanese hastily boarded the Americans at bayonet point, dividing them among the three below-the-water-line dark and hot holds. The hatches were sealed shut and there was no freshwater as the *Oryoku* moved out into Manila Bay and dropped anchor.[15]

The sun-drenched steel deck broiled to over one hundred degrees and the holds became an oven down below as the stifling heat rose in the still ship. As the prisoners yelled for fresh air and water, the Japanese guards ordered them to shut up because their noise was disturbing the Japanese women and children on the main deck—or they would begin firing into the POWs. The scene below deck was described by one POW:

> The 1,619 men comprised our group were distributed to three holds of equal size, with 611 men in number 1 hold, 189 men in hold number 2, and 819 men in number 3 hold. The hold was like a box, about 30 feet wide and fifty feet long with a ceiling height of about eight feet. The center section of the hold was an open floor, a strip about fifteen

> feet wide extending across the ship. Fore and aft of this strip, there was a shelf four feet from the floor so men could be put both on the floor and on the shelf. The only passage into and out of the hold was a ladder passing through the hatch—with the top of the hatch about fifteen feet above the floor of the hold.[16]

The infamous Japanese civilian interpreter, Shudake Wada, who often acted as if he was in command (sentenced by the postwar crimes tribunal to life imprisonment, with hard labor) told the Japanese commander in charge, "Let them die." Sundown brought a sweltering ink-black darkness filled with cries, agony, and threats as the crammed prisoners below struggled for space, water, and air. The floor soon was covered over an inch thick with vomit, urine, and excrement. The commanding officers among the POWs tried to calm the men and restore order, but the heat and stress began to literally drive men mad. By the time the guards began to allow a few men at a time on deck to get air, more than fifty bodies were removed, men having died from suffocation or being trampled in the dark confusion and filth. Among those lost on the night of December 13 to the harsh conditions in the hold was **Major Maynard G. Snell '21** of Lampasas, the former cadet commander of Company E in the Corps of Cadets and a veterinarian by training. He had served as the executive officer of the 192nd Tank Battalion prior to surrender on Bataan. Snell's body, unlike many corpses later stacked in the hold, was stripped of his scant clothing, wrapped in a straw mat, weighted down, and eased over the side of the ship. Early on December 14, shortly after the ship had pulled anchor and was sailing northward up the west side of the Bataan Peninsula, carrier planes from the *USS Hornet* and *USS Hancock* zeroed in to attack the *Oryoku*.[17]

The planes strafed and bombed the *Oryoku* repeatedly. In the dark hold, the Americans, knowing the Japanese antiaircraft gunners were being slaughtered on deck, cheered and yelled, "Pour it on!" Bullets began to ricochet in the steel-confined hold as warm blood from the killed and wounded Japanese gunners and civilians dripped through the deck into the darkness. As the air raid waned, with gaping holes in her side and a disabled rudder, the *Oryoku* limped into Subic Bay late on December 14 and beached off Olongapo Point. Throughout the night, the POWs were left in the sealed filth of the holds as the Japanese evacuated their wounded and dead. At sunrise, as the roar of American fighter planes returned, the Japanese frantically opened the hatches and ordered the naked and barefoot prisoners—most in only a thin G-string—on deck to wave at the attacking planes. As the pilots made their approach to sink the *Oryoku*, the mass of stark, white-bearded bodies averted death as the navy pilots pulled up, circled, and returned to wag their wings at the cheering POWs.[18]

Nearly 280 prisoners were killed, along with hundreds of killed and wounded Japanese. In addition to the loss of Major Snell, three Texas Aggies died in the bombing: **Orman L. Fitzhugh '40**, **Lt. James R. Davis '42**, and **Captain Jack W. Kelley '29** from Texarkana. Some twenty-one survived the initial attacks on the *Oryoku* and swam ashore, including **Captain Travis E. Perrenot '36** from San Antonio, **Captain Sidney R. Greer '35** of Tyler, **George H. Peets '30**, **Cary M. Abney Jr. '34**, **Captain Charles Dempwolf '35** of Cleburne, **Lt. Eugene G. Lewis '27**, and **Captain Wilber Adair Calvert '38** from Archer City. After swimming some three hundred yards to the beach, the surviving group of some 1,300 exhausted POWs was herded at bayonet point by the guards, yelling "Speedo! speedo!," onto a concrete tennis court (78 by 36 ft., for a total of 2,808 sq. ft.) surrounded by chicken wire until the Japanese could decide what to do. Diarrhea and dysentery continued to weaken the men and the more than 200 wounded received no medical care. During the weeklong confinement, in which the POWs received limited food in the form of raw, uncooked rice and only a small amount of water, Captain Peets died of his wounds on December 22, 1944. Captain Greer was transferred to Moji, Japan, where he died of the harsh conditions on February 8, 1945.[19]

The prison ship journey to Japan via Formosa for Abney, Perrenot, and Calvert resumed on December 27, 1944, when the three, along with Aggies John V. King '22 and H. P. Hardegee '36, were loaded on the old rusty-looking *Enoura Maru* along with 1,050 additional POWs. Hundreds of Japanese civilians and soldiers from the *Oryoku* covered the open deck. The wounded, weak, and starved Americans were once again packed into the dark hell hold of the ship, which had been carrying artillery horses—the floor was covered in fresh manure. While fighting back swarms of enormous, vicious horseflies, one POW recalled, "Scattered in the manure was a small amount of millet and oats that had been spilled in feeding the horses. This was picked out, grain by grain, and eaten." On the third day, the POWs were given a handful of rice each and a few spoons of water. As with the other Hell Ships, the heat soared above 120 degrees and the Japanese, true to form, were completely indifferent to the slimy filth, heat, starvation, and wounds of the prisoners, who were dying hourly below deck. Overflowing *benjo* buckets of excrement littered the floor. Untreated wounded and delirious men lay all around, and the dead bodies were left in the hold with the POWs for days.[20]

A second ship, the *Brazil Maru*, was also loaded in Luzon and sailed with the *Enoura*, both reaching Takao Harbor, Formosa, in four days. The POWs were held in the wreckage of the holds of both ships in the harbor until January 6, 1945, when about 235 men from the *Brazil* were transferred to the already overcrowded *Enoura*. On January 9, Allied bombers struck Takao Harbor, hitting the unmarked *Enoura* at anchor, killing more than 200 American POWs, including Aggie officers King and Hardegee. The dark-blue, emaciated American corpses were piled in the holds and on the deck, and after more than forty-eight hours of decomposition—and after much pleading by the American officers—the dead were removed by a cargo sling, hauled by crane to a barge, and buried on a nearby beach in a mass grave. As one American noted,

> This was one of the most gruesome experiences I have ever known. I was put in charge of a twenty man detail which boarded a barge alongside the ship. A large cargo net was lowered into the hold of the ship, thirty bodies were piled in the net, and then it was hoisted out over the barge. As the net was lowered to the barge, the winch operator amused himself and the guards by jerking the cable to make the bodies jump grotesquely. The guards laughed when the jerking shook blood and pieces of flesh and parts of bodies on us as we stood on the barge reaching up to catch the net to steady it. Our cloths were soaked with blood and excrement.[21]

After repeated roll calls, or *tenko*, the survivors of the *Enoura Maru* bombing were transferred back to the *Brazil*, which then sailed for Japan in a convoy of twelve ships on January 13. Abney, Perrenot, and Calvert survived the *Enoura* bombing and were transferred to the *Brazil*. That first night, more than forty-five POWs died from their wounds and exposure, and deaths continued at about the rate of twenty-five per day. The *Brazil Maru* was the last POW Hell Ship to leave the Philippines with American POWs. By early 1945, most able-bodied POWs had been shipped, while the sick and wounded were left behind to die. But before the Japanese could carry out their plans to eradicate all POWs in the face of the oncoming Americans, the camps were saved. As the American forces landed, the Japanese ran out of time to implement mass executions, as both Cabanatuan and Bilibid were dramatically liberated by US Army Rangers in February 1945. The same week as the Ranger raids on Luzon, the shipbound, starved POWs, many of them wounded, were destined on a two-week journey to Moji, Japan, zigzagging by night and hiding in the coastal islands during daylight. As they sailed northward toward Japan, there was a radical drop in temperature and the once "baked" prisoners now faced cold air and snow. Food and water was not provided until January 15—and the death rate continued to escalate. By the time the *Brazil* docked in Moji on Kyushu on January 30, 1945, more than 450 POWs had died. The extended journey from Manila had taken forty-six days, three ships, starvation, freezing temperatures, and death. Of the 1,621 men that left Manila on December 13, only about 550 survived to reach Japan. Within six weeks, due to their weakened physical condition from the harsh voyage, an additional 176 died![22]

The arrival of the *Brazil* in Moji and the poor physical condition of the brutalized prisoners shocked even the local Japanese onlookers: "It was bitterly cold when the men disembarked the ship. They were walking skeletons. The Japanese corpsmen seemed to have a look of astonishment on their faces and there were shocked expressions on the faces of the people at Moji as the prisoners were marched through the streets. Men shuffled, some walked with the support of others. The men were infested with lice and had not shaved since 13 December."[23]

Texas Aggie POWs Travis Perrenot, Cary Abney, Charles Dempwolf, and Wilbert Calvert were among the few who survived the sinking of the *Oryoku* and the bombing of the *Enoura*, yet all four died en route to Japan on a third ship, the *Brazil.* The Hell Ships were the primary cause of death among the American POWs in general and the Texas Aggie officers in particular.

THE END OF THE NIGHTMARE

The journey of Captain Jerome McDavitt '33 from Clark Field to Bataan, Corregidor, Camp O'Donnell, and Cabanatuan and his hellish transfer on July 1, 1944, by ship aboard the *Canadian Inventor II* concluded with his internment at Camp Omine Machi. Located near Hiroshima, the coal mining work camp held some 472 enlisted American soldiers (288) and British POWs (184) and only a couple of commissioned officers, including McDavitt, who was the senior officer. The twelve-hour days of forced labor in the coal mines and imprisonment seemed to never end as the POWs were used as labor by the Sanyo Muentan Coal Mining Company. However, by mid-1945, the POWs knew the end of the war was growing near as repeated B-29 raids bombed near the camp. And on August 6, 1945, the first atomic bomb was dropped on downtown Hiroshima, followed in two days by another dropped on Nagasaki. One Camp Omine POW recalled, "On that day, at the very same time that they dropped the atomic bomb, we were in formation . . . as we heard this rumble and rumble and rumble, Oh, it just kept rumbling and rumbling, and we thought that it would never end!"

Dropping the atomic bomb saved the lives of not only the surviving POWs but also hundreds of thousands of American and Allied troops that would have landed in Japan. Within days, the Emperor addressed a shocked nation, humiliated by the realization that the war was lost and surrender the only course of action. POW camps across Japan, Manchuria, the Philippines, and Korea were liberated. Although it had already been determined by the military command in Tokyo that if the Allies landed on the Japanese home islands, all POWs would be executed, the Emperor's solemn yet stern message to the nation probably averted a wave of potential mass execution of prisoners.[24]

At Camp Omine, Captain McDavitt recalls:

> I was called into the Japanese commander's office. Captain Omura told me, "I have been instructed by the Imperial Japanese Army to turn this camp over to the senior American commander. That is you. What do you want me to do?" Just as plain as that. I had to do some pretty fast thinking. My brain wasn't too sharp, but I said, "Captain Omuru, the first thing I want is for you to remove all the Japanese and Koreans who have been supervising my men and forcing them to work. I want them taken someplace where they cannot again be seen by my men. Second, I want you to start bringing food into this camp, the kind and quantity that I designate, including fresh meat, even if it's on a rope. I want you to bring it until I tell you to stop."[25]

The sudden shock of the reversal of roles was sobering. The enemy was now the captive—yet still armed. McDavitt recorded the moment of truth and his response in one of the most pungent moments of his life as Captain Omura stepped forward "and unbuckled his samurai sword and handed it to me by the handle. 'No, Captain Omura,' I said, 'I know what that sword means to you and your family, and I hereby give you another order. Take that sword home with you and don't ever give it to any American.' Right then, for the first time in my life, I saw tears in the Jap's eyes. I knew then I had him on my hip. Anything I asked for I knew I'd get, and it turned out exactly that way."

Within days, the US Army Air Corps began air drops to all 130 POW camps, with roofs painted by the freed POWs with a large white "PW." At Camp Omine Machi, the former prisoners stood in amazement as the low-flying planes opened their bomb doors to release twenty-four double-decked fifty-gallon drums, welded and stacked together full of food, medicine, and supplies. At the POW camp in Inchon, Korea, troops were so excited about the air drops of supplies,

T.Sgt. William W. Anthony '71 at the western entrance of Malinta Tunnel in late 1945. Note sign to warn of live unexploded ordinance. (Courtesy of William Anthony '71.)

many were hit by the heavy falling drums, including Aggie veterinarian **Major Oliver "Stud" Orson '32**, Vet Corps, who was hit by a parachute-borne package (after surviving three camps and three Hell Ships), breaking his leg—he was happy to be going home. McDavitt recalled each load "floated down to us on sixteen red, white and blue parachutes. I stood there amazed, and whatever words you want to use would describe my feelings." By sunrise the next morning, a huge American flag flew over the camp, fashioned overnight by the American GIs from the silk of the parachutes.[26]

By shortwave radio, McDavitt made contact with the US Naval fleet off the coast, who ordered them to stay where they were—help was on the way. The prisoners at Omine remained in the camp for nearly a full month, due to the ongoing transfer of prisoners from camps scattered across Japan, as arrangements were made to free them. At last, they boarded a train to the port, to be picked up by ships. The emergency medical cases were moved first and the balance of the American and British disinfected and given new uniforms. American prisoners of war across Asia were released in generally the same pattern. At Mukden, a standoff—soon resolved—occurred between Russians troops and American OSS agents rushing to ensure the safety of the camp. Most Japanese guards fled for fear of the Russians, and more than three weeks was needed to arrange the land and air evacuation of the Americans.[27]

Accounting for the toll the captivity took on the POWs would take decades.

THE LAST FULL MEASURE

The toll had been very heavy. Of the eighty-nine Texas Aggies on active duty in the Philippines Islands on December 7–8, 1941, six were killed in action prior to the May 9, 1942, surrender on the Rock and five escaped or were evacuated—the others would be held as prisoners of war. In more than thirty-nine months of imprisonment, fifteen died in the POW camps, thirty-one died at sea on the Hell Ships, and two Aggies, **Captain Floyd Buchel '36** and **Lt. James B. Whitley '38**, were

Postwar trial in December 1945 of General Tomoyuki Yamashita, former command of Japanese forces in the Philippines. Both Generals Yamashita and Homma were found guilty of war crimes against both Americans and Filipinos and executed. (Courtesy of the author's collection.)

both officially confirmed as missing in action in January 1946. Malnourished, some wounded, and underweight on average by fifty pounds, their transition back to Texas included extensive medical exams, dental work, and debriefings by Army intelligence, the OSS, and the FBI. They were told not to discuss the conditions of their imprisonment unless with a government official. The Army at once began the collection of data, camp rosters, and interviews for the war crimes tribunal that followed in 1946–47. Unfortunately, many of the Japanese troops and tormentors involved in the torture and brutality fled to China or Korea, while tons of documents on the treatment of the American POWs were destroyed by the Japanese prior to the US occupation of the Japanese mainland.[28]

On the morning of September 2, 1945, Major Tom Dooley, following a visit with Lt. Col. Ormond Simpson '36 on MacArthur's staff, accompanied General Wainwright aboard the battleship *USS Missouri*

General Douglas MacArthur, center, on the main deck of the *USS Missouri* in Tokyo Bay, Japan, September 2, 1945. The only known Texas Aggie to attend the formal surrender was Major Tom Dooley '35, not pictured, aide to General Wainwright. (Courtesy of NARA.)

anchored in Tokyo Bay to be a part of the official delegation to witness the formal Japanese surrender. Dooley, Wainwright, and Moore were flown back to Manila to witness the Japanese surrender in the Philippine Islands of General Yamashita and his staff at Baguio. For the liberated Texas Aggies, the welcoming party in Manila was a who's who of Aggies and friends, helping to smooth the long road home to Texas: Major General Edward H. Leavey '15, Major General Percy W. Clarkson '15, Colonel Henry C. Wendler '34, Colonel Joseph A. Aston '34, and on the flight home, meetings with Colonel Joe C. McHaney '35, Colonel William R. Large '36, and Major William R. Manor '45 in Guam.[29]

★ CHAPTER 7 ★

PER UNITATEM VIS

THROUGH UNITY STRENGTH

The isles of Pacific stand smould'ring and red;
Smell of blood and of fire, of the gutted and dead.
For the Spirit of Aggieland raged through the night,
Slashing foe with its fury—the Free and the Right!

John Holman '44

The passing of time should not allow the world to forget the first great American battle of World War II and the fate of those who suffered and died for liberty and freedom. The Battle of the Philippines, noted most for the late 1941 to April 1942 defense of both Bataan and Corregidor, has been somewhat overlooked due to the focus on early war events at Pearl Harbor and in Europe. In the devastating aftermath of the massive Japanese attacks across the Pacific in December 1941, Washington focused on supporting allies in Europe against Germany, prior to allocating military assets to stop the onslaught of the Imperial Japanese Army and Navy across the Pacific. Unable to fight a two-ocean war, the cost for this direction of priorities was the inability to reinforce and provide relief for the embattled armed forces and civilians in the Philippines.

Captured Japanese propaganda photo of Corregidor in late 1944 taken at the "Bottomside" dock looking inland at the mouth of Malinta Tunnel, center. The extensive Japanese aerial bombing and artillery barrage from Bataan and Cavati during the siege nearly cleared all foliage from the island. (Courtesy of the author's collection.)

The Imperial Japanese invaders initially planned to take Luzon, Manila, and Corregidor in as little as 50 days; however, for some 120 days, the combined forces of the Americans and Filipinos managed to slow down what was one of the most extensive air, land, and sea military offensives on record. Already engaged during the 1930s in a lengthy war of occupation and vital resource grab in China, Korea, and Indo-China, the Japanese sought to neutralize the United States and its allies before pursuing a truce that recognized their rights in the so-called Greater East Asia Co-Prosperity Sphere, planning to militarily and economically dominate the Pacific region. By late 1941, the Japanese war machine was well trained, tested, armed, and prepared to inflict maximum force and destruction on all they came in contact with. Despite intelligence reports from China in the late 1930s, the West had greatly ignored, underestimated, and even discounted the ability of the Japanese to exercise the violent air, land, and sea power they were to demonstrate in the early months of the war.

The rapid sweep and capture of China, Hong Kong, Singapore, and Indo-China; the attack on Pearl Harbor; and the great assault on the Philippines was planned to gain control of the region in order to prevent any disruption of Tokyo's grand "prosperity" objectives. From the time that the first bomber wiped out the US Far East Air Force at Clark Field and the US Navy on December 8–10, 1941, in Manila, the operational plan was to conquer the Philippines by February 15, 1942. The swiftness and accuracy of the Japanese Air Force to control the skies and the overwhelming landing of hardened troops on December 23 allowed the Imperial Army under General Masaharu Homma to march virtually unopposed to Manila by New Year's Day 1942. The rapid shock of the invasion seemed to foretell the fate of the island nation and beleaguered American and Filipino forces thrown back on their heels in retreat. Yet the original Japanese objectives and timeline did not go as planned.

Realizing his inability to mobilize the poorly trained Philippine beach defense to halt the Japanese landing on North Luzon, General Douglas MacArthur invoked War Plan Orange-3, a defensive holding strategy that had been in the making for more than three decades. He commanded his forces to make their stand on the Bataan Peninsula and on the Isle of Corregidor. What followed would be a dramatic and bloody defense of the foothold in the Philippines, as all other forces and supplies, air cover, and naval support were drawn back to either Pearl Harbor or Australia, thus leaving "the Battling Bastards" of Bataan with their backs against the wall in a fight that was, at best, a costly delaying action and ultimate defeat.

It would be years before the full story of the brutality of the Japanese on the Bataan Death March; in the POW camps; and on the many Hell Ships that attempted to transfer hundreds of Americans, including more than forty Texas Aggies, to forced labor units in Japan, Korea, and Manchuria, would be fully known. More Allied prisoners of war, by percentage of those captured, died at the hands of the Japanese Imperial Army than any other group of POWs held by other Axis powers. Thousands of Texas Aggies served on duty in locations worldwide. However, the Aggie citizen soldiers, some eighty-nine who fought both during and after Bataan and Corregidor, would suffer an over 60 percent loss.

General Douglas MacArthur, center, returns to Corregidor with a "Topside" flag ceremony on March 5, 1945. The Americans surrounding the flagpole are the paratroopers of the 503rd Parachute Infantry Regiment who recaptured the Rock. In the top center are the destroyed "mile-long barracks." (Courtesy of the author's collection.)

As American forces gradually began to roll back the Japanese in the Pacific, the campaign for the liberation of Bataan and Corregidor got under way in December 1944. American forces entered Manila on February 4, 1945, and launched an attack on Corregidor on February 12,

1945. The major assault was led by the 503rd Parachute Infantry Regiment, which included Texas Aggie Private William D Walker '44 and Lt. Charles L. Stover '44, who jumped from C-47s from a height of only four hundred feet onto the center of the Rock under heavy enemy fire. When Walker was asked what surprised him the most about the dangerous jump, he replied, "I was still alive after landing!" Within days, the island was secure and the saga of Corregidor came to a costly end with lost and wounded men.[1]

The strategic importance of the bold defense of Bataan and Corregidor to the overall Allied victory should never be forgotten and was memorialized by General MacArthur in late February 1945:

> Bataan, with Corregidor the citadel of its integral defense, made possible all that has happened since. History, I am sure, will record it as one of the decisive battles of the world. Its long protracted struggle enabled the United Nations to gather strength to resist in the Pacific. Had it not held out, Australia would have fallen with incalculably disastrous results. Our triumphs of today belong equally to that dead army. Its heroism and sacrifices have been duly acclaimed, but the great strategic results of the mighty defense are only now becoming fully apparent. The Bataan garrison was destroyed due to its dreadful handicaps, but no army in history more thoroughly accomplished its mission. Let no man henceforth speak of it other than as magnificent victory.[2]

THE ROLL CALL

The stand on Corregidor launched the worldwide observation of San Jacinto Day and Texas Aggie Muster each April 21. Association of Former Students executive Director E. E. McQuillan '22 made sure the "roll call" and the gallant message from the Rock in April 1942 would never be forgotten. Beginning in 1943, he prepared and sent notice to hundreds of Aggie Musters that were yearly held worldwide. Even while the fates of thousands of Texas Aggies at locations around the world were in question, banner headlines across the masthead of the *Texas Aggie* in mid-February 1944 boasted, "1944 Muster Will Follow

The famous 1946 Texas Aggie Muster gathering at the mouth of Malinta Tunnel at Corregidor on April 21, 1946. Aggies travel from all over the Pacific Theater to attend this memorial ceremony to those who had defended the "Rock." (Courtesy of the Association of Former Students.)

the Sun: Meetings Circle Globe." These Muster gatherings included a number of famous meetings on Guadalcanal, New Zealand, Fiji, Corsica, and Sicily and in North Africa and China. There was an impromptu meeting on the war-torn Corregidor by three Texas Aggies in 1945—Lt. Tommy Martin '40, Major Ormond Simpson '36, and Lt. Richard Conolly '37—and a postwar meeting of 127 Aggies on April 21, 1946, at the mouth of the Malinta Tunnel on Corregidor. An emotional 1946 gathering was held in the lobby of the Imperial Hotel in downtown Tokyo across from the Emperor's residence and the former high command of the Japanese army. Capping them all was the 1946 Homecoming Muster held in Texas A&M's Kyle Field featuring General of the Army Dwight Eisenhower as the keynote speaker—the stage set up for the presentation on the exact end zone site where in May 1937 President Roosevelt praised the military contribution of the Aggie corps of citizen soldiers during World War I. And two of the defenders of Bataan and Corregidor were honored as keynote speakers at the annual campus Muster: Clift Chamberlain '40 (1945) and Tom Dooley '35 (1978).[3]

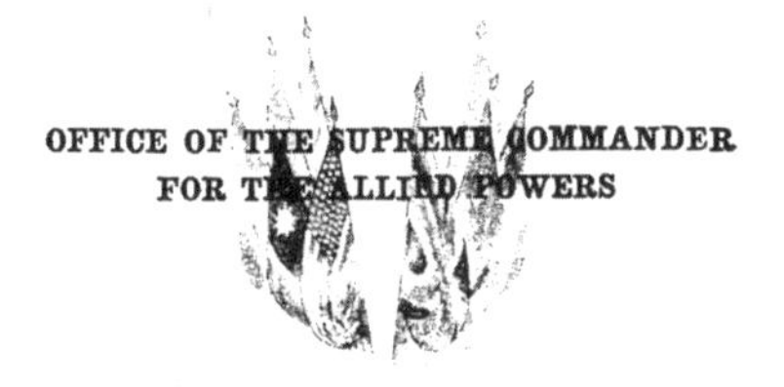

OFFICE OF THE SUPREME COMMANDER
FOR THE ALLIED POWERS

Sons of Texas A & M
on Corregidor - 21 April 1946.

In this hallowed soil lie the mortal remains of many men who here died that liberty might live. Among the bravest of these brave are twenty officers, sons of Texas A & M, unable themselves to answer this year's annual muster. It is for us, therefore, to do so for them -- to answer for them in clear and firm voice -- Dead on battle-swept Corregidor where their eternal spirit will never die but will march on forever, inspiring in those who follow the courage and the will to preserve well that for which they bled.

Of them and those of their fellow alumni who lie in hallowed soil of other lands and those who survive them, may it truly be said that in the noble teachings of their Alma Mater -- in the tradition of the great American leader, Sam Houston, who this day, one hundred and ten years ago, wrested Texas from foreign dominion by defeating Santa Ana on the historic battlefield of San Jacinto -- they stood steadfast, unyielding and unafraid through those dark days of our country's gravest peril -- and by inspiring example helped point the way.

Douglas MacArthur
DOUGLAS MacARTHUR

Letter sent by General Douglas MacArthur to honor the April 21, 1946, Texas Aggie Muster on Corregidor. (Courtesy of the author's collection.)

The war forever changed the lives of those engaged in the conflict. Of the eighty-nine Texas Aggies involved in the defense of Bataan and Corregidor, only thirty men returned home to Texas—and while all stood in harm's way, fourteen Texas Aggies were decorated for valor. Prior to the surrender of all troops in May 1942, six Aggies were killed in action, two were confirmed as missing in action, and five escaped to Australia. A total of seventy-nine Aggies were held as prisoners of war and fifteen died in POW camps of starvation and beatings—all in POW camps in the Philippines. Troops in the POW camps in the colder, nontropical climates had distinctly higher chances of survival than those being held in the Philippines. All those Texas Aggie POWs sent to nontropical locations, including three sent to Inchon, Korea, and seven sent to the cold interior of China at Mukden, all lived to return home.

An alarming thirty-one Texas Aggies died on the high seas (or onshore of wounds sustained during the attack) in the sinking of unmarked Japanese POW Hell Ships attempting to move them away from the Philippines and deeper into enemy territory in Japan and

The Texas Aggie Corregidor Muster Memorial dedicated at "Topside" near the main flag pole in memory of the Fightin' Texas Aggies who Mustered on the Rock in 1942 and 1946. (Courtesy of the Association of Former Students.)

China. The majority of those lost at sea were shipped from Manila after mid-1943 when Allied naval interdiction activity increased in the western Pacific.

After the war, all returning Aggies were processed through medical centers around the country and debriefed on their time and conditions of captivity. Many of the formal debriefings were used as evidence at the postwar tribunals in Tokyo and Manila. The ranking Texas Aggie officer, Major General George Moore, returned to Fort Monroe in Virginia for R&R and to write a detailed after-action report. In early 1946, he was ordered back to Manila on his fourth and final tour in the Philippines to command the postwar drawdown of forces. After a brief assignment, he returned to California and died a tragic death. In General Moore's honor, since 1947, the Corps of Cadets' most outstanding cadet unit selected annually is recognized and awarded the General Moore Award, in remembrance of one of Texas A&M's most distinguished World War II commanders.[4]

A number of the Aggies remained on active military duty, including Colonel Tom Dooley '35; Major Stockton Bruns '35; Colonel Henry Dittman '39; Lt. Commander Jackson L. Grayson '37; Tech Sergeant Walter Lee '41, who transitioned to the newly created US Air Force; Major Jack K. Walker '36; and Major Jerome McDavitt '33, who was assigned to Fort Riley and became a leader in the formation of the American Defenders of Bataan and Corregidor (ADBC). Colonel Edwin Aldridge '16 retired in San Antonio.

Most, after concluding a brief tour of duty and medical evaluation, left the military to return home and go back to college or to work. Robley D. Evans '40 became eastern regional sales manager for Phillips Petroleum; Clifton Chamberlain '40 returned home to Marlin; Captain John Cole '27 returned to teaching; Roy Davidson '40 to Midland; Frank Gensberg '38 to Big Spring; William Hamilton '40 became an engineer with the Gulf Colorado and Santa Fe Railroad; Urban Hopmann '39 opened a machinery company in San Antonio; Hugh Hunt '38 returned to Carthage; William E. Lewis '38 became a district agent with Republic National Life Insurance in Wellington; and Tull Louder '41 went to Talpa.

The flag fashioned by American POWs from silk parachutes dropped at Camp Omine Machi following the Japanese surrender. The flag is held by Richard "Buck" Weirus '42, executive director (1964–80) of the Texas A&M Association of Former Students, and Colonel Jerome A. McDavitt '33, Omine Machi POW commander in 1943–45 and national commander of the American Defenders of Bataan and Corregidor, 1974–75. The plaque above the flag hangs in the main entrance of the Memorial Student Center, listing the names of the eighty-nine Texas Aggies on duty in the Philippines in 1941–45 as well as the additional names of former students that served in the Pacific Theater. (Courtesy of Jerry C. Cooper '63.)

John J. Moseley '36 returned to his prewar job as a landscape architect with the National Park Service in Santa Fe, New Mexico; Oliver Orson '32 returned to his veterinarian practice in Seminole; Joe Revak '30 returned to Beaumont; Robert Robbins '41 returned to enroll in dental school at Baylor; Travis J. Smith '40 went to Waco; David M. Snell '37 went to Dallas as owner of General Insurance Agency; and Charlton J. Wimer '39 opened an engineering company in Dallas.

The defenders of Bataan and Corregidor will always hold a special place in the annals of American military history. The price for underestimating a potential enemy and for not being prepared and able to support troops in the field was a dark chapter for those who failed to address the threat that was clearly before them. Being prepared to fight through unity and strength is the best means to ensure peace—and if conflict does come, be prepared to support and defend those who have gone forward to protect the interest of the nation and freedom.

Per Unitatem Vis

APPENDIX 1

★ ★ ★

LEXICON OF TERMS

AAA—antiaircraft artillery
ADC—aide-de-camp
binta—strong, punishing slap on the face
bongo—roll call of POWs by numbers
cow-towing—low Oriental bow; sign of subservience
Dapecol—Davao Penal Colony (POW prison on Mindanao)
FDR—Franklin D. Roosevelt
FEAF—Far East Air Force
geta—wooden clogs worn by POWs
IGHQ—Imperial General Headquarters
IJA—Imperial Japanese Army
IMTFE—International Military Tribunal for the Far East
lugao—watery gruel like rice soup
MLR—main line of resistance
NCO—noncommissioned officer
***nipa* huts**—bamboo-framed structures covered with palm branches
NLF—North Luzon Force
POW—prisoner of war
PS—Philippine Scouts
SNAFU—situation normal all fouled up
speedo—Japanese Army slang; "to move faster"
the Rock—nickname for the Island of Corregidor

USAAF—United States Army Air Force
USAFFE—United States Army Forces Far East
USFIP—United States Forces in the Philippines
WPO-3—War Plan Orange-3
Zero—high performance Japanese fighter plane

APPENDIX 2

★★★

BATAAN AND CORREGIDOR AWARDS AND HONORS

Name	Award	Date	Location
Col. Edward E. Aldridge '16	Bronze Star and Purple Heart with Oak Leaf Cluster	April 1944	Bataan
Capt. Paul A. Brown '29	Silver Star	March 25, 1942	Corregidor
Lt. Lewis B Chevaillier '39	Silver Star	April 30, 1942	Bataan
Maj. Henry C. Dittman '39	Distinguished Service Cross	March 1942	Bataan
Capt. Tom Dooley '35	Silver Star	December 8, 1941	Clark Field
Lt. Robley D. Evans '40	Silver Star	March 1942	Bataan
Capt. Rudyard Kipling Grimes '38	Distinguished Service Cross	January 12, 1942	Bataan
Lt. Clifford G. Hardwicke Jr. '37	Silver Star	January 17, 1942	Bataan
Capt. James Russell Holmes '36	Silver Star	1942	Corregidor
Lt. Urban C. Hopmann '39	Silver Star	G.O. 365	Bataan

Name	Award	Date	Location
Capt. Ross I. Miller '39	Silver Star	April 30, 1942	Mindanao
Maj. Gen. George F. Moore '08	Distinguished Service Cross	April 29, 1942	Corregidor
Lt. Col. Rufus H. Rogers '26	Legion of Merit and Purple Heart	September 7, 1944	Davao
Maj. Hervey H. Whitfield '34	Distinguished Service Cross with Oak Leaf Cluster	May 6, 1942	Corregidor

Postwar Honors

The Pipkin Memorial US Army Reserve Training Center in Beaumont, Texas, is named for **Carl H. Pipkin '40**.

Gary Air Force Base in San Marcos, Texas, today Gary Training Center, is named for B-17 pilot **Lt. Arthur "Tex" E. Gary '40**, killed in the first hours of the Japanese bombing at Clark Field, December 8, 1941.

The annual outstanding Cadet Unit at Texas A&M is awarded the General Moore Award and dorm named in honor of **Maj. Gen. George Moore '08**.

Bergstrom Air Force Base in Austin, Texas, is named for B-17 pilot **Captain John August Bergstrom '29**, killed in action at Clark Field on December 8, 1941.

The Grimes Memorial US Army Reserve Center in Abilene, Texas, is named for **R. K. Grimes '38**.

APPENDIX 3

★★★

TEXAS AGGIE POWS ON JAPANESE HELL SHIPS, 1942-45

August 12, 1942: *Nagara Maru* **(or** *Suzuya Maru***)**
From Manila to Takao Harbor, Formosa
Total POWs: 179; Deaths: 0
Gen. George Moore '08
Col. Edwin Aldridge '16
Capt. Tom Dooley '35
Later, this group of three was moved to Mukden via Japan.

October 28, 1942: *Erie Maru*
From Manila to Davao
POWs: 1,000; Deaths: 2
Capt. George H. Peets '30
Capt. Gus H. Froebel '35
Capt. Travis Perrenot '36
Capt. Donald W. Peterson '40

November 7, 1942: *Nagato Maru*
From Manila to Moji, Japan
Total POWs: 1,600; Deaths: 50
Capt. John S. Coleman '29 (sent to the Yogogawa Steel Mill in Osaka)

Capt. Burt O. Griffin '41 (died December 13, 1942, in Moji)
Capt. Robert C. Robbins '41

August 2, 1944: *Sekiho Maru*
From Manila to Japan; 62-day voyage
Total POWs: 1,024; Deaths: 6
Capt. Jerome McDavitt '33

September 7, 1944: *Shinyo Maru*
From Davao to Manila
Total POWs: 750; Deaths: 667
Capt. Rufus H. Rogers '26
Major Harry O. Fischer '29
Capt. Gus H. Froebel '35
Lt. Maxey C. Chenault '37
Capt. Ross I. Miller '39
Lt. Donald W. Peterson '40
Lt. Roy D. Russell '42
Major Harry O. Fischer '29 and Lt. Roy D. Russell '42 escaped after the sinking and were rescued by the *USS Narwhal.*

October 21, 1944: *Arisan Maru*
From Manila to Japan
Total POWs: 1,800; Deaths: 1,792
M.Sgt. William G. Boyd '27
Capt. William M. Curtis '32
Capt. Roy M. Vick Jr. '35
Lt. James R. Holmes '36
Lt. John B. McCluskey '36
Lt. Edger B. Bugress '38
Lt. James M. Henry '39
Capt. Henry J. Schutte Jr. '39
Lt. Melvin R. Millard '40
Lt. John D. Stakenberg '40
Lt. Charles E. Gaskell '41

Lt. Andy M. James '41
All twelve Texas Aggies were lost—the largest loss of Aggie life in one single wartime event.

December 13, 1944: ***Oryoku Maru*** **(sunk on December 15, 1944)**
From Manila to Japan
Total POWs: 1,620; Deaths: 300
Major Maynard G. Snell '21
Capt. Paul A. Brown '28
Capt. Jack W. Kelley '29
Capt. G. H. Peets '30 (died in the Battle of Tennis Court on December 22, 1944)
Capt. Joseph A. Revak '30
Capt. Cary M. Abney Jr. '34
Capt. Sidney R. Greer '35 (died February 8, 1945)
Capt. Travis E. Perrenot '36
Capt. Wilbert Calvert '38
Lt. Hugh A. Derrick '39
Lt. Ormon L. Fitzhugh '40

December 27, 1944: ***Enoura Maru*** **(sunk on January 9, 1945)**
From Luzon to Formosa
Total POWs: 1,069; Deaths: 316
Major John V. King '22
Capt. Cary M. Abney Jr. '34
Capt. T. E. Perrenot '36
Capt. W. Calvert '38
Lt. H. P. Hardegree '39

January 28, 1945: ***Brazil Maru***
Arrived in Moji, Japan
Total POWs: 236
Lt. Col. Eugene. T. Lewis '27
Capt. Cary M. Abney '34
Capt. Charles M. Dempwolf '35

Capt. Wilber Calvert '38
Capt. T. E. Perrenot '39
Abney (3), Perrenot (4), and Calvert (6 or 7) were on multiple ships. Capt. Wilber Calvert '38 was shipped on and survived six Hell Ships before he was killed on *Brazil Maru*. Before *Brazil*, he endured *Eire*, an unknown ship, *Singoto*, *Augsberg*, *Oryoku*, and *Enoura*.

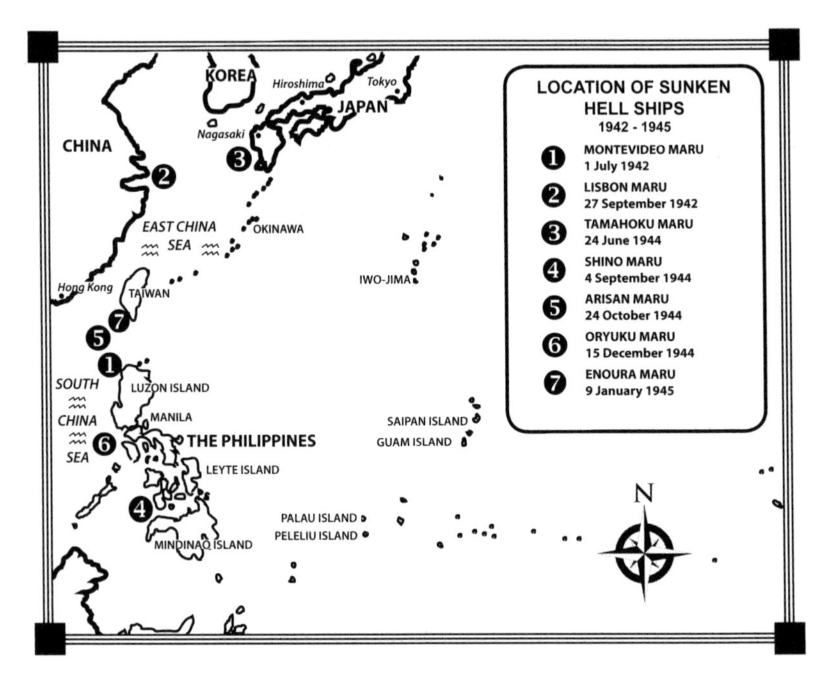

Locations of sunken Hell Ships, 1942–45.

APPENDIX 4

★ ★ ★

TEXAS AGGIES AT BATAAN AND CORREGIDOR

FINAL STATUS OF AGGIE TROOPS

	Number of troops	*Number of troops in Corregidor*
RH: Returned home	30	11
KIA: Killed in action	6	2
HS: Died on Hell Ships	31	0
CD: Died in Camp	15	13
MIA: Missing in action	2	0
ES: Escaped	5	1
Total	89	27

ROSTER OF AGGIES ON BATAAN AND CORREGIDOR

Name/class	*Unit*	*Camp/ship*	*Comment*
Capt. Cary M. Abney '34	FA	Caban/Brazil	POW/D 26 Jan 1945 HS
Col. Edwin E. Aldridge '16	61st Inf. Div.	T/Nagara/ Mukden	RH

(*continued*)

Name/class	*Unit*	*Camp/ship*	*Comment*
Lt. James Alexander '38	131st Inf.	Thailand	POW/ D 29 Aug 1943 HS
Capt. John A. Bergstrom '29	19th Bomb Gp.	Clark Field	8 Dec 1941 KIA
M.Sgt. William Giles Boyd '27	194th Tank	Cabanatuan/ Arisan	24 Oct 1944 HS
Capt. Paul A. Brown '28	4th USMC	Corr/Cab/ Oryoku/ Fuk No. 1	POW/D 11 Feb 1945 CD
Capt. George C. Brundrett '33	19th BG	Caban/Inchon	4 July 1945 CD
Capt. D. Bruns '35	59th CA	Hoten Camp/ Mukden	RH
Capt. Floyd Buchel '36	0-342155	Unknown	2 Feb 1946 (generic date) MIA
Lt. Edgar B. Burgess '38	19th BG	Caban/ Mariveles	24 Oct 1944 HS
Capt. Wilbert A. Calvert '37	60th CA	Corr/Oryoka	POW/D 22 Jan 45 CD
Lt. Clifton H. Chamberlain Jr. '40	59th CA	Ft. Drum/ Caban	Liberated 20 Jan 1945 RH
Lt. Maxey C. Chenault '37	19th BG	Davao/Shinyo	7 Sept 1944 HS
Lt. Lewis B. Chevaillier '39	60th CA	Corr/Zentsuji, Shikoku	RH
Capt. John S. Coleman '27	19th BG	O'Donnell/ Cab/ Rokuroshi	RH
Lt. W. P. Culp III '38	24th PGp	O'Donnell/ Caban	24 Aug 1972 RH
Capt. William M. Curtis '32	CAC Eng.	Caban/ Mariveles	KIA 24 Oct 1944 HS
Lt. Roy H. Davidson Jr. '40	19th BG	Osaka Camp	RH

Name/class	*Unit*	*Camp/ship*	*Comment*
Lt. Clarence R. Davis '27	19th BG	Clark	8 Dec 1941 KIA
Lt. James R. Davis '42	19th BG	Caban/Oryoku	13 Dec 1944 HS
Capt. Charles M. Dempwolf '35	14th Eng.	Caban/ POW/D	23 Jan 1945 HS
Lt. Hugh A. Derrick '39	71st Eng. Bn.	Cabantuan/HS	POW/D 23 Jan 1945 HS
Lt. Henry Dittman '39	19th BG	Clark/B/C	Escaped to Australia RH
Capt. Thomas Dooley '35	26th Cav./ HQ	Clark/B/T/ Mukden	RH
Lt. Robley D. Evans '40	45th Inf. Reg.	Rokorshi/ Osaka	RH
Major Harry O. Fischer '29	Eng.	Survived Shinyo/ Escaped *USS Narwhal*	ES
Lt. Orman L. Fitzhugh '40	AC	Caban/ Bilibid/HS	D 15 Dec 1944 HS
Lt. Stanley Friedline '40	60th CA/ AA	Corregidor	29 Apr 1942 KIA
Capt. Gus Froebel '35	86th FA Reg.	Davao/Shinyo	7 Sep 1944 HS
Lt. Arthur "Tex" Gary '40	19th Bomb Gp.	Clark Field	8 Dec 1941 KIA
Lt. Charles E. Gaskell '41	24th PGp	O'Donnell/ Caban/Arisan	10 Oct 1944 HS
Capt. Frank Gensberg '38	86th FA Reg.	Nagato/ Rokoroski	RH
Capt. Adolph H. Giesecke '26	Inf.	Caban/ Oryoku/ Fukuoka	POW/D 6 Feb 1945 HS

(*continued*)

Name/class	*Unit*	*Camp/ship*	*Comment*
Lt. Jackson L. Grayson '37	USN/ aviator	Unknown	RH
Capt. Sidney R. Greer '35	59th CE	Camp Moji/ KMH	POW/D 8 Jan 1945 HS
Capt. Paul R. Gregory '40	14th Eng.	Lipa Batanges	D 5 Dec 1942 CD
Capt. James R. Griffin '39	19th BG	Nichols/B/ Corr/Del Monte	Evac. to Australia, ES KIA New Guinea
Lt. Burt O. Griffin '41	31st Eng. Bn.	Corregidor/ KMH	6 Dec 1942 CD
Capt. Rudyard Grimes '39	57th Inf. (PS)	O'Donnell	POW/D Oct 1942 CD
Lt. William A. Hamilton Jr. '40	60th AA	Corr/Caban/3 HShips O, E, B/Fukuoka	RH
Lt. Howard P. Hardegree '39	24th PGp	Caban	POW/D 9 Jan 1945 CD
Lt. Clifford Hardwicke Jr. '37	26th Cav.	Bataan	17 Jan 1942 KIA
Capt. Graham M. Hatch Jr. '31	Inf.	Fukuaka	POW/D 9 Feb 1945 CD
Lt. James M. Henry '39	24th PGp	O'Donnell/ Arisan 24	Oct 1944 HS
Capt. James R. Holmes '36	60th CA	O'Donnell/ Arisan	24 Oct 1944 HS
Lt. Urban C. Hopmann '39	22nc Inf. Reg.	Unknown	RH
Sgt. Hugh D. Hunt '38	6971014	Sendai/ Hanatua Camp, J	RH
Lt. Andy M. James Jr. '41	CAC/HQ	Caban/Arisan	24 Oct 1944 HS

Name/class	*Unit*	*Camp/ship*	*Comment*
Capt. Jack W. Kelley '29	19th BG	Clark/B/O/ Caban Oryoku	12 Dec 1944 HS
Lt. Marshall H. Kennady Jr. '40	192nd Tank	O'Donnell/ Fukuaka 19	Jan 1945 CD
Major John V. King '27	AdjGen	Enoura	9 Jan 1944 HS
WO Walter M. Lee '41	QMC	Tokyo/ Hanawa	POW/RH
Lt. John L. Lester '29	Unknown	Corregidor	8 May 1942 KIA
Lt. Col. Eugene T. Lewis '27	43rd Inf. (PA)	Fukuaka/ KMH D/ Moji Hosp.	31 Jan 45 HS
Lt. William E. Lewis Jr. '38	92nd CAC	Osaka/Nagato/ Rokuroshi	RH
Lt. Tull Ray Louder '41	60th CA HQ	Osaka	RH
Lt. John B. McCluskey Jr. '36	59th CAC	Corr/Caban/ Arisan	24 Oct 1944 HS
Capt. Jerome McDavitt '33	24th FA	Clark/B/Corr/ Caban/Omine, Japan D 3	May 82 RH
Lt. Melvin R. Millard '40	CAC 5/5 Bn.	Caban/ Mariveles	24 Oct 1944 HS
Capt. Ross I. Miller '39	101st Eng.	O'Donnell/ Shinyo 9	July 1944 HS
Maj. Gen. George Moore '08	CG	Corregidor B/T/Mukden	RH
T.Sgt. John J. Moseley '39	515th HQ/ CAA	Tottori/ Mukden	RH
Lt. John W. Muse '40	27th BG	Caban/Cleb malaria	25 July 1942 CD

(continued)

Name/class	*Unit*	*Camp/ship*	*Comment*
Lt. John R. Noles '39	19th BG	Clark/B Japan D/25	Jan 1996 RH
Lt. James R. Oppenheim '35	803 Eng. Bn.	Cabanatuan	16 July 1942 CD
Major Oliver W. "Stud" Orson '32	AC Vet. Med.	Jinsen, Korea Inchon	RH
Capt. H. Peets '30	31st Inf.	Davao/Oryoku	22 Dec 1944 HS
Capt. Travis E. Perrenot '36	24th FA Reg.	Davao	POW/D 22 Jan 1945 HS
Lt. Donald W. Petersen '40	27th BG	Davao/ Skinkyo	7 Aug 1944 HS
Capt. Chester A. Peyton '33	57th Inf. Reg.	Fukouka	POW/D 17 Feb 1943 CD
Capt. Carl H. Pipkin '40	60th CAC	Osaka/Umeda	POW/D 2 Feb 1943 CD
Capt. Joseph R. Revak '30	192nd Tank	Oryoku/ Fukouka/ Inchon	RH
Lt. Robert C. Robbins '41	14th Eng. CE	Rokuroshi, Honshu	RH
Lt. Col. Rufus H. Rogers '26	81st Div.	Davao/Shinyo	7 Sept 1944 HS
Lt. James N. Roland '30	Unknown	Unknown	Unknown
Lt. Roy D. Russell '42	19th BG	Caban/Davao/ survived Shinyo/ escaped *USS Narwhal*	ES
Lt. Harry J. Schreiber '36	19th BG B-17 Nav.	D	20 July 1995 ES
Capt. Willis A. Scrivener '37	60th CAC	Fukouka	POW/D 7 Feb 1945 CD

Name/class	*Unit*	*Camp/ship*	*Comment*
Capt. Henry J. Schutte Jr. '39	59th CAC	O'Donnell/ Tarlac/Arisan	24 Oct 1944 HS
Lt. Travis J. Smith '40	131st FA	Osaka/Tofuku/ Rokuroski	RH
Major Maynard G. Snell '27	192nd Tank	Caban/Oryiku	13 Dec 1944 HS
Lt. David M. Snell '37	192nd Tank	Keijo, Seoul	Fuk No. 1 RH
Lt. John D. Stukenburg '40	81st Div. CE	Davao/Arisan	24 Oct 1944 HS
Capt. Roy M. Vick Jr. '35	91st CA Reg. (PS)	Arisan	24 Oct 1944 HS
Capt. Jack K. Walker '36	24th FA	Caban/ Mukden	RH
Capt. Hervey H. Whitfield '34	19th BG	Del Monte/ escaped to Australia	ES
Capt. John T. Whitfield '37	Unknown	Died at sea on return to United States after 15 Aug 1945 surrender	CD
Lt. Charlton J. Wimer '39	AWS Sig.	Omori Tokyo Base Camp	RH
Lt. James B. Whitley '38	0-385216	MIA on Bataan, declared 1 Feb 1946	MIA

CD—camp death

ES—escaped

HS—Hell Ship

KIA—killed in action

MIA—missing in action

POW—prisoner of war

RH—returned home

AGGIE HEADSHOTS

Maj. Gen. George Fleming Moore
1908

Col. Edwin E. Aldridge
1916

Capt. Adolph H. Giesecke
1926

Lt. Col. Rufus H. Rogers
1926

M.Sgt. William G. Boyd
1927

Capt. John S. Coleman
1927

Lt. Clarence R. Davis
1927

Maj. John V. King
1927

Maj. Maynard G. Snell
1927

Capt. Paul A. Brown
1928

Capt. John A. Bergstrom
1929

Maj. Harry O. Fischer
1929

Capt. Jack W. Kelley
1929

Capt. Joseph R. Revak
1930

Capt. Graham M. Hatch
1931

Capt. William M. Curtis
1932

Capt. George C. Brundrett
1933

Capt. Jerome A. McDavitt
1933

Capt. Chester Alan Peyton
1933

Capt. Cary M. Abney Jr.
1934

Capt. Hervey H. Whitfield
1934

Capt. Stockton D. Bruns
1935

Capt. Charles Martin
Dempwolf
1935

Capt. Thomas Dooley
1935

Capt. Sidney Robert Greer
1935

Lt. James R. Oppenheim
1935

Capt. Roy McMahon Vick
1935

Capt. Floyd McRae Buchel
1936

Lt. John B. McCluskey Jr.
1936

Capt. Travis E. Perrenot
1936

Capt. Wilbert A. Calvert
1937

Lt. Maxey C. Chenault
1937

Lt. Jackson L. Grayson
1937

Lt. Clifford G. Hardwicke
1937

Capt. Willis A. Scrivener
1937

Lt. David M. Snell
1937

Lt. William Boyd
1938

Lt. Edgar B. Burgess
1938

Lt. Willis P. Culp III
1938

Capt. Frank Gensberg
1938

Lt. William D. Lewis
1938

Lt. James B. Whitley
1938

Lt. Lewis B. Chevaillier
1939

Lt. Henry Dittman
1939

Lt. Urban C. Hopmann
1939

T.Sgt. John J.
Moseley
1939

Lt. John R. Noles
1939

Capt. Henry J. Schutte Jr.
1939

Lt. Charlton J. Wimer
1939

Lt. Clifton H. Chamberlain
1940

Lt. Roy H. Davidson Jr.
1940

Lt. Robley D. Evans
1940

Lt. Orman L. Fitzhugh
1940

Lt. Stanley Friedline
1940

Capt. Paul R.
Gregory
1940

Lt. William A. Hamilton
1940

Lt. Marshall H.
Kennady
1940

Lt. Melvin Ray Millard
1940

Lt. Donald W. Petersen
1940

Capt. Carl H. Pipkin
1940

Lt. John Darrell
Stukenburg
1940

Lt. Andy M. James
1941

Not pictured:

1927
Lt. Col. E. T. Lewis

1929
Lt. John L. Lester

1930
Capt. George H. Peets
Lt. James M. Roland
Lt. James N. Roland

1932
Maj. Oliver W. Orson

1935
Capt. Gus H. Froebel

1936
Capt. James R. Holmes
Lt. Harry J. Schreiber
Capt. Jack K. Walker

1937
Capt. John T. Whitfield

1938
Lt. James Alexander
Sgt. Hugh Hunt

1939
Lt. Hugh A. Derrick
Capt. James R. Griffin
Capt. Rudyard Grimes
Lt. Howard P. Hardegree
Lt. James M. Henry
Capt. Ross I. Miller

1940
Lt. Arthur "Tex" Gary
Lt. John W. Muse
Lt. Travis J. Smith

1941
Lt. Tull Ray Louder
Lt. Charles E. Gaskell
Lt. Burt O. Griffin
WO Walter M. Lee
Lt. Robert C. Robbins

1942
Lt. James R. Davis
Lt. Roy D. Russell

NOTES

CHAPTER 1

1 Text of President Roosevelt's May 11, 1937, address in President's Personal File, Master Speech File, Box 32, Number 1053, Franklin D. Roosevelt Papers, Hyde Park, NY; *Battalion*, May 11, 1937; *Bryan Eagle*, May 11, 1937; *Longhorn*, 1938, pp. 2–3, 38; John A. Adams Jr., *Keepers of the Spirit*, College Station: Texas A&M University Press, 2001, pp. 98–99; *New York Times*, July 14, 1918; "A. & M. Furnished 2233 Officers [and Former Students]: Half Graduates Serve," *Reveille*, February 26, 1919, pp. 1, 4.

2 "Sixty Years of Growth," *The Bryan News*, September 21, 1936, p. 1; Kenneth Davis, *FDR: The War President 1940–1943*, New York: Random House, 2000, pp. 9–16; Robert S. McElvaine, *The Great Depression: America, 1929–1941*, New York: Time Books, 1993, p. 320. Here is a sample of New Deal "alphabet" agencies: AAA, Agricultural Adjustment Administration; WPA, Works Project Administration; RFC, Reconstruction Finance Corporation; CCC, Civilian Conservation Corps; and TVA, Tennessee Valley Authority.

3 Adams, *Keepers of the Spirit*, College Station: Texas A&M University Press, 2001, pp. 133–34. There were a total of thirty-nine Aggies that saw FDR in May 1937 and later served on Bataan or Corregidor: four from 1937, nine from 1938, thirteen from 1939, and thirteen from 1940.

4 Minutes of the Board of Directors, Texas A&M, October 17, 1936, p. 71; "Governor Appoints Elliott Roosevelt as A. & M. Director," *Texas Aggie*, December 15, 1936, p. 1; Steven Fenberg, *Unprecedented Power: Jesse Jones, Capitalism, and the Common Good*, College Station: Texas A&M University Press, 2011, pp. 270, 340. Elliott Roosevelt was a resident of Fort Worth and was appointed to the board by Governor James V. Allred in November 1936. Jesse Jones, a Houston

businessman, was the primary force behind the increased facilities investment at Texas A&M; in November 1939, Texas A&M honored Jones by dedicating the annual Thanksgiving Day football game against the University of Texas to him—Texas A&M won 20–0 and went on to the 1940 New Year's Day Sugar Bowl to beat Tulane 14–13 and capture the Texas Aggies' first national football championship.

5 Adams, *Keepers of the Spirit*, pp. 144–47. For detailed organization charts and strength reports of the Corps of Cadets from 1876 to the present, see Pamela W. Johnson, *The Corps: The Core of A&M*, College Station: Texas A&M University Press, 2005.

6 Interview with Joe Utay '08, May 21, 1976; "Corregidor Commander," *Texas Aggie*, January 31, 1942; Wilbur Evans and H. B. McElroy, *The Twelfth Man*, Huntsville, AL: Strode, 1974, pp. 45–51.

7 Adams, *Keepers of the Spirit*, pp. 136–37; Jim Woodall, "Gen George Moore," unpublished manuscript; Henry C. Dethloff and John Adams, *Texas Aggies Go to War*, College Station: Texas A&M University Press, 2006, pp. 80–84.

8 Russell F. Weigley, *History of the United States Army*, New York: Macmillan, 1967, pp. 398–408; James H. Belote and William M. Belote, *Corregidor*, New York: PEI Books, 1980, p. 9; Edward J. Drea, *Japan's Imperial Army: Its Rise and Fall, 1853–1945*, Lawrence: University Press of Kansas, 2009, 190–222.

9 Forrest C. Pogue, *George C. Marshall: Ordeal and Hope*, New York: Viking, 1965, pp. 19–79; Bob Welch, *Resolve: From the Jungles of World War II Bataan*, New York: Berkley Caliber, 2012, pp. 16–18.

10 W. O. Thompson, "Military Training at Educational Institutions," *Infantry Journal*, May 1929, pp. 496–502; Richard M. Ketchum, *The Borrowed Years, 1938–1941: America on the Way to War*, New York: Random House, 1989, p. 539, 542; Keith E. Eiler, *Mobilizing America: Robert P. Patterson and the War Effort, 1940–1945*, Ithaca, NY: Cornell University Press, 1997, p. 43; Thomas E. Ricks, *The Generals*, New York: Penguin Books, 2012, pp. 30–37; John A. Glusman, *Conduct Under Fire*, New York: Viking, 2005, p. 51; George C. Marshall, "A Survey of the Army Program since July 1939," statement before the Senate Special Committee Investigating the National Defense Program, 77th Cong., 2nd sess., April 22, 1941, in H. A. DeWeerd, ed., *Selected Speeches and Statements of General of the Army George C. Marshall*, Washington, DC: Infantry Journal Press, 1945, pp. 101–16.

11 Maury Klein, *A Call to Arms: Mobilizing America for World War II*, New York: Bloomsbury Press, 2015, pp. 13–62; Weigley, *History of the United States Army*, pp. 411, 418; US Army, War Plans Division, "The Most Serious Weakness in Our National Defense System," Tab B, Army Chief of Staff, WPD, February 2, 1939; Adams, *Keepers of the Spirit*, p. 133; Clay Blair, *MacArthur*, New York:

Nelson Doubleday, 1977, pp. 35–41; Douglas MacArthur, *Reminiscences*, New York: McGraw-Hill, 1964, pp. 102–3; William Manchester, *American Caesar: Douglas MacArthur 1880–1964*, Boston: Little, Brown and Company, 1978, pp. 171–72; FDR Speech, Roosevelt Library, Box 32, Number 1053, College Station, Texas, May 11, 1937. The US Army War Plans Division recommended the "need for Five Divisions" and noted in the report the Germans had fielded ninety divisions, Italy had forty-five, and Japan had fifty on the China mainland alone.

12 *Longhorn*, 1941, pp. 266–69, 316–24; "First Time in History of School Majority U.S. Officers Stationed at A&M Are Ex-Students," *Texas Aggie*, March 1, 1941; Adams, *Keepers of the Spirit*, pp. 142–46.

13 *Battalion*, October 14, 1941, and March 7, 1942; "First Time in History of School Majority U.S. Officers Stationed at A&M Are Ex-Students," *Texas Aggie*, May 1, 1941; Henry C. Dethloff, *A Centennial History of Texas A&M University 1876–1976*, vol. 2, College Station, Texas: A&M University Press, 1975, p. 451; Adams, *Keepers of the Spirit*, pp. 136–44; Ricks, *The Generals*, pp. 8–9; McElvaine, *The Great Depression*, pp. 314–20; *Dallas Morning News*, April 2, 1942. By the fall of 1941, the United States and partners in the Dutch East Indies controlled and supplied some 90 percent of Japan's imported oil. Japan's first phase of planning began as early as April 17, 1941, with the signing of a nonaggression pact with Russia, and placed the Imperial High Command in high gear soon after the American and British froze Japanese assets on July 24, 1941, in Indo-China.

14 Interview with former Cadet Corps Commander William Becker '41, October 5, 1998; *Longhorn*, 1941, p. 24; Manchester, *American Caesar*, pp. 195–204; "Defenders of Philippines," *LIFE*, December 22, 1941, pp. 26–35; Ian W. Toll, *Pacific Crucible*, New York: W. W. Norton & Company, 2012, p. 61; "A.& M. Men Ready," *Texas Aggie*, November 1, 1940; R. W. Steen, "The Various Polls," *Battalion*, September 20, 1941.

15 Craig Shirley, *December 1941: 31 Days that Changed America and Saved the World*, Nashville: Thomas Nelson, 2011, pp. 109–10; Walter Lord, *Day of Infamy*, New York: Henry Holt and Company, 1957, pp. 3–20; Site visit to USS Arizona Memorial by author, Pearl Harbor, April 17, 1991. Dates are difficult to cite because of the fact that the Philippines is essentially a day ahead of the United States because of the International Date Line. For example, it was December 8 in Japan when Pearl Harbor was attacked on the morning of December 7, 1941, in Hawaii.

16 AM to Mother, Daddy, and all, "Somewhere in the Philippines," in Andy Marmaduke James Jr. Papers, Cushing Library, Texas A&M University, n.d.; "Lt. A. M. James First to Learn of Jap War," *Dalhart Texas*, April 2, 1942; Eric Morris, *Corregidor: The American Alamo of World War II*, New York: Cooper Square Press, 2000, pp. 77–109.

17 Jonathan M. Wainwright, "General Jonathan M. Wainwright's Own Story of the Battle and Fall of Bataan and Corregidor and His Years as a Prisoner of the Japanese," St. Joseph (Missouri) *Gazette* series from October 7, 1945, until November 17, 1945, in forty-two installments (hereafter referred to as Wainwright, "Own Story," *Gazette*, with installment number). There are numerous accounts of who received the first notice of the Japanese attack on the US Asiatic fleet in Hawaii. Furthermore, MacArthur and his army staff failed to notify Admiral Hart at Cavite, eight miles southwest of Manila, and when Admiral Husband Kimmel radioed Hart of the attack at Pearl Harbor, Hart "neglected" to inform MacArthur; see Manchester, *American Caesar*, p. 205.

18 US Army, "The Moore Report," Wainwright Papers, Part C, http://www.corregidor.org; Pogue, *George C. Marshall*, pp. 200, 233–35. See also background data in Major A. M. Santos, "The 1st Regular Division in the Battle of the Philippines," Fort Leavenworth, KS: Command and General Staff College, 1949, pp. 1–23, and Stephen A. Kwiecinski, *Honor, Courage, Faith: A Corregidor Story*, Manila: Anvil, 2012, p. xvi.

19 Edward S. Miller, *War Plan Orange: The U.S. Strategy to Defeat Japan, 1897–1945*, Annapolis: Naval Institute Press, 1991; John A. Glusman, *Conduct Under Fire*, New York: Viking, 2005, p. 61. See also Steven T. Ross, *American War Plans, 1890–1939*, New York: Frank Cass, 2000, and Andrew Roberts, *The Storm of War*, New York: Harper, 2011, pp. 187–89.

20 "Walton, Welty Urge Cadets to Continue Studies as Usual," *Battalion*, December 9 and 11, 1941; Adams, *Keepers of the Spirit*, p. 150.

21 Wainwright, "Own Story," *Gazette*, installment 3; William H. Bartsch, *Doomed at the Start*, College Station: Texas A&M University Press, 1992.

22 Major William R. Nealson, "The Operations of a Provisional Battalion, 41st Division," Fort Benning: The Infantry School, 1948, p. 5; Manchester, *American Caesar*, p. 167.

23 W. L. While, *Queens Die Proudly*, New York: Harcourt Brace, 1943, pp. 5–10, 34; Wainwright, "Own Story," *Gazette*, installment 5; Edgar D. Whitcomb, *Escape from Corregidor*, Chicago: Henry Regnery Company, 1958, pp. 21, 269; Hanson W. Baldwin, *Battles Lost and Won: Great Campaigns of World War II*, Old Saybrook, CT: Konecky & Konecky, p. 117. For the Japanese perspective of the war, *Fading Victory: The Diary of Admiral Matome Ugaki*, translated by Masataka Chihaya (University of Pittsburgh Press, 1991), is the best documentation of the Japanese road to war in the Pacific; in early entries, Ugaki expresses surprise and pleasure at the rapid success of the Japanese military during the early months of the war.

24 White, *Queens Die Proudly*, p. 34.

25 William H. Bartsch, *December 8, 1941: MacArthur's Pearl Harbor*, College Station: Texas A&M University Press, 2003, p. 410; Bartsch, *Doomed at the Start*,

pp. 201–4; Richard Connaughton, *MacArthur and Defeat in the Philippines*, Woodstock, NY: Overlook Press, 2001, pp. 166–70; Toll, *Pacific Crucible*, pp. 48–49, 58; Morris, *Corregidor: The American Alamo of World War II*, p. 92. The official USAAF figure (which often underestimated the number killed) was given at 55 dead; however, Captain Jerry McDavitt's battery of Philippine Scouts logged in 189 bodies. Body counts would be in conflict during the entire Philippine Campaign. Capt. Tom Dooley '35, aide to General Wainwright, noted in his diary the "announced" figures, for example, shortly after the attack and before the official count of dead and wounded, were 82 dead and 110 wounded; *The Dallas News*, October 2, 1945, and Wainwright, "Own Story," *Gazette*, installment 5 in his postwar memoir, estimated there were 193 dead and wounded in the first attack on Clark field and the enemy only lost two planes during the raid.

26 Royal Gunnison, "Blitz over the Philippines," *Collier's*, January 17, 1942, pp. 17, 49; Toll, *Pacific Crucible*, pp. 50–53; Lewis H. Brereton, *The Brereton Diaries*, New York: William Morrow and Company, 1946, p. 52. See also Antony Best, *British Intelligence and the Japanese Challenge in Asia, 1914–1941*, New York: Palgrave Macmillan, 2002, and Roberts, *The Storm of War*, p. 87.

27 "Aid to Defenders: Attack on Philippines Pressed from Many Directions," *New York Times*, December 13, 1941; Brereton, *Brereton Diaries*, p. 51; Grace C. Nash, *That We Might Live*, Scottsdale: SHANO, 1984, p. 66; Belote and Belote, *Corregidor*, pp. 28–30; Bill Sloan, *Undefeated: America's Heroic Fight for Bataan and Corregidor*, New York: Simon and Schuster, 2012, pp. 3, 40, 43.

28 Louis Morton, *War in the Pacific: The Fall of the Philippines*, Washington, DC: Center for Military History, US Army, 1953, pp. 64–70; Brereton, *Brereton Diaries*, pp. 58–67; Hanson W. Baldwin, "The Fall of Corregidor," *American Heritage*, August 1966, pp. 17–18. General Jonathan Wainwright is reported to have echoed MacArthur's orders, stating, "We must die in our tracks, falling not backward but forward toward the enemy," with one senior officer responding, "Don't believe everything you hear."

29 Wainwright, "Own Story," *Gazette*, installment 3.

30 Bartsch, *December 8, 1941*, p. 373; Toll, *Pacific Crucible*, p. 51; Sloan, *Undefeated*, pp. 26, 36.

31 White, *Queens Die Proudly*, 55–64; "Harry Schreiber," http://lanbob.com.

32 *Longhorn*, 1927, p. 45; http://www.7th-material.org; AFS, *Directory of Former Students*, 1949, p. xxviii.

33 Bartsch, *December 8, 1941*, pp. 244, 324, 410.

34 Jerry Cooper, "Lest We Forget: Jerome McDavitt '33 Recalls WWII POW Camps," *Texas Aggie*, April 1989, pp. 6–7; Donald Knox, *Death March: The Survivors of Bataan*, New York: Harcourt Brace Jovanovich, 1981, pp. 15, 104; John A. Glusman, *Conduct Under Fire*, New York: Viking, 2005, p. 81; Eric Morris,

Corregidor: The End of the Line, New York: Stein and Day, 1981, pp. 96, 146, 405–6.

35 Knox, *Death March*, pp. 106–7; Eunice C. Hatchitt, "Bataan Nurse," *Collier's Weekly*, August 1, 1942, p. 13. See also Juanita Redmond, *I Served on Bataan*, Philadelphia: J. B. Lippincott Company, 1943, pp. 19, 152.

36 Celedonio A. Ancheta, ed., "Report of Operations of USAFFE and USFIP in the Philippine Islands 1941–1942," in *The Wainwright Papers*, vol. 1, Quezon City, Philippines: New Day, 1980, pp. 1–62 (hereafter "Wainwright Report"); John S. Coleman Jr. '29. *Bataan and Beyond: Memories of an American POW*, College Station: Texas A&M University Press, 1978.

37 "Japanese Pounded in Luzon," *New York Times*, December 13, 1941, p. 1; Thomas C. Hart, "War on the Horizon," pp. 17–22, in John T. Mason Jr., ed. *The Pacific War Remembered*, Annapolis: Naval Institute Press, 1986; Meirion Harries and Susie Harries, *Soldiers of the Sun: The Rise and Fall of the Imperial Japanese Army*, New York: Random House, 1991, pp. 315–25; Roberts, *The Storm of War*, p. 213. Morale of the British defenders at Singapore was greatly shattered following the sinking of the pride of the British Navy, the *HMS Prince of Wales* and the *HMS Repulse*, the greatest maritime disaster of the war for the Royal Navy. By late January 1942, the Japanese had captured a vast area of some 32 million square miles and controlled 70 percent of the world's tin supply, 80 percent of the quinine supply, and more than 90 percent of all natural rubber sources.

38 Connaughton, *MacArthur and Defeat in the Philippines*, pp. 170–71; Manchester, *American Caesar*, p. 206; Herman S. Wolk, "When Arnold Bucked FDR," *Airforce Magazine*, November 2001; Thomas M. Huber, "The American Bataan Campaign, December 1941 to April 1942," *Army History*, Winter 1991–92, pp. 4–5; Kemp Tolley, "Army Snubs Navy in the Philippines," in Mason, *The Pacific War Remembered*, pp. 23–30; Bartsch, *December 8, 1941*, pp. 263, 410–15; Brereton, *Brereton Diaries*, p. 50; *New York Times*, September 1946; Pogue, *George C. Marshall*, 232–37. Bartsch notes, "Arnold went to his grave without ever receiving as adequate answer to his question." In an article (Robert F. Futrell, "Air Hostilities in the Philippines, 8 December 1941," *Air University Review*, January 1965), Futrell clearly lays the confusion and delay in ordering bombers to attack Formosa on MacArthur's chief of staff General Southerland who served as "gatekeeper," preventing General Brereton from talking directly to MacArthur. See Mark Perry, *The Most Dangerous Man in America: The Making of Douglas MacArthur*, New York: Basic Books, 2014, pp. 80–81.

39 *Longhorn*, 1938 and 1939, n.p.; Frank Graham, "Setting the Pace: Young Man from Goose Creek, Texas," *New York Sun*, August 13, 1943, p. 18; AFS, *Directory of Former Students of the A&M College of Texas 1876–1949*, 1949, pp. xxxii, 111.

40 Shirley, *December 1941*, p 273; "Attack on Hawaii," *LIFE*, December 29, 1941; "The US at War," *TIME*, December 29, 1941; Robert L. Dennison, "The Philippines: Prelude to Departure," in Mason, *The Pacific War Remembered*, pp. 31–37; Matthew S. Klimow, "Lying to the Troops: American Leaders and the Defense of Bataan," *Parameters*, December 1990, pp. 48–60.

41 Major Kary C. Emerson, "The Operations of the II Philippine Corps of Bataan, 10 January–8 April 1942," Fort Benning: Advanced Infantry Officers Course, 1950, p. 26; Major Donald G. Thompson, "Operations of Company 'L,' 31st Infantry Regiment, PA, in the Battle of Layac Junction, Bataan, P.I., 6–7 January 1942," Fort Benning: Advanced Infantry Officers Course, 1948, pp. 16–17; Major Everett V. Mead, "The Operations and Movements of the 31st Infantry Regiment, 7 December 1941–9 April 1942," Fort Benning: Advanced Infantry Officers Course, 1948, p. 28; Sloan, *Undefeated*, pp. 49, 53–54.

42 Thomas Dooley '35, "The First United States Tank Action in World War II," monograph written for the Advanced Officers Course, May 1, 1948, and reprinted in "The U.S. Tank Action in World War II," *Armor*, July–August 1983 (hereafter Dooley, "First Tank Action"); Richard Sassaman, "The Battling Bastards of Bataan," http://www.americanwwii.com. See also Nealson, "The Operations of a Provisional Battalion," pp. 4–6. More than sixty-five dialects were spoken in the islands, with Philippine officers usually speaking Tagalog and the Americans understanding none of the dialects.

43 Morton, *Fall of the Philippines*, pp. 145–57; Samuel E. Morison, *The Rising Sun in the Pacific*, Boston: Little, Brown and Company, 1951, p. 195; Richard C. Mallonee, *Battle for Bataan*, Novato, CA: Presidio Press, 1997, pp. 28–29.

44 Emerson, "Operations of the II Philippine Corps of Bataan," pp. 6–8; Baldwin, "The Fall of Corregidor," *American Heritage*, pp. 19–23.

45 MacArthur, *Reminiscences*, p. 124; Tom Dooley '35, Bataan and Corregidor Notebooks, Cushing Library, Texas A&M University, December 1941 to April 9, 1942 (hereafter Dooley Diary), Alcala, December 22, 1941; Wainwright Report, pp. 22–24; Shirley, *December 1941*, p. 442; Major M. T. Flores, "An Analytical Study of the Defense of Bataan," Fort Leavenworth, KS: Command and General Staff College, 1949, pp. 1–12; Mallonee, *Battle for Bataan*, p. 33. Some estimates paced the invading Japanese force as high as 200,000 troops, which in fact was not true; also Brereton, *Brereton Diaries*, p. 59, published in 1946, uses the Japanese estimated troop number of 80,000, quite possibly the source of the figure used by MacArthur (or his ghostwriter) in his 1964 memoir.

46 General Order Number 5, N.L.F., in Personnel Record Thomas Dooley (CAV) ADC, 1941–42, p. 14, Colonel Thomas Dooley WWII Collection, Cushing Library, Texas A&M; Duane Schultz, *Hero of Bataan: The Story of General Jonathan M. Wainwright*, New York: St. Martin's Press, 1981, p. 78; Peter S. Wainwright,

"Memorial Address of November 11, 1996," Walla Walla, WA: 1996, comments on Dooley's first Silver Star.

47 Personnel Record Thomas Dooley (CAV) ADC, p. 24, Dooley Collection; Lt. Col. T. J. H. Trapnell, "The Operations of the 26th Cavalry (P.S.) Personal Experience of a Squadron Commander," Fort Leavenworth, KS: Command and General Staff College, 1947, pp. 1–7; Wainwright, "Own Story," *Gazette*, installment 4. The famed 26th Cavalry (PS) is one of the last operational mounted units in the US Army. While a modern cavalry regiment numbered 1,261 men, the 26th listed at its peak 889 men, yet the actual combat strength was 682 men. Wainwright's after-action report by G-1 gave a misleading inflated strength of 850 men as of April 3, 1942. By early March, the 26th had been reduced by over half of its men and its mounts ordered slaughtered for food.

48 Dooley, "First Tank Action"; Jeffery W. Woodhall, "26th Cavalry in the Philippines," *Armor*, January–February 1983, pp. 8–16; "Operations of the Provisional Tank Group: USAFFE 1941–1942," p. 8, http://www.memorialmuseum.org; Emerson, "The Operations of the II Philippine Corps on Bataan," p. 11; Morton, *Fall of the Philippines*, pp. 174–77. There are five defensive lines in WPO-3:

D1—Aguilar to San Carlos to Urdaaneta City (beachhead)
D2—Argo River
D3—Santa Ignacia to Gerona to San Jose
D4—Tarlac to Cabanatuan City
D5—Bamban to Sibul Springs

49 Morton, *Fall of the Philippines*, 161–89; Sloan, *Undefeated*, pp. 83–85; Jeremy Black, *The Age of Total War*, Lanham: Rowman & Littlefield, 2006, p. 134.

50 Trapnell, "The Operations of the 26th Cavalry (P.S.)," pp. 9–12; Bartsch, *Doomed at the Start*, pp. 123–25; Morton, *Fall of the Philippines*, pp. 157, 187–89, 232–34; Sloan, *Undefeated*, pp. 55–56; "Old Area in Ruins," *New York Times*, December 28, 1941.

51 Dooley Diary, December 3, 1941; George C. Marshall, *Biennial Report of the Chief of Staff of the United States Army: July 1, 1943–June 30, 1945*, Washington, DC: Infantry Journal Press, 1946, pp. 8–10; Stanley Weintraub, *Pearl Harbor Christmas*, Cambridge, MA: Da Capo Press, 2011, pp. 20, 33, 37, 69; Andrew Roberts, *Masters and Commanders*, New York: Harper, 2009, pp. 66–72. See also Mark A. Stoler, "George C. Marshall and the 'Europe-First' Strategy, 1939–1951: A Study in Diplomatic as Well as Military History," *Journal of Military History*, April 2015, p. 299; Charles Barman, *Resist to the End: Hong Kong, 1941–1945*, Hong Kong: Hong Kong University Press, 2009; Klimow, "Lying to the Troops," pp. 4860.

52 Weintraub, *Pearl Harbor Christmas*, p. 69; Allison Ind, *Bataan: The Judgment Seat*, New York: Macmillan, 1944, pp. 174–77; Welch, *Resolve*, pp. 44–45; Jonathan W. Jordan, *American Warlords*, New York: NAL Caliber, 2015, pp. 136–38.

53 Wainwright Report, pp. 25–28; Wainwright, "Own Story," *Gazette*, installment 6 and 7; Morison, *The Rising Sun in the Pacific*, p. 195; Wainwright, "Philippine Mistakes Bared by Wainwright," *Baltimore News-Post*, October 8, 1945. US Naval operations in the Philippines halted most operations after December 24, 1941. See also Major A. M. Santos, "The 1st Regular Division in the Battle of the Philippines," CGSC, 1947, pp. v, 52–57.

54 Schultz, *Hero of Bataan*, p. 256; Perry, *The Most Dangerous*, pp. 80–81; "Australia's MacArthur," *TIME*, March 30, 1942; "MacArthur," *Newsweek*, March 9, 1942; Weintraub, *Pearl Harbor Christmas*, pp. 39–40. MacArthur's communiques from his HQ in Malinta Tunnel became headlines in papers across the nation; of the 142 issued before he departed for Australia in March 1942, 109 identified only one person—General MacArthur.

55 Wainwright, "Own Story," *Gazette*, installment 8. In Ugaki, *Fading Victory*, p. 51, the Japanese admiral reacts to radio reports that the US commanders at Pearl Harbor faced possible court-martial with some satire, "This tells us so much about the shock they received [on December 7]. It is a gross error for the authorities to want to punish their subordinates when some misfortune occurs, when a state wants to force its national politics, that state must be sufficiently prepared for war to carry them out. It is natural that he be defeated when he is not fully prepared to back up his braggadocio, and responsibility always rests on the president. Shall we send our judge advocates there to defend those [American] officers, saying that Japan should be accused instead, since it was Japan that attacked there? Ha! Ha!" (entry from December 10, 1941).

CHAPTER 2

1 Colonel Andres Lopez, "The Fall of the Philippines," *Military Review*, August 1946, pp. 11–12; Santos, "The 1st Regular Division in the Battle of the Philippines," pp. 35–36; Major Clarence R. Bess, "Operations of Service Company, 31st Infantry, 5 January 1942–9 April 1942," Fort Benning: Advanced Infantry Officers Course, 1948, pp. 10–11; Richard Connaughton, John Pimlott, and Duncan Anderson, *The Battle for Manila*, Novato, CA: Presidio Press, 1995, pp. 39–47, 115–16, 120–21.

2 Harrison Salisbury, "Japs Start All-Out Assaults," *Sweetwater Reporter*, January 7, 1942, p. 1; Harries and Harries, *Soldiers of the Sun*, pp. 314–15; Morton, *Fall of the Philippines*, pp. 208–9; Morris, *Corregidor*, pp. 178–80; Lawrence Taylor, *A Trial of General: Himma, Yamashita, MacArthur*, South Bend: Icarus Press, 191, pp. 53–57. From the time General Homma was notified in Tokyo he would command the 14th Army for the invasion of the Philippines on November 2, 1941, he was constantly second guessed by the Imperial Japanese general staff and eventually recalled

and retired in mid-1943. While under direct orders to capture Manila by January 1, 1942, many questioned his "oversight" in letting the defenders escape into Bataan.

3 Diary, "Lecture Note Book," December 31, 1941, Colonel Edwin E. Aldridge '16 Papers, Cushing Library, Texas A&M University. See also Trapnell, "The Operations of the 26th Cavalry (P.S.)," pp. 11–13. See also John W. Whitman, "Delaying Action in the Philippines," *World War II*, November 1998, pp. 42–48.

4 *Armor*, January–February 1989, http://www.benning.army.mil/armor/armor magazine/content/Issues/1989/ArmorJanuaryFebruary1989web.pdf; Lew H. Wallace, "The 192nd Tank Battalion in the Philippines," *Armor*, January 2011, pp. 26–32. For a detailed review of US tank operations in the Philippines, see Lt. Col. Thomas Dooley, "The First United States Tank Action in World War II," Advanced Officers Class, May 1, 1948, and "Operations of the Provisional Tank Group, United States Army Forces in the Far East 1941–1942," http://www.memorialmuseum.org.

5 Knox, *Death March*, pp. 46–47; Gene E. Salecker, *Rolling Thunder Against the Rising Sun*, Mechanicsville, PA: Stackpole Books, 2008, pp. 40–41; David Sears, "The U.S. Cavalry's Last Charge," *World War II*, March 2015, pp. 48–55.

6 MacArthur, *Reminiscences*, pp. 126–27; Captain Robley D. Evans '40, "Statement of Mistreatment while a Prisoner of War of Imperial Japanese Government," Ft. Worth, February 13, 1947, Annex I, Evans Family Papers.

7 Captain Harry J. Stempin, "The Operations of Company G, 57th Infantry P. S. on Luzon," December 7, 1941–January 30, 1942, Fort Benning, AOC, 1947, p. 8; Roberts, *The Storm of War*, p. 198. The total numbers of both American and Filipino combatants has never been confirmed, and to this day, numbers vary. I have used so-called official statistics estimated by the US Army during postwar reconstruction of data.

8 Wainwright, "Own Story," *Gazette*, installment 8; Mead, "Operations and Movements of the 31st Infantry Regiment," p. 21; Bess, "Operations of Service Company, 31st Infantry," p. 13; Morton, *Fall of the Philippines*, pp. 254–57; Sloan, *Undefeated*, p. 70. More than 250,000 gallons of gasoline were destroyed at Fort Stotsenburg because there was no time or advanced planning to remove supplies to Bataan!

9 Beverly N. Skarden, "The Operations of Company A, 92D Infantry, Philippine Army: 3 January 1942, 24 March 1942," Fort Benning: Advanced Infantry Officers Course, 1946, pp. 5–6; Glusman, *Conduct Under Fire*, pp. 64–65.

10 Vince Taylor, *Cabanatuan*, Waco: Texian Press, 1985, p. 36; Harries and Harries, *Soldiers of the Sun*, p. 315.

11 "Bataan Hospital Is Bombed by Foe: Causalities—Building, Plainly Marked," *New York Times*, March 31, 1942; "Bombs on Bataan Hit Hospital: Scatter Wounded 'Like Toys,'" *New York Times*, April 8, 1942.

12 Ugaki, *Fading Victory*, p. 72, January 9, 1942, as the Japanese admiral reports in his daily diary, "The enemy on the Bataan Peninsula is resisting stubbornly . . . yet they seem to be running short of foodstuff . . . how long will it last with the enemy who is used to a luxurious life?"

13 US Army, Maj. Gen. George M. Parker Jr., "Report of Operations of South Luzon Force, Bataan Defense Force, and II Philippine Corps in the Defense of South Luzon and Bataan from 8 December 1941 to 9 April 1962," December 12, 1946 (declassified 2/16/2012), Report of Operations, Box 1157, RG 407, NARA, College Park, Maryland (hereafter "Parker, 'Report of Operations'"). Those major divisions listed in the text are the major commands and do not include the many units that compose these forces yet are outlined in General Parker's after-action report.

14 Donald J. Young, *Battle for Bataan*, Jefferson, NC: McFarland & Company, 1992, pp. 43, 57, 73–74; Morton, *Fall of the Philippines*, pp. 261–63.

15 Dooley Diary, West Sector, January 10 and 15, 1942; Wainwright, "Own Story," *Gazette*, installment 8; Edwin P. Ramsey and Stephen J. Rivele, *Lieutenant Ramsey's War*, Washington: Brassey's, 1990, pp. 60–62.

16 Connaughton, *MacArthur and Defeat in the Philippines*, p. 234; Elizabeth Norman, *We Band of Angels*, New York: Random House, 1999, p. 73; Michele Manning, "Angels of Mercy: The Army Nurse Corps on Bataan and Corregidor," *Parameters*, Spring 1992, p. 91.

17 John W. Whitman, "US Army Doctrinal Effectiveness of Bataan, 1942: The First Battle," Fort Leavenworth, KS: Command and General Staff College, 1984, pp. 8–24.

18 Wainwright, "Own Story," *Gazette*, installment 9; Lt. Sheldon H. Mendelson, "Operations of the Provisional Air Corps Regiment in the Defense of Bataan Peninsula, P.I., 8 January–10 April 1942," pp. 14–15; Mead, "Operations and Movements of the 31st Infantry Regiment," pp. 28–29; Emerson, "Operations of the II Philippine Corps of Bataan," pp. 18–19; Parker, "Report of Operations"; Mallone, *Battle of Bataan*, p. 52. One company commander recalled, "There were plenty of maps at the G-3 office, some of them Spanish dating from 1892, most of them 1907 editions—and not one was worth a tinkers damn."

19 Nealson, "The Operations of a Provisional Battalion," pp. 5–20.

20 Ibid.; Mendelson, "Operations of the Provisional Air Corps Regiment in the Defense of Bataan," pp. 14–16; Morton, *Fall of the Philippines*, pp. 274–46.

21 Tom Dooley '35, Bataan Notebook, Cushing Library, Texas A&M University, January 17, 1942, and February 27, 1942; "Posthumous Awards for Sheranite," *Sherman Democrat*, March 25, 1943; World War II veterans file, Association of Former Students Papers, Cushing Library; Ramsey and Rivele, *Lt. Ramsey's War*, pp. 68–70; "GIs and Generals," *The Dallas News*, October 5, 1945; Sears, "The U.S. Cavalry's Last Charge," *WWII*, pp. 48–55.

22 MacArthur, *Reminiscences*, pp. 132–33.

23 Letter, Capt. John S. Coleman to Lt. Sheldon H. Mendelson, December 31, 1946, in Mendelson, "Operations of the Provisional Air regiment in the Defense of Bataan Peninsula, P.I. 8 January–10 April 1942," Fort Benning: Advanced Infantry Officers Course, 119147, p. 10.

24 Whitman, "US Army Doctrinal Effectiveness of Bataan," pp. 25–37; William R. Nealson, "The Operations of a Provisional Battalion, 41st Division (PA) at Abucay Hacienda (Bataan), 15–25 January 1942," Fort Benning: Advanced Infantry Officers Course, 1947, pp. 16–18; Huber, "The American Bataan Campaign," *Army History*, 10–11. See also Parker, "Report of Operations."

25 Wainwright, "Own Story," *Gazette*, installment 9 and 17. War correspondent Frank Hewlett would become the primary nonmilitary observer of the combat actions on Bataan and Corregidor. He was embedded with Wainwright staff and accompanied the general on numerous dangerous trips to the frontlines. Hewlett was on one of the last flights to leave Corregidor prior to its fall.

26 A. Skarden, "The Operations of Company A, 92D Infantry," pp. 11–12.

27 Bartsch, *Doomed at the Start*, pp. 212–18; Salecker, *Rolling Thunder*, pp. 57–64. See also Edward Malikowski, *A Brother's Hero*, West Chester, PA: n.p., 2011, pp. 49–54.

28 Brereton, *Brereton Diaries*, p. 59.

29 Bartsch, *Doomed at the Start*, pp. 105, 107, 117, 132, 145, 240–42; Roberts, *Masters and Commanders*, pp. 160–61; MacArthur, *Reminiscences*, p. 127. General Marshall's communique with MacArthur was mainly the result of a strategic planning session in Washington called the Arcadia Conference, attended by the US Joint Chiefs of Staff and their British counterparts for the purpose of advising both Roosevelt and Churchill. The planners concluded "with ruthless severity and overstatement" it would be "an entirely unjustifiable diversion of forces from the principle theater—the Atlantic."

30 "The Moore Report," Conduct of the Campaign, Wainwright Papers, Part C, http://www.correigidor.org; Whitman, "US Army Doctrinal Effectiveness of Bataan," pp. 41–43; Colonel William C. Braly, "Corregidor: A Name, A Symbol, A Tradition," n.d., http://www.philippine-defenders.lib.wv.us, p. 10; Wainwright, "Own Story," *Gazette*, installment 9. Captured Japanese soldiers attested to the fierce nature of the shelling and wondered where the intense shelling came from, with many jumping off the cliff into the sea to escape the terrible fire.

31 Dooley Diary, West Sector, January 21, 22, 1942; "Japanese Scheme to Capture Fortress Crushed by MacArthur," *The Denison Press*, February 2, 1942, p. 1; General Wainwright, "Report of Operations of North Luzon and I Philippine Corps," August 10, 1946, pp. 36–37; "Desperate Bataan Fighters," *The Dallas News*, October 7, 1945.

32 Lt. Col. Harold K. Johnson, "Defense of the Philippine Islands, Anyasen and Silaiim Points, Bataan," Fort Leavenworth, KS: Command and General Staff College, 1947, pp. 13–14; Dooley Diary, West Sector, January 28, 1942; Bartsch, *Doomed at the Start*, pp. 272–94; Robert Conroy, *The Battle of Bataan*, Toronto: Macmillan, 1969, pp. 33–35; Whitman, "US Army Doctrinal Effectiveness of Bataan," pp. 44–56. For details of the Points battle, see Morton, *Fall of the Philippines*, pp. 296–324. Then Lt. Col. Johnson—later general and chief of staff of the US Army (1964–68)—noted in his 1947 paper that it was a mystery why the Japanese did not march inland after their landing on the Points; the thin US defense during the first six days could not have stopped them, concluding, "My only explanation is another instance of the Japanese out fumbling us, not the first time, and certainly not the last."

33 Morton, *Fall of the Philippines*, p. 323; Drea, *Japan's Imperial Army*, p. 231. The case of mass suicide by Japanese troops is best highlighted in May 1943 on Attu Island in the Aleutians when Japanese doctors purposely killed the sick and wounded before a last bloody charge "in order to preclude any stain on the so-called Japanese warrior spirit." Similar mass suicide followed at Iwo Jima, Okinawa, and Bougainville.

34 Inazo Nitobe, *The Way of the Samurai*, London: Arcturus, 2011, pp. 7, 90–95; Peter Thompson, *The Battle of Singapore*, London: Piatkus, 2006, pp. 528–29; John Toland, *But Not in Shame: The Six Months after Pearl Harbor*, New York: Random House, 1961, pp. 197–218.

35 Major William E. Webb, "Operations of the 41st Infantry Regiment (P.A.) of the 41st Infantry Division in the Defense of the Abucay Line, Bataan, Philippine Islands, 10–18 January 1942," Fort Benning: Advanced Infantry Officers Course, 1950, p. 26; Morton, *Fall of the Philippines*, pp. 350–52; Schultz, *Hero of Bataan*, p. 193; Taylor, *Cabanatuan*, pp. 36–37; Welch, *Resolve*, pp. 69–71.

36 "Corregidor Guns Blast Japs on Bataan," *The Mexia Weekly Herald*, April 17, 1942, p. 1; "Japs Fought to Standstill by US Defenders, Bataan," *Denison Press*, March 31, 1942; "Hunger, Sickness—Japs Allies Enter Grim Battle for Bataan," *The Dallas News*, October 10, 1945.

37 Morton, *Fall of the Philippines*, p. 352; "Bataan Hospital is Bombed by Foe: 'Number of Casualties' Result—Building, Plainly Marked," *New York Times*, April 1, 1942; Knox, *Death March*, 103–6; Mallone, *Battle of Bataan*, p. 109; Baldwin, *Battles Lost and Won*, p. 123. See also Rab Paterson, "The Fall of Fortress Singapore: Churchill's Role and the Conflicting Interpretations," *Sophia International Review*, pp. 31–68, and Karl Hack and Kevin Blackburn, *Did Singapore Have to Fall? Churchill and the Impregnable Fortress*, London: Routledge, 2004.

38 Emerson, "Operations of the II Philippine Corps on Bataan," pp. 22–23; Mead, "Operations and Movements of the 31st Infantry Regiment," p. 18; Huber, "The American Bataan Campaign," p. 10; William B. Breuer, *The Great Raid on*

Cabanatuan: Rescuing the Doomed Ghost of Bataan and Corregidor, New York: John Wiley & Sons, 1994, p. 24.

39 Redmond, *I Served on Bataan*, p. 86. Following the attack on Pearl Harbor, the American public was afraid the Japanese would attack the West Coast. A survey by Gallup asked, "Do you think there is any chance that your [West Coast] city will be bombed?" and 49 percent responded yes, 40 percent no, and 11 percent "unready to guess." George Gallup, "Air Raid Sentiments Sounded by Gallup Poll," *New York Times*, December 13, 1942.

40 Morton, *Fall of the Philippines*, pp. 387–94; Glusman, *Conduct Under Fire*, p. 127; "Japan First," *Battalion*, June 2, 1942; Colonel Braly, "Corregidor," p. 15; FDR quote in Linda G. Holmes, *Guests of the Emperor: The Secret History of Japan's Mukden POW Camp*, Annapolis: 2010, p. 3. One lone editorial was found in the Texas A&M campus newspaper, the *Battalion*, titled "Japan First"—calling for a focus on the Pacific front as the first priority and Europe second.

41 Wainwright, "Own Story," *Gazette*, installments 10 and 11; "Tense Drama of Command Change Marks Yanks' Fate in Philippines," *The Dallas News*, October 9, 1945; Breuer, *The Great Raid*, p. 25; "Tense Drama of Command Change," *The Dallas News*, October 9, 1945; *Longhorn*, 1934 and 1935. Upon the transfer of Wainwright and HQ to Corregidor, Dooley was promoted to major.

42 Morton., *Fall of the Philippines*, p. 401; Manning, "Angels of Mercy," *Parameters*, pp. 92–93.

43 Coleman, *Bataan and Beyond*, p. 41; "Bataan in Grave Peril," *Boston Herald*, April 8, 1942, p. 8; Aldridge Diary, pp. 6–7. See also Michele Manning, "Angels of Mercy: The Army Nurse Corps on Bataan and Corregidor," *Parameters*, Spring 1992, p. 92; Schultz, *Hero of Bataan*, p. 228. Direct bombing of the hospitals began on April 5, and there were more Japanese apologies for attacking these open targets, creating very heavy casualties among the already wounded.

44 "Bataan's Eleventh Hour: Bitter Trial of Defenders Near Climax—Corregidor in Reserve for Final Stand," *New York Times*, April 8, 1942; Coleman, *Bataan and Beyond*, p. 48; Morton, *Fall of the Philippines*, p. 421. See also Sidney Stewart, *Give Us This Day*, New York: Popular Library, 1958, pp. 40–42.

45 "Bombs on Bataan Hit Hospital, Cots Scatter Wounded 'Like Toys,' Injure Many Doctors and Nurses: Enemy Ignores Crosses," *New York Times*, April 8, 1942; Wainwright, "Own Story," *Gazette*, installment 12; Salecker, *Rolling Thunder*, pp. 74, 75; Coleman, *Bataan and Beyond*, p. 45; Morton, *Fall of the Philippines*, pp. 445–50; Chris Schaefer, *Bataan Diary*, Houston: Riverside, 2004, p. 35; "Asian Pacific Americans in the US Army," http://www.army.mil; Huber, "The American Bataan Campaign," p. 11.

46 Morton, *Fall of the Philippines*, 404; Dooley Diary, Bataan, April 1, 1942; Edward E. Aldridge Jr., ed., "The Diary of Colonel Edward E. Aldridge," pp. 6–7; Wainwright, "Own Story," *Gazette*, installment 11.

47 HQ USFP, "Pan for movement of units to Corregidor," April 8, 1942 (declassified per JCS LTR of August 20, 1975), in Robley Evans Family Papers; "Order Not Disobeyed at Bataan," *The Mercury*, Hobart, Australia, January 1, 1949; "US Orders Ignored," *Sidney Morning Herald*, December 31, 1948; John M, Beebe, ed. *Prisoner of the Rising Sun: The Lost Diary of BG Lewis Beebe*, College Station: Texas A&M University Press, 2006, p. 70. During the chaos of April 7–8, orders were issued and soon revoked, all communications broke down, and stragglers poured into the rear—the organized army "evaporated into thin air." Til his dying day in 1964, General MacArthur remained adamant that he "utterly opposed the ultimate capitulation of Bataan" and felt the army should have fought to the end and reverted to guerrilla warfare. General Dwight Eisenhower, who at the time was a brigadier in the War Department Operations Division in Washington, recalls in early 1952 that news flooded in and clearly on April 7 "the surrender of Bataan was becoming hourly more imminent"; Eisenhower, *Crusade in Europe*, New York: Doubleday, 1952, p. 36. See also MacArthur, *Reminiscences*, p. 146; Schultz, *Hero of Bataan*, pp. 234–36; Glusman, *Conduct Under Fire*, pp. 156–58; and for a Japanese perspective, Hiroshi Masuda, *MacArthur in Asia*, Ithaca, NY: Cornell University Press, pp. 128–31.

48 Whitman, "US Army Doctrine Effectiveness on Bataan, 1942," pp. 108–11; Letter from Coleman to Mendelson, December 31, 1946; Salecker, *Rolling Thunder*, pp. 75–78; Dooley, Notebook, April 6, 1942. Brig. Gen. Clifford Bluemel confirmed King's concern for the condition of the troops: "Our units were now so reduced in strength and so utterly exhausted that prolonged resistance was impossible." See also Bluemel, "Report of BG Clifford Bluemel, US Army on 31st Division, Philippine Army, Mt. Samat, Bataan, P.I., November 18, 1941, to April 9, 1942."

49 Morton, *Fall of the Philippines*, pp. 451–56; Dooley, Notebook, April 6, 7, 8, 1942; Aldridge Diary, April 1–9, 1942, pp. 6–7; Knox, *Death March*, 109–10; MacArthur, *Reminiscences*, p. 146; William M. Huffman '53, ed., "Notebook and Diary of Captain Cary McClure Abney Jr. '34," Marshall, TX: Privately printed, 2011, p. 41. Following the fall of Bataan, MacArthur was quick to laud the troops; see "M'Arthur Praises Bataan Defenders," *New York Times*, April 9, 1942; yet postwar articles by Wainwright ("Philippines Mistakes Bared by Wainwright," *Baltimore News-Post*, October 8, 1945) bluntly questioned the "defeatist plan" to defend the Philippines. Furthermore, in postwar interviews with veterans of the Battle of Bataan, there is clearly a mixed response to General MacArthur's "order" to "fight to the last man," with most supporting the halting of the fighting by General King. See interview with Albert N. Brown, April 14, 2007, and Alfred McGrew, April 15, 2007, Rutgers Oral History Archives, New Brunswick: Rutgers University.

50 "Ballad of the Bastards," anonymous, August 10, 1942, stanza num. 11, in Colonel Edward E. Aldridge Papers, Cushing Library. See also Wainwright, "Own Story," *Gazette*, installment 13.

51 "Bataan Line Broken" and "U.S. Troops to 'Expand to Europe'—Gen. Marshall," *Boston Evening Globe*, April 8, 1942, p. 1; Paul D. Bunker, *Bunker's War: The World War II Diary of Col. Paul D. Bunker*, New York: Presidio Press, p. 120; "Foes Take Outpost in Bataan Attack," *New York Times*, April 2, 1942, and "Marshall and Hopkins Arrive in London to Discuss American 'Expansion' in Europe; Japanese Forces Pound New Line on Bataan," *New York Times*, April 9, 1942, p. 1.

52 Dooley Diary, April 5, 6, 1942; Taylor, *A Trial of Generals*, pp. 53–57.

53 Jonathan M. Wainwright, *General Wainwright's Story: The Account of Four Years of Humiliating Defeat, Surrender, and Captivity*, New York: Modern Library Editions, 1945, pp. 86–87; Salecker, *Rolling Thunder*, p. 76; Gwinn U. Porter, "Anti-aircraft Defense of Corregidor," Fort Leavenworth, KS: Command and General Staff College, 1947, p. 12; Morton, *Fall of the Philippines*, pp. 466–67; Connaughton, *MacArthur and Defeat in the Philippines*, pp. 293–96; "Hell-Torn Yanks of Bataan Perplexed," *The Dallas News*, October 12, 1945; Baldwin, *Battles Lost and Won*, pp. 138–39. Only the 2nd Battalion of the 60th CA (AA) was able to cross the channel; most of the other AA units destroyed their equipment, barely escaping to the Rock. The War Department in Washington attempted to downplay the Bataan surrender, reporting to the news media "*only* 36,000 [almost exactly half the actual number?] Filipinos and American troops [were] captured, fighting to the end of it flickering forlorn hope." See "Japanese Capture 36,000 Troops," *New York Times*, April 10, 1942, and "Bataan Falls Troops 36,800," *Pittsburg Sun-Telegraph*, April 9, 1942. The refugees from Bataan increased the size of the Corregidor garrison to more than 11,600 men. More than a thousand wounded and hundreds of sick filled Malinta Tunnel; due to overcrowding, some patients were moved outside into the open. In addition to malaria, there was an epidemic of acute gastroenteritis, an outbreak of tonsillitis, and many cases of jaundice.

54 "Epic of Bataan," *Reader's Digest*, June 1942, p. 7.

55 Dorothy Cave, *Beyond Courage: One Regiment Against Japan 1941–1945*, Las Cruces: Yucca Free Press, 1992, p. 149; Sloan, *Undefeated*, pp. 176–78; Harries and Harries, *Soldiers of the Sun*, pp. 314–16; Glusman, *Conduct Under Fire*, pp. 154–64; Schultz, *Hero of Bataan*, pp. 240–43.

56 Norman and Norman, *Tears in the Darkness*, p. 153; Edward P. King, "General King's Own Story: Exhausted Yanks Buried Alive by Japanese on Bataan Death March," *Atlanta Constitution*, September 26, 1945; Falk, *Bataan*, p. 21. In 1948, Louis Morton, chief of the historical division on the US Army's Pacific section, claimed that General King had disobeyed Wainwright's orders to continue defending Bataan in early April 1942. General Wainwright quickly responded, rejecting the comment and "strongly resent[ing] such a comment," calling General King "a gallant soldier, a brave and courageous man." See "General Defends

'Gallant Soldier' of Bataan Fame," *The Daily News*, December 31, 1948. Note that Gen. Homma was convicted of war crimes and executed on April 3, 1946.

CHAPTER 3

1 John W. Dower, *Embracing Defeat: Japan in the Wake of World War II*, New York: W. W. Norton & Company, 1999, pp. 456–58, 504–8; Morison, *The Rising Sun in the Pacific*, pp. 164–83; Bartsch, *Doomed at the Start*, p. 387; H. J. Timperley, "What War Means: The Japanese Terror in China," *Foreign Affairs*, January 1939; Coleman, *Bataan and Beyond*, p. 72; Mallonee, *Battle of Bataan*, p. 15; John W. Dower, *War without Mercy: Race and Power in the Pacific War*, New York: Pantheon, 1986. See also Timperly, "From Tokyo to Washington," deciphered telegram transmitted to US Intelligence, February 1, 1938, NARA; *The Rape of Nanking*, film available at http://www.brainmind.com and http://rapeofnanking.info; B. V. A. Roling and C. F. Ruter, eds., *The Tokyo Judgment: The International Tribunal for the Far East (I.M.T.F.E.), 29 April 1946–12 November 1948*, 2 vols., Amsterdam: APA-University Press, 1977; Tim Maga, *Judgment at Tokyo: The Japanese War Crimes Trials*, Lexington: University of Kentucky Press, 2001; Philip Snow, *The Fall of Hong Kong: Britain, China and the Japanese Occupation*, New Haven: Yale University Press, pp. 79–83; A. Frank Reel, *The Case of General Tamashia*, Chicago: University of Chicago Press, 1949, p. 99. For example, over ten thousand Chinese women, from their early teens to their sixties, were raped or gang raped in the Japanese sack of Hong Kong.

2 "Anglo-Americanism Must Be Wiped Out," *Japan Times*, November 5, 1942; Edwin P. Hoyt, *Japan's War*, New York: Da Capo Press, 1986, p. 251. See also Gregory F. Michno, *Death on the Hellships: Prisoners at Sea in the Pacific War*, Annapolis: Naval Institute Press, 2001, pp. 130–33, and Yuki Tanaka, *Hidden Horrors: Japanese War Crimes in World War II*, New York: Westview Press, 1996, pp. 206–24.

3 "Incredible Record: In Contest to Cut Down 100 People: Mukai 106, Noda, 105," *Tokyo Nichi-Nichi Shimbun*, December 6, 1937; "Jap Atrocities at Hong Kong Are Confirmed," *Denison Press*, March 23, 1942, p. 1; NARA for the Nazi War Crimes and Japanese Imperial Government Records Interagency Group, Washington, DC, 2006; "Jap Slaughter of Prisoners Described by Escaped Fliers," *Boston Herald*, April 8, 1942, p. 7; Manny Lawton, *Some Survived*, Chapel Hill: Algonquin Books, 1984, p. 14; Breuer, *The Great Raid*, pp. 32, 52; Gavan Daws, *Prisoners of the Japanese: POWs of World War II in the Pacific*, New York: William Morrow and Company, 1994, pp. 70–83; Brian MacArthur, *Surviving the Sword: Prisoners of the Japanese in the Far East, 1942–1945*, New York: Random House,

2005, pp. 14–15. See also Bernard Edwards, *Blood and Bushido: Japanese Atrocities at Sea, 1941–1945*, New York: Brick Tower Press, 1997; Ronald Searle, *To the Kwai and Back*, Boston: Atlantic Monthly Press, 1986, pp. 66–67; and Yamamoto Tsunetomo, *Hagakure*, Tokyo: Kodansha International, 1979.

4 "Story of Atrocities by Japs on Hapless Prisoners Is Released by U.S.: Deliberate Starvation, Torture, Death," January 28, 1944, http://www.angelfire.com/nm/bcmfofnm/atrocities/atrocities01.html; Ramon Farolan, "Mariveles Massacre," *Philippine Daily Inquirer*, April 11, 2011; Michno, *Death on the Hellships*, pp. 130–33; Breuer, *The Great Raid*, p. 32. Very little of the American POW atrocities were known at the time they occurred back in America, as the military kept what they knew a top secret, ordering those that had escaped not to tell their horrific stories. By late 1943, POW stories from other countries began to leak out to the public. Not until January 1944 was the full magnitude of the horrific torture and killing made known to the public.

5 Roling and Ruter, *The International Tribunal for the Far East*, pp. 1–515. See also Tanaka, *Hidden Horrors*, 1996; Mallonee, *Battle of Bataan*, p. 143.

6 Michno, *Death on the Hellships*, p. 1; Connaughton, *MacArthur and Defeat in the Philippines*, pp. 296–97; "US Defense of Bataan Collapses, 36,000 Exhausted Men Face Capture," *The Evening Bulletin*, Philadelphia, April 9, 1942; Toland, *But Not in Shame*, pp. 310–12. Exact data on the total number of POWs is unlikely to be compiled. Many American and Filipinos were unaccounted for because they were killed during the final Japanese offensive of April 3–8, 1942, and their bodies were never recovered. Also, before and during the Death March, many thousands of Filipinos and hundreds of Americans escaped to the jungle—most did not survive. Another group of defenders that were hard to account for were the wounded and sick in the Bataan field hospitals, as well as those that were lost at sea attempting to swim to Corregidor.

7 Falk, *Bataan*, pp. 21–55, 68; Michno, *Death on the Hellships*, pp. 130–33; Drea, *Japan's Imperial Army*, p. 224. The US War Department grossly underestimated the number of troops and for some reason was not sure until late March 1942 how many troops were on Bataan, constantly reporting only about 36,800, fewer than half of those fighting.

8 Roling and Ruter, *The International Tribunal for the Far East*, pp. 49–52, 385–427; "1,500-Mile Trail of Butchery, Rape," *The Mercury*, September 6, 1945, p. 2; Colonel William Dyess, *The Dyess Story*, New York: G. P. Putnam's Sons, 1944, pp. 10–50; Hoyt, *Warlord: Tojo Against the World*, Lanham: Scarborough, 1993, pp. 98–100; Tanaka, *Hidden Horrors*, pp. 17–22. One argument made by the Japanese military in the 1930s for opposing the Convention was that prisoners of war could not be punished as severely as Japanese soldiers for infractions of Japanese army discipline; for example, a Japanese soldier who deserted was subject

to the death penalty, while a POW who escaped could not be punished under the Geneva Convention.

9 Roling and Ruter, *The Tokyo Judgment*, pp. 1–515; Tanaka, *Hidden Horrors*, pp. 2–3; Lawrence Taylor, *The Trial of Generals*, South Bend: Icarus Press, 1981, pp. 92–100. See also the partial list of eighty-eight Texas Aggie POWs that appears in "War Recorded—Prisoners," *Texas Aggie*, February 15, 1944; Jim Nelson, "The Causes of the Bataan Death March Revisited," April 22, 2005, http://www.us-japandialogueonpows.org.

10 Huffman, "Notebook and Diary of Captain Cary McClure Abney Jr. '34," p. 9; Falk, *Bataan*, p. 171; Richard M. Gordon, "Bataan, Corregidor, and the Death March: In Retrospect," Burnt Hills, New York, http://battlingbastardsbataan.com/inretro.htm; Lester I. Tenney, *My Hitch in Hell: The Bataan Death March*, Washington: Brassey's, 2000, pp. 42–65.

11 Affidavit of Captain Robley Evans '40, Ft. Worth, August 20, 1946; Cave, *Beyond Courage*, pp. 157–60; Breuer, *The Great Raid*, p. 33; Toland, *But Not in Shame*, pp. 306–8; Stewart, *Give Us This Day*, pp. 51–59; "Aggie Muster," *Texas Aggie*, August 1992, p. 11; Bert Bark, *Back from the Living Hell*, Tuscaloosa: n.p., 1945, pp. 19–20; Lawton, *Some Survived*, p. 17, quoted a captured American colonel: "These Japs are running around like crazy men." Evans's 1940 Aggie class ring and watch were taken by the Japanese soldiers.

12 Huffman, "Notebook and Diary of Captain Cary McClure Abney Jr. '34," pp. 8–9; Santos, "The 1st Regular Division in the Battle of the Philippines," pp. 45–46; R. Jackson Scott, *90 Days of Rice*, Pioneer, California: California Traveler, 1975, pp. 42–49.

13 Letter, Roy H. Davidson '40 to C. C. Taylor '51, Houston, November 15, 2006, Lt. Edger B. Burgess '38 File, Association of Former Student Papers, Cushing Library.

14 Coleman, *Bataan and Beyond*, p. 69; Tenney, *My Hitch in Hell*, pp. 46–52. Coleman recalls the water had a bad smell and taste due to the chlorine tablets he had added.

15 Statement by Major Hugh Harwood, October 28, 1945, in Paul R Gregory File, AFS World War II Papers, Cushing Library; *Longhorn*, 1940, n.p.; AFS, *Directory of Former Students*, 1949, p. xxxiii. Gregory was first listed by the War Department as missing in action and given a "generic" date of death as August 3, 1944, until his status was officially changed to *died while escaping*. A statement by Lt. Robert Kramer, who escaped with Gregory and helped bury him, helped clear the case along with the 1945 investigation by Major Hugh Harwood.

16 Col. Floyd Marshall, "Reports of Operations of Luzon Force, 12 March–9 April 1942," in Ancheta, ed., *The Wainwright Papers*, pp. 162–78; Lt. Col. Jack Williams, "Affidavit Regarding Bataan Hospital #2," NARA RG 331, Box 920,

http://www.mansell.com; Schultz, *Hero of Bataan*, pp. 161, 236; Falk, *Bataan*, pp. 83–90.

17 Dr. Jack Schwartz, "Affidavit Regarding Bataan Hospital #2 and Cabanatuan," November 21, 1946, http://www.mansell.com; Norman, *We Band of Angels*, pp. 39–49, 85–96; Glusman, *Conduct Under Fire*, pp. 168–70; Falk, *Bataan*, pp. 87–90.

18 "POWs Sing as They Die," *The Daily News*, September 8, 1945; Coleman, *Bataan and Beyond*, p. 72; Schultz, *Hero of Bataan*, p. 250. There is some dispute as to when Corregidor, April 12 or 15, opened fire on the Japanese artillery.

19 Coleman, *Bataan and Beyond*, pp. 69–72; Cave, *Beyond Courage*, p. 158; Lawton, *Some Survived*, pp. 20–21; Toland, *But Not in Shame*, pp. 288–91; Falk, *Bataan*, p. 35.

20 Coleman, *Bataan and Beyond*, pp. 70–72; Affidavit of Captain Robley Evans, August 20, 1946, and Statement of the mistreatment of the prisoners of war by the Imperial Japanese Government, February 13, 1947; Arvil Steel, *Report on Japanese Torture and Murder of American and Filipino Prisoners of War*, Washington, DC: Bureau of Naval Personnel Informational Bulleting, March 1944; Tenny, *My Hitch in Hell*, p. 52; Falk, *Bataan*, p. 81.

21 "Itinerary of Travel after Capture on Bataan April 1942," Colonel Edward E. Aldridge '16 Papers, Cushing Library; Toland, *But Not in Shame*, pp. 314–18; Glenn D. Frazier, *Hell's Guest*, n.p.: eGen Co., 2007, pp. 77–79; Bert Bank, *Back from the Living Dead*, n.p.: 1945, pp. 18–26.

22 Bartsch, *Doomed at the Start*, pp. 380–81, 431–32.

23 "19th Bombardment Group," http://www.historyofwar.org; White, *Queens Never Die*, pp. 35–36; Morris, *Corregidor*, pp. 90–92.

24 Daws, *Prisoners of the Japanese*, pp. 75–79; Breuer, *The Great Raid*, pp. 37–38; Adrian R. Martin, *Brother from Bataan: POWs, 1942–1945*, Manhattan: Sunflower University Press, 1992, pp. 26–29.

25 Toland, *But Not in Shame*, pp. 321–22.

26 Coleman, *Bataan and Beyond*, p. 72; Morris, *Corregidor*, pp. 417, 423.

27 Morris, *Corregidor*, pp. 417–18; Falk, *Bataan*, pp. 46, 64–68, 107–9.

28 Coleman, *Bataan and Beyond*, pp. 83–85; Gene S. Jacobsen, *We Refused to Die*, Salt Lake City: University of Utah Press, 2005, pp. 93–106.

29 Cave, *Beyond Courage*, pp. 173–74; Falk, *Bataan*, pp. 47–48. See also Aldridge Diary and papers.

30 Lawton, *Some Survived*, pp. 22–25; Stewart, *Give Us This Day*, p. 59; Falk, *Bataan*, pp. 162–70; Knox, *Death March*, pp. 150–53; Coleman, *Bataan and Beyond*, pp. 83–84.

31 Harries and Harries, *Soldiers of the Sun*, pp. 475–80. As this author notes, "The atrocities committed by the Imperial Japanese Army are impossible to catalog.

The number and the hideous variety of the crimes defy even the most twist[ed] imagination: murder on a scale amounting to genocide; rapes beyond counting; vivisection; cannibalism; torture; American prisoners of war allowed to drown in excrement in the 'hell ships,' with the lame statement that the cruelties against the Bataan Death Marchers was 'partly due to Japanese inexperience as herdsmen.' Hogwash!"

32 Tanaka, *Hidden Horrors*, p. 15; Falk, *Bataan*, pp. 172–76; Daws, *Prisoners of the Japanese*, p. 80; "Camp O'Donnell," Aldridge Diary.

33 Charles Morehouse, GHQSWP to W. W. Evans (father of Robley D. Evans '40) May 9, 1942, Evans Family Papers; "No Philippine News," *Texas Aggie*, May 25, 1942; "The World Turns On: From Bataan," *Battalion*, June 16, 1942. One Army chaplain, Robert Taylor, held prisoner "wondered what the reaction would be if the nations of the world could see Cabanatuan Compound" (in Billy Keith, *Days of Anguish, Days of Hope*, Garden City: Doubleday, 1972, p. 111).

34 Letter, Lucille G. Moore to W. W. Evans, July 27, 1943, Evans Family Papers.

CHAPTER 4

1 Junald Dawa Ango, "The Cebu-Acapulco Galleon Trade," *Philippine Quarterly of Culture and Society*, 38, 2010, pp. 147–73; US Army, The Combat History Division, G-1, AFWESPAC, "Corregidor of Eternal Memory," n.p., January 1946, pp. 1–2; Belote and Belote, *Corregidor*, pp. 7–10.

2 "A Pronouncing Gazetteer and Geographical Dictionary of the Philippine Islands: Corregidor and Adjacent Islands, Luzon," U.S. Senate, 57th Cong., 1st sess., Doc no. 280, Washington, DC: GPO, 1902; Morton, *Fall of the Philippines*, p. 471; Evan Thomas, *The War Lovers: Roosevelt, Lodge, Hearst, and the Rush to Empire, 1898*, New York: Back Bay Books, 2011, pp. 254–61, 275–76, 371–73. Other sources for the origin of the name for Corregidor include "alderman." See also "Dewey's Victory: Corregidor Island Forts Reduced," *Shinner Gazette*, May 11, 1898, p. 1, and "The Great Battle of Manila," *Brownsville Daily Herald*, May 3, 1898, p. 1.

3 Thomas, *The War Lovers*, pp. 148, 177–79, 389; "Foreign Spies Here," *Brownsville Daily Bulletin*, August 11, 1911; "On a War Footing: Corregidor Fortifications to Protect Manila from Attack," *The Bastrop Advertiser*, February 20, 1914; "Philippines Weak in Lame Defense," *The Washington Times*, December 18, 1914; Tanaka, *Hidden Horrors*, pp. 210–11; Hoyt, *Japan's War*, pp. 53–186; Kwiecinski, *Honor, Courage, Faith*, p. xvi. Concern with the militarization of Japan is reflected in the expansion of the Imperial Army and Navy from 68,720 men in 1905 to 103,784 in 1912 and more than 136,000 in 1921. See also Drea, *Japan's Imperial Army*, pp. 190–222.

4 Morton, *Fall of the Philippines*, 471–72; Wainwright, "Own Story," *Gazette*, installment 16; Major Fred M. Green, "Coast Artillery Life in the Philippines," *Journal of the U.S. Artillery*, January 1922, pp. 444–52; Porter, "Anti-aircraft Defense of Corregidor," pp. 1–4; Charles S. Small, *Rails to Doomsday: The U.S. Army's Corregidor and Manila Bay Railroads*, Canton: Railhead Publications, 1998, pp. 1–70; Fred Stolley, "The Fall of Corregidor," *History of the Second World War*, part 31, n.p.: 1972, pp. 864–65.

5 Manchester, *American Caesar*, pp. 64–66; Ed Cray, *General of the Army: George Marshall*, New York: W. W. Norton & Company, 1990, pp. 32–46. Douglas MacArthur contracted malaria on Bataan in mid-1904. When asked by a colonel in Manila during a war game exercise what he would do if left with a small force to defend the Manila Harbor, he replied, "I'd send a rumor the harbor was mined, then I'd go out and fight like hell."

6 Manchester, *American Caesar*, p. 67; Michael Schaller, *Douglas MacArthur: The Far Eastern General*, New York: Oxford University Press, 1989, pp. 7–8. See also Fumio Takahashi, "The First War Plan Orange and the First Imperial Japanese Defense Policy: An Interpretation from the Geopolitical Strategic Perspective," *NIDS Security Reports*, 5, March 2004, pp. 68–103.

7 Eric Morris, *Corregidor: The American Alamo of World War II*, New York: Cooper Square Press, p. 4. See also Steven T. Ross, *American War Plans, 1890–1939*, New York: Frank Cass, 2000.

8 Charles H. Bogart, "The Doomed Philippine Island Seas Defense Project," http://www.corregidor.org; Belote and Belote, *Corregidor*, pp. 17–22; Connaughton et al., *The Battle of Manila*, pp. 25–26.

9 Morison, *The Rising Sun in the Pacific*, pp. 40–56, 149–54; Joint Army and Navy Basic War Plan, "Rainbow 5," March 1941, printed in part 32, p. 70.

10 Combat History Division, G-1, "Corregidor of Eternal Memory," AFWESPAC, January 1946; John Moffitt, "The Malinta Tunnel from Concept to Completion," Field notes, December 24, 2012, http://www.corregidor.org; Morton, "Harbor Defenses of Manila Bay," http://www.corregidor.org; Baldwin, *Battles Lost and Won*, p. 115.

11 *Longhorn*, 1941, pp. 188–89; Adams, *Keepers of the Spirit*, pp. 142–45.

12 George Fuermann, "Anne Moore, Passenger on the Ill-Fated *Athenia*," *Battalion*, October 7, 1939. The sinking of the *S.S. Athenia*, commanded by Captain Fritz Julius Lemp, was among the very first shots fired in the Atlantic following the declaration of war—Nazi U-boats (submarines) would account for more than 1,000 sinkings by August 1945. Quick action by the crew of the *Athenia* and rescue parties saved most of the 1,100 passengers, including 311 Americans, with the loss of only 118 souls.

13 Belote and Belote, *Corregidor*, p. 85; "Corregidor Aggie Meeting Thrills Nation," *Texas Aggie*, May 6, 1942, p. 1.

14 "The Moore Report," Part B, December 15, 1945, http://www.corregidor.org (hereafter "Moore Report"); Porter, "Anti-aircraft Defense of Corregidor," p. 4. See also Belote and Belote, *Corregidor*, pp. 27–41.

15 US Army, Corregidor Eternal, p. 7; Belote and Belote, *Corregidor*, p. 25.

16 Moore Report, February 24; Morris, *Corregidor*, pp. 292–93; Morton, *Fall of the Philippines*, p. 367; Schultz, *Hero of Bataan*, pp. 192–95. See also Richard B. Frank, *MacArthur*, New York: Palgrave Macmillan, 2007, pp. 40–50; Michael Schaller, *Douglas MacArthur: The Far East General*, New York: Oxford University Press, 1989, 55–64; Manchester, *American Caesar*, 1978, pp. 169–230.

17 Dooley, Notebook, March 13, 1942.

18 Wainwright, "Own Story," *Gazette*, installment 27.

19 Manchester, *American Caesar*, pp. 253–58; Morton, *Fall of the Philippines*, pp. 356–60; Shirley, *December 1941*, pp. 331, 542; Schultz, *Hero of Bataan*, 200–204. Bitter poems and jokes were passed from foxhole to foxhole, as the departed general was now commonly referred to as "Dugout Doug." One senior officer noted that MacArthur's departure "put an end to any further talk of help being on the way."

20 Toland, *But Not in Shame*, p. 270; Morton, *Fall of the Philippines*, p. 361; Moore Report, Harbor Def., p. 42; Mallonee, *Battle of Bataan*, pp. 109–10; W. L. White, *They Were Expendable*, New York: Harcourt Brace, 1942, and John Ford, Director, *They Were Expendable*, Metro-Goldwyn-Mayer, 1945. MacArthur awarded the entire PT boat crew the Silver Star for the daring operation. An article titled "General to Make Stern Taskmaster for Japan" on the front page of the August 26, 1945, edition of the *San Antonio Light* shows a different yet similar quote from MacArthur to Gen. Moore: "Don't give up the fort, George. I'll be back."

21 Moore Report, March 21; Morton, *Fall of the Philippines*, pp. 362–66.

22 Morton, *Fall of the Philippines*, p. 360; Wainwright, *General Wainwright's Story*, pp. 2–6.

23 *Bryan Eagle*, July 12, 1947; *Longhorn*, 1934 and 1935.

24 Manila, The Corregidor Historic Society, Roster, Personnel, 59th and 60th Coast Artillery, as of March 31, 1942; Porter, "Anti-aircraft Defense of Corregidor," pp. 6–14; Belote and Belote, *Corregidor*, pp. 55–59, 78–80. See also Arthur E. Huff, "Boston," http://www.corregidor.org.

25 Report, Lt. Col. E. L. Barr, "Mobile—Battery 'M' 60th Coast Artillery (AA)," http://www.corregidor.org; "Ex-Aggie Killed in Action on Corregidor," *Battalion*, May 8, 1942; Belote and Belote, *Corregidor*, p. 136.

26 "Silver Star," http://www.militarytimes.com; Huff, "Boston"; Baldwin, *Battles Lost and Won*, pp. 140–41. Texas Aggies held POW at Zentsuji Camp include Chevaillier, Culp, Evans, Gensberg, Hopmann, Noles, Lewis, and Robbins. See Sam Kinch, "Train Trip across Japan Is Strange," *Fort Worth Star Telegram*, August 13, 1945, in Robley Evans Papers.

27 Interview with William Hamilton '40, October 21, 1991, and October 26, 2013; *Longhorn*, 1941, p. 150; Hamilton paper/interview.

28 Belote and Belote, *Corregidor*, pp. 24–25. See also Breuer, *The Great Raid.*

29 Dooley, Notebook, March 22, 1942; "Honored: Moore and Moses Halls," *Battalion*, March 17, 1942; "DSC Awarded General Moore," *Texas Aggie*, May 5, 1942; "Major General George F. Moore," *Longhorn*, 1943, pp. 65–67.

30 Corregidor Eternal, p. 17; Porter, "Anti-aircraft Defense of Corregidor," pp. 10, 14; Belote and Belote, *Corregidor*, p. 133; Moore Report, January 13 to April 1. See also Morris, *Corregidor*, pp. 379–400. Porter estimates 92 planes were shot down and about 135 others "visibly damaged."

31 Schultz, *Hero of Bataan*, p. 315.

32 Toland, *But Not in Shame*, p. 268. See also John Keegan, *The Mask of Command*, New York: Viking, 1987, pp. 318–22, and Richard B. Meixsel, "Major General George Grunert, WPO-3 and the Philippine Army, 1940–1941," *Journal of Military History*, April 1995, p. 303.

33 Belote and Belote, *Corregidor*, pp. 114–17. There was little chance General King would be court-martialed; until his death, he was admired by his men and recognized as the honorary commander of the "American Defenders of Bataan and Corregidor, Inc." Also, according to the Moore Report, plans were already under way on April 8 "in anticipation of the early fall of Bataan" to give priority to withdrawing antiaircraft batteries to Corregidor.

34 Moore Report, April 9.

35 Beebe, *Prisoner of the Rising Sun*, p. 73.

36 Ted W. Lawson, *Thirty Seconds over Tokyo*, New York: Penguin, 1944, pp. 44–52, 155–62; John A. Adams Jr., *Softly Call the Muster*, College Station: Texas A&M University Press, 1994, p. 22; "Major Hilger Adds Personal Vengeance to Nat'l Revenge in First Bombing of Japanese," *Texas Aggie*, May 25, 1942; Donald B. Duncan, "Secret Planning for the Tokyo Raid," pp. 63–69; Henry L. Miller, "Training the Doolittle Fliers," pp. 70–76; Hoyt, *Japan's War*, pp. 270–78.

37 "Major Hilger, Ex-Aggie Led US Bombers Over Japan," *Battalion*, June 2, 1942; Bill J. Leftwich, *The Corps at Aggieland*, Lubbock: Smoke Signal, 1976, p. 103; Duncan, "Secret Planning for the Tokyo Raid," p. 69; Hoyt, *Japan's War*, p. 274.

38 Roling and Ruter, *The Tokyo Judgment*, p. 408; Edwin P. Holt, *Warlord: Tojo Against the World*, Lanham: Scarborough House, 1993, pp. 94–95, 103, 109; John Bradley, *Flyboys*, New York: Little, Brown and Company, 2003, pp. 121–22, 133–34; Drea, *Japan's Imperial Army*, p. 226. Five of the fliers were given life imprisonment, and three were executed on October 15, 1942. Additionally, in the weeks after the Doolittle Raid, more than two hundred thousand Chinese were systematically murdered by the Japanese as a reprisal for the assistance given to the American fliers and as a bloody message to the Chinese not to aid any further Americans.

39 Combat History Division, "Corregidor of Eternal Memory," pp. 14–21.

40 Adams, *Softly Call the Muster*, pp. 1–27.

41 Interview with Tom Dooley '35, October 21, 1991; John C. Adams, *The Voices of a Proud Tradition: A Collection of Aggie Muster Speeches*, Bryan: Brazos Valley Printing, 1978 Muster speech by Tom Dooley '35 in College Station, April 21, 1978. The Moore Report, April 18–24, notes, "During this period there usually were three or four raids daily combined with a great deal of enemy shelling, especially from Bataan."

42 Interview with Colonel Tom Dooley, October 21, 1991.

43 "Aggie Spirit on Corregidor" and "Corregidor Aggies Meeting Thrills Nation and Brings High Tribute in Congress," *Texas Aggie*, May 5, 1942; Adams, *Softly Call the Muster*, pp. 22–23; "Corregidor 1946," *Texas Aggie*, March 1996, pp. 37–40; Bill Cunningham, "Great College Story Needs No Glamorizing," *Seattle Times*, April 17, 1943. A second informal gathering was held on the recaptured island on April 21, 1945, by Major R. N. "Dick" Conolly '37, Lt. Tommy Martin '40, and Lt. Col. Ormond Simpson '36. In April 1946, 127 Aggies posed at the mouth of Malinta Tunnel in what has become the most recognized photo (and often confused and mislabeled as 1942) of the Texas Aggies Muster tradition. There are no known pictures of the April 21, 1942, Corregidor Muster.

44 Stewart, *Give Us This Day*, pp. 58–62; MacArthur, *Surviving the Sword*, p. 13.

45 Letter from Col. Ray T. Elsmore to Lt. Col. Frank Kurtz, June 30, 1943, http://lanbob.com; Bartsch, *Doomed at the Start*, p. 348; Miami *The Morning Herald*, May 27, 1944, p. 8; "The 'Bamboo Fleet' Shuttle Service to Corregidor," http://www.defensemedianetwork.com; Diane L. Hamm, ed., *Military Intelligence: Its Heroes and Legends*, Honolulu: University Press of the Pacific, 2001, pp. 34–36; "Flew Unarmed Planes," *The Courier Mail*, Queensland, Australia, July 11, 1942, p. 5; Felix McKnight, "Life Is Rationed in Pacific, So Fighter [H. H. Whitfield] Can't Find Cause for Grumbling by Home Folks," *Dallas Morning News*, January 1, 1943. In addition to the Waco UC-72, the "Bamboo Fleet" flew a Bellanca "Pacemaker" and a Beech "Staggerwing" biplane. The training aircraft being used in Venezuela were PT-19s and AT-21s.

46 Logbook, *USS Spearfish*, "U.S. Submarine War Patrol Reports, 1941–1945," NARA, Pub. M1752, Fiche 986, 2050 hrs., May 3, 1942; Belote and Belote, *Corregidor*, p. 153; Morton, *Fall of the Philippines*, pp. 401–4; Lt. Cmdr. Brian J. Haggerty, *Conduct and Support of Amphibious Operations from United States Submarines in World War II*, Command and General Staff College, Fort Leavenworth, KS. p. 3, http://www.dtic.mil/dtic/tr/fulltext/u2/a536666.pdf. Two damaged small observation planes did fly a few missions from Kindley Field to Mindanao, landing at night only as a searchlight was briefly dipped to mark the runway. War correspondents Frank Hewlett, United Press (author of B*attling Bastards of Bataan)*,

and Dean Schedler, Associated Press, were among the last few evacuated by the island's crude air taxi. The last PBY took off on April 28 from the south bay, with fifty "selected" passengers, including thirty-eight American nurses. By April 29, all lifelines by air with the outside were cut. In the case of US Navy submarines, they made eight trips to Corregidor between January to May 1942, evacuating 186 military personnel and, in February, President Quezon and his family.

47 Moore Report, April 25–May 4; Wainwright, "Own Story," *Gazette*, installments 17 and 18. See also Beebe, *Prisoner of the Rising Sun*, pp. 81–84, and Adams, *Softly Call the Muster*, pp. 26–27; Baldwin, *Battles Lost and Won*, p. 142. Porter, "Anti-aircraft Defense of Corregidor," p. 13, noted that "Japanese reports indicate that more than 200,000 rounds were fired onto Corregidor between 29 April and 6 May."

48 Brig. Gen. Steve Mellnik, *Philippine Diary 1939–1945*, New York: Van Nostrand Reinhold Company, 1969, pp. 135–36.

49 Moore Report, May 3–6; Wainwright, "Own Story," *Gazette*, installments 18 and 19; J. Michael Miller, "From Shanghai to Corregidor: Marines in the Defense of the Philippines," http://1stbn4thmarines.com; Kazumaro Uno, *Corregidor: Isle of Delusion*, Shanghai: Mercury Press, 1942, p. 17; Captain Paul A. Brown, http://www.militarytimes.com; Schultz, *Hero of Bataan*, p. 282; Wainwright, "Report of Operations," August 10, 1946, pp. 51–59; Stolley, "The Fall of Corregidor," pp. 866–68.

50 "Story of Atrocities by Japs on Hapless Prisoners Is Released by the U.S.; Deliberate Starvation, Torture, Death," http://www.angelfire.com/nm/bcmfofnm/atrocities/atrocities01.html.

51 Belote and Belote, *Corregidor*, pp. 142–43, 183–85; Connaughton, *MacArthur and Defeat in the Philippines*, pp. 296–308. See also Colonel Braly, "Corregidor."

52 Ugaki, *Fading Victory*, p. 121; Tanaka, *Hidden Horrors*, pp. 206–11; Michno, *Death on the Hell Ships*, pp. 130–33. As Admiral Ugaki made his diary entries, his task force sailed into the Coral Sea, where the US Navy lost the *USS Lexington* and had the *USS Yorktown* seriously damaged but able to escape sinking.

53 "Japs Land on Corregidor," *Boston Herald*, May 6, 1942; Morris, *Corregidor*, pp. 459–64; Bunker, *Bunker's War*, pp. 146–51; AFA, *Directory of Former Students of the A&M College of Texas, 1876–1949*, College Station: September 1949, p. xxviii; Baldwin, *Battles Lost and Won*, pp. 143–50. See also Stephen M. Mellnik, "How the Japs Took Corregidor," *Coast Artillery Journal*, March 1945; Wainwright, "Own Story," *Gazette*, installments 19 and 20. A few days after the battle, the Japanese raised another previously captured US flag and staged the production of a propaganda film for Tokyo showing the troops lowering and denigrating the US flag.

54 KCB, editorial, "On the Level," *Brownwood Yellow Jacket*, May 14, 1942.

55 Wainwright, "Own Story," *Gazette*, installment 23; Uno, *Corregidor: Isle of Delusion*, p. 24; Robert E. Lee, *Recollections and Letters*, New York: Barnes and Noble Books, 2004 (org. pub. 1904), p. 136. As one observer recalled on April 9, 1865, "As he [Lee] rode slowly along the lines, hundreds of his devoted veterans pressed around the noble chief, trying to take his hand, touch his person, or even lay their hands upon his horse, thus exhibiting for him their great affection. The General then with head bare, the tears flowing freely down his manly cheeks, bade adieu to the army."

56 Moore Report, May 6; Col. William C. Bradley, "Corregidor: A Name, A Symbol, A Tradition," n.d., n.p., http://www.philippine-defenderes.lib.wv.us; Baldwin, *Battles Lost and Won*, pp. 424–25, n. 26. See also Mellnik, "How the Japs Took Corregidor," *Coast Artillery Journal*, pp. 3–11, 17.

57 Wainwright, "Own Story," *Gazette*, installment 18; Schultz, *Hero of Bataan*, p. 31; Uno, *Corregidor*, pp. 72–73. See also "More Than 11,000 Americans Are Corregidor Jap Prisoners," *Denison Press*, May 7, 1942, p. 1.

58 Beebe, *Prisoner of the Rising Sun*, p. 71; Cooper, "Lest We Forget," *Texas Aggie*, April 1989, p. 7; Commander Melvyn H. McCoy and Lt. Col. S. M. Mellnik, *Ten Escape from Tojo*, New York: Farrar & Rinehart, 1944, pp. 20–23; John M. Wright Jr., *Captured on Corregidor: Diary of an American P.O.W. in World War II*, Jefferson, NC: McFarland & Company, 1988, pp. 4–11.

59 Drew Pearson, "The Washington Merry-Go-Round," *The Cass County Sun*, Linden, Texas, April 30, 1942; "MacArthur Remembers Corregidor," *Sweetwater Reporter*, May 6, 1942; Ancheta, ed., *The Wainwright Papers*, pp. 60–62. With the decision to transfer the American general officers and their immediate staffs to a new camp at Tarlac on June 9, 1942, the authorities informed General Wainwright that the Imperial Japanese Army had declared "organized resistance [in the PI] has ended."

CHAPTER 5

1 Samuel B. Moody, *Reprieve from Hell*, Orlando: n.p., 1991, pp. 86–88; "Bled Prisoners to Death to Get Transfusions," *Singleton Argus*, September 17, 1945, p. 1.

2 Daws, *Prisoner of the Japanese*, pp. 83–85; Coleman, *Bataan and Beyond*, p. 84; Robert S. LaForte, R. E. Marcello, and Richard L. Hummel, eds., *With Only the Will to Live: Accounts of Americans in Japanese Prison Camps 1941–1945*, Wilmington: SR Books, 1994, pp. 29, 50; Taylor, *Cabanatuan*, p. 57; Preston J. Hubbard, *Apocalypse Undone*, Nashville: Vanderbilt University Press, 1990, p. 94; Sloan, *Undefeated*, pp. 233–34. For a detailed official after-action report on the treatment of American POWs and camps, see US Army, Office of the Provost Marshall General, "Report on American Prisoners of War Interned by the Japanese in the Philippines,"

n.p., November 19, 1945, http://www.mansell.com (hereafter "US Army POW Report 1945").

3 Quote as seen in Sloan, *Undefeated*, p. 235; Taylor, *Cabanatuan*, p. 59; US Army POW Report 1945, pp. 6, 10. One justification for the use of the term "captive" is that the Japanese claimed that until all the rouge guerrilla units in the hills surrendered in accordance with General Wainwright's offer of unconditional surrender, none of the Americans would be treated as prisoners of war.

4 Roling and Ruter, *The Tokyo Judgment*, pp. 422–25; Glusman, *Conduct Under Fire*, p. 76; Roberts, *Masters and Commanders*, p. 177; "No Philippine News," *Texas Aggie*, May 25, 1942, p. 1.

5 Daws, *Prisoners of the Japanese*, pp. 84–86; Sloan, *Undefeated*, pp. 230–36; Taylor, *Cabanatuan*, pp. 61–62.

6 "Japanese WWII POW Camp Fukuoka #17," http://www.lindavdahl.com; Colonel Irvin Alexander, *Surviving Bataan and Beyond*, Mechanicsburg, PA: Stackpole Books, 2005.

7 See detailed map, Medical Research Committee of American Ex-Prisoners of War, "Japanese Prisoner of War Camps During World War II, 1941–1945," Brownsville, Texas, January 1980. Of the more than one hundred thousand prisoners (military and civilian Americans, Filipinos, native Indians, and Allied troops), approximately fifty thousand were sent into exile in other lands. See also Dr. Marcel Junod, *Warrior without Weapons*, New York: Macmillan, 1951.

8 MacArthur, *Surviving the Sword*, pp. 3–40; "Japs Lie about U.S. Heroes," *LIFE*, September 14, 1942, p. 25; Hoyt, *Warlord: Tojo Against the World*, pp. 115–16, 120–21. A few weeks before the Bataan Death March, over ninety thousand troops—British, Australians, and Indians—had surrendered in the fall of Singapore, the worst and largest capitulation in British history. For details of the location of camps across Asia from 1939–45, see "Prisoner of War of the Japanese 1939–1945," http://www.forces-war-records.co.uk, and "POW Camps in Japan Proper," http://www.powresearch.jp.

9 Sloan, *Undefeated*, pp. 235–37; Norman and Norman, *Tears in the Darkness*, pp. 234–37; Bill Keith, *Days of Anguish, Days of Hope*, Longview: Stonegate, 2011, pp. 99–109; Stewart Wolf and Herbert S. Ripley, "Reactions among Allied Prisoners of War Subjected to Three Years of Imprisonment and Torture by the Japanese," *American Journal of Psychiatry*, September 1947, p. 182; Hubbard, *Apocalypse Undone*, pp. 96–99. See also Schwartz, "Affidavit Regarding Bataan Hospital #2," and US Army Report 1945, pp. 1–5. It is important to remember that determining the number of prisoners of war, both living and dead, either on the Bataan Death March or in the POW camps is at best an estimated guess. The US Army realized this as early as its first extensive postwar investigation and report of POW conditions in November 1945. Following both the fall of Bataan

and then Corregidor, records were either destroyed or lost, and the figures used today are those rosters that have been reconstructed from after-action reports, some meager camp records, and materials compiled by the postwar judge advocate general's office. The records of the dead and those interned while moved between the various POW camps or lost on the Hell Ships are also difficult to confirm.

10 Texas A&M WWII Files, Cushing Library.

11 Statement of Robley Evans, February 13, 1947, Evans Family Papers; Sloan, *Undefeated*, p. 238; Roling and Ruter, *The Tokyo Judgment*, pp. 402–7; John Henry Poncio and Marlin Young, *Girocho: A GI's Story of Bataan and Beyond*, Baton Rouge: LSU Press, 2003, pp. 120–26; Waterford, *Prisoners of the Japanese*, pp. 251–61; McCoy and Mellnik, *Ten Escape from Tojo*, p. 64; Office of the Provost Marshal General, "Report of American Prisoners of War Interned by the Japanese in the Philippines," November 19, 1945, http://www.mansell.com. For a detailed overview of the POW casualties, see Lisa Beckenbaugh and Heather Harris, "Casualties of the Philippines POW Camps O'Donnell and Cabanatuan and the History of their Burials," Archival Research Memo, Washington, DC: Defense Prisoner of War—Missing Personnel Office, March 2, 2010. Also, civilian internment camps were established at Los Banos, Santo Tomas, and Camp John Hay, holding some eight thousand men, women, and children.

12 Beckenbaugh and Harris, "Casualties of the Philippines POW Camps," p. 6; Mallonee, *Battle of Bataan*, pp. 154–56; Office of the Provost Marshal General, Report on American Prisoners of War Interned by the Japanese in the Philippines, Camp O'Donnell, November 19, 1945, in the Evans Family Papers. In late August 1942, the Japanese allowed grave markers.

13 John D. Lukacs, *Escape from Davao*, New York; Penguin, 2010, p. 93; Taylor, *Cabanatuan*, pp. 71–73; Melvyn McCoy and S. M. Mellnik, "Death Was Part of Our Life," *LIFE*, February 7, 1943, p. 29; Tenney, *My Hitch in Hell*, pp. 108–10; Sloan, *Undefeated*, 243–45.

14 Beckenbaugh and Harris, "Casualties," pp. 3–6; US Army POW Report 1945, pp. 7–9.

15 Knox, *Death March*, p. 203.

16 McCoy and Mellnik, "Death Was Part of Our Life," pp. 30–31. See also Office of the Provost Marshal General, Report on American Prisoners of War Interned by the Japanese in the Philippines, Camp Cabanatuan, May 27, 1942, in Evans Family Papers.

17 Testimony of Captain Robley Evans, May 21, 1946, Evan Family Papers; J. E. Nardini, "Survival Factors in American Prisoners of War of the Japanese," AJP, October 1952, pp. 241–44; Sloan, *Undefeated*, p. 247; Tenney, *My Hitch in Hell*, p. 107. See also Hampton Sides, *Ghost Soldiers: The Forgotten Epic Story*, New York: Doubleday, 2011; Adrian R. Martin and Larry W. Stephenson, *Operation Plum*, College Station: Texas A&M University Press, 2008, pp. 265–67.

18 Coleman, *Bataan and Beyond*, pp. 92–93; Glusman, *Conduct Under Fire*, 254–63. See also Schwartz, "Affidavit Regarding Bataan Hospital #2."

19 Sloan, *Undefeated*, p. 251; Keith, *Days of Anguish, Days of Hope*, p. 113; Wolf and Ripley, "Reactions among Allied Prisoners of War Subjected to Three Years of Imprisonment," AJP, pp. 182–83; McCoy and Mellnik, "Death Was Part of Our Life," p. 96. Not until December 15, 1942, did Camp No. 1 at Cabanatuan celebrate its first "zero death" day!

20 Texas A&M, AFS, Veteran's Records, Cushing Library; Bemis, "Boys of the Cave—Men of Bataan," pp. 50–51.

21 Keith, *Days of Anguish, Days of Hope*, p. 110; Wright, *Captured on Corregidor*, p. 58; Lukacs, *Escape from Davao*, pp. 105–6; "Conquerors Show Animal Ways," *The Dallas News*, October 17, 1945; Nardini, "Survival Factors in American Prisoners of War of the Japanese," AJP, p. 246; Glusman, *Conduct Under Fire*, p. 258; "Abilene Officer, Survivor of Bataan Dies a Prisoner," *Abilene Reporter-News*, July 5, 1943, and "Bataan Hero's Posthumous Award Presented to Father," *Abilene Reporter-News*, January 19, 1947. Nardini concludes that prisoner suicide (active self-inflicted injury) per se was rare. Captain Grimes finished his entire freshman year at Texas A&M and then transferred to West Point.

22 Dooley, "The First U.S. Tank Action in World War II," *Armor*, July 1983; Harries and Harries, *Soldiers of the Sun*, pp. 353–54.

23 Breuer, *Great Raid*, 60–62; Daws, *Prisoners of the Japanese*, p. 132; Tenney, *My Hitch in Hell*, pp. 110–13; Schwartz, "Affidavit Regarding Bataan Hospital #2."

24 Glusman, *Conduct Under Fire*, p. 270; US Army POW Report 1945, p. 6.

25 Sloan, *Undefeated*, p. 244; US Army POW Report 1945, pp. 8, 11; Mallonee, *Battle of Bataan*, pp. 160–62, 171–76; "Japs Ignore Pledge to Keep War Rules," *The Dallas News*, October 18, 1945. While at Tarlac, there was only one American death of a colonel who died of exposure shortly after the Death March.

26 James W. Erickson, "*Nagara Maru*," n.d., and "*Nagara Maru* POW roster," n.d., http://sites.google.com/site/powsofthejapanese; Wainwright, *General Wainwright's Story*, pp. 157, 169–75, 181–82; "Nips Make Officers, GIs Stand Naked in Heat," *The Dallas News*, October 19, 1945; E. Bartlett Kerr, *Surrender and Survival: The Experience of American POWs in the Pacific, 1941–1945*, New York: William Morrow and Company, 1985, pp. 107–8; Michno, *Death on the Hellships*, pp. 34–36.

27 Michno, *Death on the Hellships*, p. 36; Mallonee, *Battle of Bataan*, pp. 178–79; Michno, *Death on the Hellships*, p. 310; Wainwright, "Own Story," *Gazette*, installments 30 and 31.

28 Nardini, "Survival Factor in American Prisoners of War of the Japanese," AJP, p. 242.

29 Michno, *Death on the Hellships*, p. 311.

30 Lukacs, *Escape from Davao*, pp. 110–17.
31 McCoy and Mellnik, "Death Was Part of Our Life," pp. 97–98; LaForte et al., *With Only the Will to Live*, p. 123.
32 Capt. Sydney R. Greer '35, AFS World War II file, TAMU Archives; Dyess, *The Dyess Story*, pp. 148–60; William D. Miner, *Surrender on Cebu: A POW's Diary—WWII*, Paduch, KY: Turner, 2001, pp. 149–50, 180–83. Rogers was held in the local Cebu jail for six months before transfer to Dapecol.
33 Dyess, *The Dyess Story*, pp. 25, 34, 52; Poncio and Young, *Girocho*, p. 115; Mellnik, *Philippine Diary*, pp. 179–81.
34 Dyess, *The Dyess Story*, pp. 162–63. In 1944, two escapees chronicled a vivid account of camp conditions and torture in McCoy and Mellnik, *Ten Escaped from Tojo*, 1944.
35 Mark Sandrich, director, *So Proudly We Hail*, Paramount Pictures, June 22, 1943; Tay Garnett, director, *Bataan*, Metro-Goldwyn-Mayer, June 1943; Redmond, *I Served on Bataan*. Additional movies during the period include *Corregidor*, 1943; *The Purple Heart*, 1944; *Back to Bataan*, 1945; *Cry "Havoc"*, 1943; and *Orders from Tokyo*, 1945.
36 Dethloff, *Centennial History of Texas A&M 1876–1976*, vol. 2, p. 454; Dyess, *The Dyess Story*, pp. 200, 210–11; Stewart, *Give Us This Day*, p. 86.
37 US Army Provost Marshall General, "Report on American Prisoners of War," pp. 5–30; Beckenbaugh and Harris, "Casualties of the Philippines POW Camps," pp. 3–8; Daws, *Prisoners of the Japanese*, pp. 284–87; S. P. MacKenzie, "The Treatment pf Prisoners of War in World War II," *Journal of Modern History*, September 1994, pp. 514–19; "Prisoner of War," *Texas Aggie*, January 5, 1943.
38 Mannie Bemis, ed., "Boys of the Cave—Men of Bataan," Carlsbad Caverns National Park, 2013, pp. 50–51; Holmes, *Guests of the Emperor*, pp. 6–9, 24; "Mukden Prisoner of War Remembrance Society," http://www.mukdenpows.org; Phone interview with Mannie Bemus, November 20, 2014; T.Sgt. to Mrs. Ed Gossett, from Mukden, Manchukuo, September 1, 1945, Moseley Papers; Interview with Kay Moseley Hilliard, Houston, November 23, 2014. Moseley was shipped from Manila to Mukden via Pusan, Korea, arriving November 11, 1942, on the *Tottori Maru*. The title of the camp newspaper is lifted from a 1652 English poem by Richard Lovelace, "To Althea, from Prison": "Stone walls do not a prison make, *nor iron bars* a cage."
39 Wainwright, "Own Story," *Gazette*, installments 1–31; Papers of Colonel Edwin Aldridge '16, Cushing Library; Colonel Tom Dooley '35, Papers and Diary, Cushing Library; Huffman, "Notebook and Diary of Captain Cary McClure Abney Jr. '34."
40 Holmes, *Guest of the Emperor*, p. 50.
41 For more details, see "Section 07 Treatment of POWs Document May 18, 1944," Tom Dooley Diary, POW documents, 1944, Cushing Library.

42 Holmes, *Guests of the Emperor*, pp. 16–39; Tanaka, *Hidden Horrors*, pp. 135–65. Class action lawsuits were attempted against the Japanese manufactures for using prison slave labor during the war; see "Japanese Companies, Including Steelmakers, Sued over WWII Profits," April 11, 1999, http://www.nwitimes.com.

43 Statement of Robley D. Evans on mistreatment while a prisoner of war of the Imperial Japanese Government, Ft. Worth, February 13, 1947, and "Former POW's Asked to Tell about Atrocities of Japanese," *Ft. Worth Star Telegram*, n.d., in Evans Family Papers. See also "Research of Japanese War Crimes Records," Nazi War Crimes and Japanese Imperial Government Records Interagency Working Group, NARA: Washington, DC, 2006.

44 LaForte et al., *With Only the Will to Live*, pp. 107–10; Sides, *Ghost Soldiers*, pp. 1–28; Manning, *Hirohito*, p. 203; Bob Wilbanks, *Last Man Out: Glen McDole, USMC, Survivor of the Palawan Massacre in World War II*, Jefferson, NC: McFarland & Company, 2004; "Roster of the Victims of the Palawan Massacre," http://philippine-defenders.lib.wv.us. Palawan was not the first mass murder by the Japanese, as ninety-six American construction workers in 1943 were blindfolded and bound and then machine gunned to death on Wake Island and then dumped into a mass grave. This incident was not public knowledge until the war crimes trials in 1946.

45 "Kill-All-Order," August 1, 1944, captured in camp documents in Taiwan POW Camp HQ in Taihoku, Document 2701, Exhibit "O", NARA, War Crimes, Japan, RG 24, Box 2015; "Kill All Order" in Japanese and translated to English; see Jacobsen, *We Refused to Die*, pp. 180–81. Some have argued this was written and transmitted from the War Ministry without proper authority. That amounts to balderdash, given the fact it did come from an official Japanese government agency at the "policy level" and was sent to all camps, leaving the camp commanders with the option to decide how to carry out the annihilation "of them all." Furthermore, the Imperial Japanese Army had already developed a detailed policy to eliminate all American prisoners, especially if there was an invasion of the Japanese homeland. This order or "policy" was consistent with over a decade of kill orders used long before Pearl Harbor and only taken to a new level after December 1941. Plans were also in place to kill all noncombatant civilian internees—with no exception, all children, women, and men. In "Anglo-Americanism Must Be Wiped Out," *Japan Times*, November 5, 1942, the call was for "*annihilation*." See also "Order Telling Guards to Flee to Avoid Prosecution for War Crimes and Order to Kill All POWs," http://www.mansell.com.

46 Roling and Ruter, *The Tokyo Judgment*, pp. 408–9; Reel, *The Case of General Yamashita*, p. 99; Tanaka, *Hidden Horrors*, pp. 154–60. Quoted from Sides, *Ghost Soldiers*, p. 24.

47 Manning, *Hirohito*, pp. 105–6; Connaughton et al., *The Battle for Manila*, pp. 182–84; Conrad H. Lanza, "North Luzon," *Field Artillery Journal*, May 1945,

pp. 303–8.; "Rescue at Cabanatuan," http://www.4point2.org/cabantuan.htm; John H. Blair, "Operations of the 3D Battalion, 503D Parachute Infantry Regiment in the Landing on Corregidor, P.I., February 16–March 2, 1945," Fort Benning: The Infantry Officers School, 1950. Many planners in Washington, and especially those who had a low regard for MacArthur, lobbied to go around the Philippines and land in Formosa to establish advanced bases for the battle against Japan.

48 William B. Breuer, *Retaking the Philippines: America's Return to Corregidor and Bataan, October 1944–March 1945*, St. Martin's Press, 1986, pp. 129–46; Sloan, *Undefeated*, pp. 322–26; "Survivors of Bataan Rescued from Prison," *Abilene Reporter-News*, February 2, 1945; Interview with William Hamilton '40, November 23, 2014, Kansas City; Adams, *Softly Call the Muster*, pp. 27, 73. The official postwar count for the Cabanatuan rescue was 522 rescued: 489 POWs and 33 civilians.

49 LaForte et al., *With Only the Will to Live*, pp. 197–99, 244; Tanaka, *Hidden Horrors*, pp. 74–78; Nash, *That We Might Live*, pp. 221–23.

CHAPTER 6

1 Michno, *Death on the Hellships*, pp. 1–2; "POW Camps in Japan Proper," http://www.powresearch.jp; Map, "Japanese Prisoner of War Camps during World War II, 1941–1945," Brownsville, Texas: Medical Research Committee of American Ex-Prisoners of War, January 1980; Interview with Jim Erickson, College Station, Texas, September 15, 2014. See also Beckenbaugh and Harris, "Casualties of the Philippines POW Camps," March 2, 2010. The number of Allied soldiers captured in the western Pacific and Southeast Asia ranges from 290,000 to 310,000. Of the total number captured, some one-third, or 100,000, died in captivity. Of this number, approximately 140,000 were Western soldiers and sailors. Between 19,000 and 21,000 died at sea, many deaths the result of Allied air and submarine attacks on POW ships. The total number of POWs shipped to some 80 camps across Japan was about 36,000, of which 3,500 died in prison in Japan. Those who died in Japan were cremated and the remains entrusted to Buddhist temples in the respective regions of the camp.

2 Capt. Burt Griffin File, AFS World War II Papers, Cushing Library; AFS, *Directory of Former Students*, 1949, pp. xxxvi, 368.

3 Michno, *Death on the Hellships*, p. viii.; Daws, *Prisoners of the Japanese*, p. 297. Official Japanese figures estimate that of the some 50,000 POWs shipped, 10,800 died at sea. Again, like all phases of the conflict in and around the Philippines, numbers of combatants and casualties are hard to confirm and are still under investigation; see the work by Jim Erickson and Mansell. Also, the only documented exception of a Hell Ship being labeled as a "POW ship" was in early

October 1942, when the *Tottori Maru* had "Prisoners of War Aboard" painted in Japanese on the smoke stack. Linda Holmes (*Guests of the Emperor*, p. 10) noted that the writing in Japanese was done for the benefit of the Japanese only, not American submarines who could not read Japanese!

4 Bunker, *Bunker's War*, pp. 216–23. Not all early ships, regardless of the Japanese control of sea lanes, were as humane as the *Nagara Maru*. In January of 1942, Marines and civilian contractors from Guam (*Argentina Maru*) and Wake Island (*Nitta Maru*) were crowded below deck, and five men were decapitated by the Japanese. Before the end of 1942, most ship deaths were due to slowness and conditions on ships; however, unknown until after the war, in the weeks prior to the sailing of the *Nagara*, over one thousand Australian soldiers and civilians were killed off the coast of the Philippines in the sinking of the *Montevideo Maru* by the USS Sturgeon on July 1, 1942, sinking in eleven minutes with all on board but a few guards who jumped ship. And on October 1, 1942, the *Lisbon Maru* was torpedoed between Hong Kong and Japan by an American submarine, with over a thousand British POWs lost.

5 Daws, *Prisoners of the Japanese*, pp. 283–85; Tanaka, *Hidden Horrors*, pp. 70–78, 213–15; NARA for the Nazi War Crimes and Japanese Imperial Government Records Interagency Working Group, 2006, p. 4; Hoyt, *Japan's War*, p. 251. Tanaka notes, "The Japanese failed to take seriously the concept of 'rights'—Respect for human rights [stemming from the Judeo-Christian tradition] in Western society is an idealistic rather than a realistic concept."

6 Eugene A. Mazza, "USS Paddle: Sinking American POWs," http://www.microworks.net/pacific/personal/pattle.htm.

7 "S.A. Man [Capt. Gus H. Froebel] on Sunken Prison Ship Not Listed as Survivor," n.p., n.d.; Letter, Tillie H. Froebel to J. B. Hervey, August 7, 1950; Letter, Mrs. C. I. Miller to E. E. McQuillen, June 7, 1946; Letter, Felix C. Sharp Jr. to Mrs. Miller, March 3, 1945; Letter, Major General William F. Sharp to Clarence I. Miller, January 7, 1946, confirming award of the Silver Star to Capt. Ross Miller; "Lt. Colonel R. H. 'Bill' Rogers Is Reported Prisoner of War of Japanese," *Del Rio News-Herald*, May 16, 1943; Mrs. R. H. Rogers to E. E. McQuillen, January 18, 1946, confirming the awarding of the Legion of Merit and Purple Heart posthumously to Lt. Col. Rogers, all located in the Association of Former Students Papers, Cushing Library.

8 Harry O. Fischer Jr. '29, *Longhorn*, 1929, p. 43.

9 Cooper, "Lest We Forget," *Texas Aggie*, April 1989, p. 8; Glusman, *Conduct Under Fire*, pp. 354–56; Lawton, *Some Survived*, pp. 113–16; MacArthur, *Surviving the Sword*, pp. 298–99.

10 Michno, *Death on the Hellships*, pp. 244–52; Daws, *Prisoners of the Japanese*, pp. 292–93; William Bowen "The Arisan Maru Tragedy,"

http://www.us-japandialogueonpows.org; Lee A. Gladwin, "American POWs on Japanese Ships Take a Voyage into Hell," Winter 2003, http://www.archives.gov; Glusman, *Conduct Under Fire*, pp. 357–58; Lawton, *Some Survived*, pp. 114–18.

11 Michno, *Death on the Hellships*, pp. 252–55, p. 332, n. 74; Bill Bowen's "Arisan Maru Roster," http://www.us-japandialogueonpows.org; Lawton, *Some Survived*, pp. 121–28.

12 Michno, *Death on the Hellships*, p. 258; Glusman, *Conduct Under Fire*, pp. 366–67.

13 Letter, General Douglas MacArthur to Mr. James, August 31, 1945; Letter, Mrs. A. M. James to E. E. McQuillen, January 21, 1946; Letter to the *Battalion* from C. C. Jones, January 28, 1946; Letter, Henry J. Schutte to Mr. McQuillen, August 1, 1945; Frank Hewlett, "Death Struggle of Bataan Is Tragic Story," *Amarillo News-Globe*, April 9, 1942, all located in Association of Former Students papers, Cushing Library. To add further confusion and concern to the James family in Dalhart, a special January 1946 edition of the college newspaper, the *Battalion*, "omitted" Andy James Jr. '41 from a list of Texas Aggies killed in action.

14 Letter, "DE" to E. E. McQuillen, March 23, 1944, and Letter, Gertrude Curtis to McQuillen, July 14, 1945, Association of Former Student Papers, Cushing Library.

15 Lawton, *Some Survived*, pp. 152–53; Judith L. Pearson, *Belly of the Beast*, New York: New American Library, 2001, pp. 136–41; MacArthur, *Surviving the Sword*, p. 298.

16 Wright, *Captured on Corregidor*, p. 88.

17 "U.S. vs Junsaburu TOSHINO and Shusuke WADA, et al.," General HQ, Supreme Commander for the Allied Powers, Legal Section, File no. 014.13, Summary No. 510, February 25, 1947; Lawton, *Some Survived*, pp. 156–61; *Armor*, January–February 1989, http://www.benning.army.mil/armor/armormagazine/content/Issues/1989/ArmorJanuaryFebruary1989web.pdf; Letter, C. Snell [brother] to E. E. McQuillen, August 7, 1945, Association of Former Student Papers; *Longhorn*, pp. 67, 88; Pearson, *Belly of the Beast*, pp. 141–43.

18 Lawton, *Some Survived*, p. 163; Pearson, *Belly of the Beast*, pp. 156–63; Daws, *Prisoner of the Japanese*, pp. 298–300; MacArthur, *Surviving the Sword*, pp. 301–5.

19 *Longhorn*, 1929, p. 50; "Kelley Lost on Jap Transport," *Marshall News Messenger*, July 26, 1945; Huffman, "Notebook and Diary of Captain Cary McClure Abney Jr. '34," p. 6; "Tyler Veteran's Son to Obtain Father's [Greer] Watch; Senator Aids," *Tyler Courier Times*, September 17, 1946; Pearson, *Belly of the Beast*, pp. 178–79; Stewart, *Give Us This Day*, pp. 132–142; Letter, C. Brice Perrenot '38 to E. E. McQuillen, November 1, 1945; "Captain Travis Perrenot Killer on Transport," *Houma Courier*, August 2, 1945.

20 "Jap Prison Ship," Associated Press, Jinsen, Korea, September 9, 1945; John M. Wright, *Captured on Corregidor: Diary of an American POW in World War II*,

Jefferson, NC: McFarland & Company, 1988, p. 113; Lawton, *Some Survived*, pp. 183–88: Stewart, *Give Us This Day*, p. 124.

21 Wright, *Captured on Corregidor*, pp. 123–24

22 Lawton, *Some Survived*, pp. 198–203; MacArthur, *Surviving the Sword*, pp. 304–8; "Raiders and Guerillas Release 510 Prisoners on Luzon," *Sweetwater Reporter*, February 1, 1945, p. 1. The sole Texas Aggie officer liberated in the raid on Cabanatuan was Lt. Clifton Chamberlain.

23 "U.S. vs. Toshino, Wada, et al.," General HQ, February 25, 1947, n.p.; "POW Camps in Japan Proper," Sec. 2, No. 2, http://www.powresearch.jp.

24 Leonard Mosley, *Hirohito: Emperor of Japan*, Englewood Cliffs: Prentice-Hall, 1966, pp. 326–28; "Omine Machi (Sanyo)," http://www.mansell.com; Linda McDavitt, "An Amazing Journey: Trip to the Site of Omine Machi POW Camp," Fall 2011, http://www.us-japandialogueonpows.org; Robert C. Daniels, *1220 Days: The Story of a U.S. Marine Edmond Badler*, Bloomington: AuthorHouse, 2011, p. 101; Harries and Harries, *Soldiers of the Sun*, pp. 456–62; LaForte et al., *With Only the Will to Live*, p. 254; "POW Camps in Japan Proper," Sec. 2, No. 11.

25 Knox, *Death March*, p. 441.

26 Ibid., pp. 441, 448; "Campus Muster," *Texas Aggie*, April 1985, p. 3; Cooper, "Lest We Forget," *Texas Aggie*, April 1989, p. 9; Miner, *Surrender on Cebu*, p. 102. This famous American POW flag hangs in the lobby of the Clayton Williams Association of Former Students on the College Station campus. A commemorative plaque dedicated to the American Defenders of Bataan and Corregidor is displayed in the foyer of the Memorial Student Center. Names of the eighty-nine Texas Aggies who served in the Philippines in 1941–42 are included, along with names of additional former students of Texas A&M who served in the Pacific Theater.

27 Bill Streifer, "Operation Cardinal: OSS in Manchuria," *OSS Society Journal*, Fall 2010, pp. 22–25; LaForte et al., *With Only the Will to Live*, p. 256. See also "Mukden Rescue and Evacuation," http://www.mansell.com.

28 World War II MIA rosters at http://www.dtic.mil; Nardini, "Survival Factors in American Prisoners of War of the Japanese," *American Journal of Psychiatry*, October 1952, pp. 241–48. Extensive research, records collection, and record declassification continues in an effort to compile a more complete record, see "Implementation of the Japanese Imperial Government Disclosure Act and the Japanese War Crimes Provisions of the Nazi War Crimes Disclosure Act," 2002.

29 Colonel Tom Dooley's Diary, September 1–4, 1945.

CHAPTER 7

1 Interview with William D. Walker '44 in Hewitt, Texas, March 2, 2015; Jerry Cooper, "Aggie History Was Made on the Rock," *Texas Aggie*, June 1996,

pp. 12–13; Reel, *The Case of General Yamashita*, pp. 22–24. See also E. M. Flanagan, *Corregidor: The Rock Force Assault*, Navato, CA: Presidio Press, 1995, and Gerald M. Devlin, *Back to Corregidor: American Retakes the Rock*, New York: St. Martin's Press, 1992.

2 USAFFE, HQ, Communication No. 1048, February 19, 1945; "1944 Muster Will Follow the Sun: Meeting Circle Globe," *Texas Aggie*, February 15, 1944, p. 1.

3 Adams, *Softly Call the Muster*, pp. 42–75.

4 "Hero's Welcome Greets Gen. Moore on Campus Visit," *Texas Aggie*, November 1, 1945, p. 1; Robley D. Evans Papers, debriefing, September 1945.

BIBLIOGRAPHY

PRIMARY SOURCES

Ancheta, Celedonio A., ed. *The Wainwright Papers*, vol. 1. Quezon City, Philippines: New Day, 1980.

Bemis, Mannie, ed. *Boys of the Cave—Men of Bataan*. Carlsbad Caverns National Park, NM: National Park Service, April 2013.

Braly, Colonel William C. "Corregidor: A Name, a Symbol, a Tradition." http://www.philippine-defenders.lib.wv.us.

MacArthur, Douglas. *Reports of General MacArthur: The Campaigns of MacArthur in the Pacific*, vol. 1. Washington, DC: GPO, 1966.

Roling, B. V. A., and C. F. Ruter, eds. *The Tokyo Judgment: International Military Tribunal for the Far East (I.M.T.F.E.) 29 April 1946–12 November 1948*. Amsterdam: APA-University Press Amsterdam BV, 1977.

Roosevelt, Franklin D. "Address by the President: Texas A. & M. College, May 11, 1937." Franklin D. Roosevelt Presidential Library, Master Speech File, Box 32, 1053, "Galveston, Houston and Texas A&M Extemporaneous," Hyde Park, New York.

US Army. Blair, John H. "Operations of the 3D Battalion, 503D Parachute Infantry Regiment in the Landing on Corregidor, P.I. 16 February–2 March 1945." Fort Benning: Advanced Infantry Officers Course, 1950.

———. Combat History Division, G-1 Section, HQ AFWESPAC. "Corregidor of Eternal Memory." n.p.: GPO, January 1946.

———. Dooley, Thomas. "The First United States Tank Action in World War II." Fort Benning: Advanced Infantry Officers Course, May 1, 1948.

———. Flores, M. T. "An Analytical Study of the Defense of Bataan." Fort Leavenworth, KS: Command and General Staff College, 1949.

———. Hill, Hudson C. "The Operations of Company 'E,' 503D Parachute Regiment at Wheeler Point, Island of Corregidor, Philippine Islands, 23 February 1945." Fort Benning: Advanced Infantry Officers Course, 1948.

———. His General Staff. *Reports of General MacArthur*. Washington, DC: GPO, 1950.

———. HQ Philippines Command. "US Army Recognition Program of Philippine Guerrillas." n.p.: n.d. [circa 1945].

———. Johnson, Harold K. "Defense of the Philippine Islands, Anyasen and Silaiim Points, Bataan." Fort Leavenworth, KS: Command and General Staff College, 1947.

———. Marshall, George C. *Biennial Report of the Chief of Staff of the United States Army: July 1, 1943–June 30, 1945*. Washington, DC: Infantry Journal Press, 1946.

———. Mead, Everett V. "The Operations and Movements of the 31st Infantry Regiment, PA, 7 December 1941–9 April 1942." Fort Benning: Advanced Infantry Officers Course, 1948.

———. Mendelson, Sheldon H. "Operations of the Provisional Air Corps Regiment in the Defense of Bataan Peninsula, P.I. 8 January–10 April 1942." Fort Benning: Advanced Infantry Officers Course, 1947.

———. "The Moore [General George F. Moore '08] Report." Wainwright Papers, Part C, 1945. http://www.corregidor.org.

———. Nealson, William R. "The Operations of a Provisional Battalion, 41st Division, PA, at Abucay Hacienda, 15–25 January 1942: Personal Experience of a Battalion Commander." Fort Benning: Advanced Infantry Officers Course, 1948.

———. Office of the Provost Marshall General. "Report on American Prisoners of War Interned by the Japanese in the Philippines." November 19, 1945. http://www.mansell.com.

———. "Operations of the Provisional Tank Group: USAFFE 1941–1942." http://www.memorialmuseum.org.

———. Porter, Gwinn U. "Anti-aircraft Defense of Corregidor." Fort Leavenworth, KS: Command and General Staff College, 1947.

———. Santos, Alfredo M. "The 1st Regular Division in the Battle of the Philippines." Fort Leavenworth, KS: Command and General Staff College, 1947.

———. Skarden, Beverly N. "The Operations of Company A, 92D Infantry, Philippine Army: 3 January 1942, 24 March 1942." Fort Benning: Advanced Infantry Officers Course, 1946.

———. Smith, Magnus L. "Operations of the 'Rock Force' in the Recapture of Corregidor Island, 16 February–8 March 1945." Fort Benning: Advanced Infantry Officers Course, 1950.

———. Trapnell, T. J. H. "The Operations of the 26th Cavalry (P.S.) Personal Experience of a Squadron Commander." Fort Leavenworth, KS: Command and General Staff College, 1947.

———. Whitman, John W. "US Army Doctrinal Effectiveness on Bataan, 1942: The First Battle." Fort Leavenworth, KS: Command and General Staff College, 1984.

US Congress. *Congressional Record*, April 20, 1942, A1453.

US House of Representatives. Committee on Foreign Affairs. "Corregidor-Bataan Memorial Commission." 85th Cong., 1st sess., H.R. 973, May 8, 1957.

US Navy. "Bataan and Corregidor: World War II Commemorative Bibliography No. 3." Washington, DC: Navy Department Library, November 1992.

———. "Pacific POW Roster." http://www.mansell.com.

US Senate. "Pouncing Gazetteer and Geographical Dictionary of the Philippine Islands: Corregidor and Adjacent Islands, Luzon." 57th Cong., 1st sess., Doc. No. 280, 1902.

Texas A&M University Archives, Cushing Library

Andy Marmaduke James Jr. '41 Papers

Association of Former Students (AFS) Draft of Bataan and Corregidor Roster, October 18, 1973

Association of Former Students (AFS) Killed-in-Action Files

Association of Former Students (AFS) World War II Veteran Files

Colonel Edwin E. Aldridge '16 Papers

Colonel Thomas Dooley '35 WWII Collection

General George Moore Bio File

1942 Muster Files

US Archives

NARA. The Nazi War Crimes and Japanese Imperial Government Records Interagency Working Group, Washington, DC, 2006

National WWII Museum, "Beyond All Boundaries," New Orleans, Louisiana, visited July 23, 2014

RG-2: Records of the Headquarters of US Army Forces in the Far East (USAFFE), 1941–42; Guide to Microfilm Collection, 2006

RG-43: Papers of Weldon B. Hester, MacArthur Archives, Norfolk, Virginia

RG-407: Records of the Adjutant General's Office, 1917–

Rutgers Oral History Archives, Rutgers University, New Brunswick, New Jersey

U.S.S. Spearfish Log, "U.S. Submarine War Patrol Reports, 1941–1945," NARA, Pub. M1752, Fiche, 986

First-Person Accounts of Bataan and Corregidor

Babcock, C. Stanton. "Philippine Campaign." *The Cavalry Journal*, parts 1 and 2, March and May 1943.

Bank, Bert. *Back from the Living Dead.* Tuscaloosa: 1945, reprint.

Beebe, John M., ed. *Prisoner of the Rising Sun: The Lost Diary of Brig. Gen. Lewis Beebe.* College Station: Texas A&M University Press, 2006.

Brain, Philip S. *Soldier of Bataan.* Minneapolis: Rotary Club of Minneapolis, 1990.

Braly, William C. "Corregidor—A Name, a Symbol, a Tradition." *Coastal Artillery Journal,* July–August 1947, 2–9, 36–44.

Brereton, Lewis H. *The Brereton Diaries.* New York: William Morrow and Company, 1946.

Brougher, William Edward. *The Long Dark Road.* n.p.: 1946.

Brown, R. M. *A G.I. Named Brown.* London: Brown, Watson, 1960.

Bruns '35, Stockton D. "'Idaho'—Battery 'I', 59 Coast Artillery [Ft. Hughes, P.I.]." http://www.corregidor.org.

Chandler, William E. "The 26th Cavalry." *Armored Cavalry Journal,* March–August 1947.

Clark, Corbett W. *From Hell to Surrender.* Fayetteville, GA: Hawkeye, 2002.

Coleman, John S. *Bataan and Beyond: Memories of an American POW.* College Station: Texas A&M University Press, 1978.

Day, Kenneth W. *Forty-Nine Days in Hell: The Story of the Oryoku Maru.* Santa Fe, NM: Bataan Veteran's Organization, 1950.

DeWeerd, H. A., ed. *Selected Speeches and Statements of General of the Army George C. Marshall.* Washington, DC: Infantry Journal Press, 1945.

Dyess, William E. *The Dyess Story: The Eye-Witness Account of the Death March from Bataan and the Narrative of Experiences in Japanese Prison Camps and of Eventual Escape.* New York: G. P. Putnam's Sons, 1944.

Gay, George. *Sole Survivor: Torpedo Squadron Eight—Battle of Midway.* Jersey City: 3B Litho, 1979.

Hersey, John. *Men of Bataan.* New York: Alfred A. Knopf, 1942.

Hibbs, Ralph E. *Tell MacArthur to Wait.* New York: Carlton Press, 1988.

Huffman '53, William M., ed. "Notebook and Diary of Captain Cary McClure Abney Jr. '34." Marshall, TX: Privately printed, 2011.

Hunt, Frazier. *MacArthur and the War Against Japan.* New York: Charles Scribner's Sons, 1944.

Ind, Allison. *Bataan: The Judgment Seat Saga of the Philippine Command of the U.S.A.A.F. May 1941–May 1942.* New York: Macmillan, 1944.

Irwin, C. L. "Corregidor in Action." *Coast Artillery Journal,* January 1943.

Johnson, Harold K. "Defense along the Abucay Line." *Military Review,* February 1949.

Keith, Billy. *Days of Anguish, Days of Hope: The Story of Chaplain Major General Robert P. Taylor's Ordeal and Triumph in the Philippines.* New York: Doubleday & Company, 1972.

Lanza, Conrad H. "North Luzon." *Field Artillery Journal,* May 1945, 303–8.

Leek, Jerome B. *Corregidor G.I.* Culver City, CA: Highlands Press, 1948.

Levering, Robert W. *Horror Trek: A True Story of Bataan, the Death March and Three and One-Half Years in Japanese Prison Camps*. Dayton, OH: Horstman, 1948.

Mellnik, Stephen M. "How the Japs Took Corregidor." *Coast Artillery Journal*, March 1945.

———. *Philippine Diary 1939–1945*. New York: Van Nostrand Reinhold Company: 1969.

Merrill, Smith "Bud," with William J. Duggan. *Silence of a Soldier*. Oakwood, OR: Elderberry Press, 2003.

Miller, E. B. *Bataan Uncensored*. Long Prairie, MN: Hart Publications, 1949.

Moody, Samuel B. *Reprieve from Hell*. Orlando: Moody, 1991.

Nardini, J. S. "Survival Factors in American Prisoners of War of the Japanese." *American Journal of Psychiatry*, October 1952, 241–48.

Palmer, Bruce. "Covering the Withdrawal into Bataan." *Infantry School Quarterly*, July 1950.

Parker, T. C. "The Epic of Corregidor—Bataan," *Proceedings*, January 1943.

Raymond, Steve, and Mike Pride. *Too Dead to Die: A Memoir of Bataan and Beyond*. Concord: Plaidswede, 2006.

Redmond, Juanita. *I Served on Bataan*. Philadelphia: J. B. Lippincott, 1943.

Romulo, Carlos P. *I Saw the Fall of the Philippines*. New York: Doubleday, Doran & Co., 1943.

Schwartz, Jack W. "Affidavit Regarding Bataan Hospital #2." NARA RG 331, Box 920. http://www.mansell.com.

Scott, R. Jackson. *90 Days of Rice*. Pioneer, CA: California Traveler, 1975.

Searle, Ronald. *To the Kwai—and Back: War Drawings 1939–1945*. Boston: Atlantic Monthly Press, 1986.

Stevens, Frederic H. *Santo Tomas Internment Camp: 1942–1945*. n.p.: FHS, 1946.

Stewart, Sidney. *Give Us This Day*. New York: W. W. Norton & Company, 1956.

Tenney, Lester I. *My Hitch in Hell: The Bataan Death March*. Washington: Brassey's, 2000.

Uno, Kazumaro. *Corregidor: Isle of Delusion*. Shanghai: Mercury Press, 1942.

Wainwright, Jonathan M. *General Wainwright's Story: The Account of Four Years of Humiliating Defeat, Surrender, and Captivity*. New York: Modern Library Editions, 1945.

"Wainwright," *TIME*, May 8, 1944.

Wheeler, John. "Rearguard in Luzon." *The Cavalry Journal*, March 1943.

Wright, John M. *Captured on Corregidor: Diary of an American P.O.W. in World War II*. Jefferson, NC: McFarland & Company, 1988.

Author Interviews with Bataan and Corregidor Survivors

William Boyd '38, February 17, 1992

Tom Dooley '35, October 21, 1991, and January 19, 1992

William A. Hamilton '40, October 21, 1991, and October 26, 2014
Urban C. Hopmann '39, March 24, 1988
David M. Snell '37, March 24, 1988
William D. Walker '44, March 2, 2015

Other Interviews by Author or as Noted

William Becker '41, October 5, 1998
Jim Black '69, April 20–21, 1992, Corregidor site visit
Bob Epstein '44, April 21, 2015, Corregidor site visit
Ernest Langford '13, May 23 and 30, 1975
Affidavit by William E. Lewis, AFS WWII Veteran Files, TAMU Archives
John J. Moseley '40, by Fuyuko Mishisato, October 4, 2008
Lee Taylor, June 14, 2014, Arlington, Texas
Joe Utay '08, May 21, 1976
Richard "Buck" Weirus, May 22, 1976
J.V. "Pinky" Wilson, March 19, 1975

Period Articles: 1941-45

"Aggie Hero's Freed from Japs." *Battalion*, September 6, 1945.
Atlanta Journal Constitution, April 20, 1942.
"Bataan." *Newsweek*, May 4, 1942.
"Bataan." *TIME*, April 13, 1942.
"Bataan Epic." *Reader's Digest*, June 1942, 4–7.
Chihaya, Masataka, trans. *Fading Victory: The Diary of Admiral Matome Ugaki*. Pittsburgh: University of Pittsburgh Press, 1991.
"General Wainwright." *TIME*, May 8, 1944, cover.
"Historic Meeting Held by Texas Aggies on Corregidor." *Bryan Eagle*, November 11, 1942.
"Lt. A. M. James First to Learn of Jap War." *Dalhart Texan*, April 2, 1942.
"MacArthur at Bataan." *Reader's Digest*, April 1942, 99.
"MacArthur of Bataan: The War's No. 1 Hero." *Newsweek*, March 9, 1942.
McCoy, Melvyn, and S. M. Mellnik. "Death Was Part of Our Life." *LIFE*, February 7, 1943, 26–31, 96–102.
McKnight, Felix. "Aggies Sure Corregidor in Capable Hands." *Dallas Morning News*, April 22, 1942.
Texas Aggie, April 22, 1942, and May 5, 1942.

Movies and Documentaries

Dmytryk, Edward, director, movie, *Back to Bataan*. PKO Radio Pictures, 1945.
Ford, John, director, movie, *They Were Expendable*. Metro-Goldwyn-Mayer, 1945.

Garnett, Tay, director, movie, *Bataan*. Metro-Goldwyn-Mayer, 1943.
Griffin, David, documentary, *Orders from Tokyo*. Warner Brothers, August 1945.
Gross, Paul, director, movie, *Ghost Soldiers*. Hurbinek Productions, 2012.
Hawks, Howard, director, movie, *Air Force*. Warner Brothers, March 20, 1943.
"Japanese Sign Final Surrender," *USS Missouri*, documentary, United Newsreel Corporation, September 2, 1945.
Jolie, Angelina, director, movie, *Unbroken*. Universal Pictures, 2014.
Milestone, Lewis, director, movie, *The Purple Heart*. 20th Century Fox, February 1944.
Nigh, William, director, movie, *Corregidor*. PRC: Hollywood, 1943.
Sandrich, Mark, director, movie, *So Proudly We Hail!* Paramount Pictures, June 1943.
Sedanth, Lesley, director, movie, *I Was an American Spy*. Allied Artist, 1951.
Thrope, Richard, director, movie, *Cry "Havoc"*. Metro-Goldwyn-Mayer, 1943.

SECONDARY SOURCES

Articles

Anderson, Burton. "Company C, 194th Tank Bn in the Philippines, 1941–42." *Armor*, May 1996, 32–36.
Anselmo, Guy. "Fourth Marines: Bataan and Corregidor." *Leatherneck*, November 1988, 44–50.
Arnold, Harold A. "The Lessons of Bataan: The Story of the Bataan Quartermaster Depots." *Quartermaster Review*, November 1946.
Baldwin, Hanson W. "The Fall of Corregidor." *American Heritage*, August 1966, 17–23, 84–90.
"Bataan: Where Heroes Fell." *TIME*, April 20, 1942, 18–21.
"Battle of the Philippines." *TIME*, March 30, 1942, 25.
"Blitz over the Philippines." *Collier's*, January 17, 1942, 17, 49.
Breuer, William B. *The Great Raid on Cabanatuan: Rescuing the Doomed Ghosts of Bataan and Corregidor*. New York: John Wiley & Sons, 1994.
Bryan, Lamar. "Bataan Survivor [Tom Dooley '35] Recalls Hardship as War Prisoner." *Kentucky News Era*, April 11, 1992.
Cook, Charles O. "The Strange Case of Rainbow-5." *U.S. Naval Institute Proceedings*, August 1978.
Cooper, Jerry. "Aggie History Was Made on the Rock." *Texas Aggie*, June 1996, 12–13.
———. "Lest We Forget: Jerome McDavitt '33 Recalls WWII POW Camp." *Texas Aggie*, April 1989, 6–9.
"The Expendables." *Nation*, June 21, 1943, 829–30.
Falk, Stanley L. "Ships That Never Came In." *Journal of Military History*, Winter 1995, 43–45.
Fernandez, Marian N. "Women in Combat? Meet the Heroines of Corregidor, Bataan." *Army*, April 1979, 42.

Ford, Corey. "We Lived to Tell." *Collier's*, March 3, 1945, 11–32.

Futrell, Robert F. "Air Hostilities in the Philippines 8 December 1941." *Air University Review*, January 1965.

"Ghostly Garrison." *TIME*, May 18, 1942, 25.

Gordon, John. "The Navy's Infantry at Bataan." *Proceedings*, March 1985, 64–69.

Green, Fred M. "Coast Artillery Life in the Philippines." *Journal of the U.S. Artillery*, January 1922, 444–52.

Hagee, Florence W. "These Men Survived." *Survey*, March 1946, 67–72.

Hanson, Tim. "The Guns of Corregidor: A Close-Up Look at an Island Fortress." *Pacific Stars and Stripes*, December 29, 1991.

Holt, Thaddeus. "King of Bataan." *Journal of Military History*, Winter 1995, 32–42.

Huber, Thomas M. "The American Bataan Campaign: December 1941 to April 1942." *Army History*, Winter 1991/92, 1–13.

James, D. Clayton. "The Other Pearl Harbor." *The Quarterly Journal of Military History (MHQ)*, Winter 1995, 22–29.

"Japs Lie about U.S. Heroes." *LIFE*, September 14, 1942, 25–29.

Klimow, Matthew S. "Lying to the Troops: American Leaders and the Defense of Bataan." *Parameters*, December 1990, 48–60.

Lay, Kermit. "724th Aviation Ordnance Company: The Misplaced Company of Bataan and Corregidor." *The Quan*, June 1990, 15–16.

Lopez, Andres. "The Fall of the Philippines." *Military Review*, August 1946, 11–12.

Manning, Michele. "Angels of Mercy: The Army Nurse Corps Bataan and Corregidor." *Parameters*, Spring 1992, 86–100.

Martin, John R. "War Plan Orange and Maritime Strategy." *Military Review*, May 1989.

Meixsel, Richard B. "Major General George Grunert, WPO-3, and the Philippine Army, 1940–1941." *Journal of Military History*, April 1995, 303.

Nardidi, J. E. "Survival Factors in American Prisoners of War of the Japanese." *American Journal of Psychiatry*, October 1952, 241–48.

Paterson, Rab. "The Fall of Fortress Singapore: Churchill's Role and Conflicting Interpretations." *Sophia International Review*, 31–68.

Powell, J. B. "Prisoner of the Japanese." *Nation*, October 10, 1942, 335–37.

Prickett, William F. "Naval Battalion at Mariveles." *Marine Corps Gazette*, June 1950, 41–42.

Roland, Charles G., and Harry S. Shannon. "Patterns of Disease among World War II Prisoners of the Japanese: Hunger, Weight Loss, and Deficiency Diseases in Two Camps." *Journal of the History of Medicine and Allied Science*, 1991, 65–83.

Stoler, Mark A. "George C. Marshall and 'Europe-First' Strategy, 1939–1951: A Study in Diplomatic as well as Military History." *Journal of Military History*, April 2015, 293–316.

Stolley, Fred. "The Fall of Corregidor." *History of the Second World War*, Part 31, n.p.: 1972, 864–68.

Streifer, Bill. "Operation Cardinal: OSS in Manchuria." *OSS Society Journal*, Fall 2010, 22–25.

Takahashi, Fumio. "The First War Plan Orange and the First Imperial Japanese Defense Policy: An Interpretation from the Geopolitical Strategic Perspective." *NIDS Security Reports*, No. 5, March 2004, 68–103.

"Thunder from the Rock." *TIME*, April 27, 1942, 21.

"The 26th Cavalry in the Philippines" *The Cavalry Journal*, January 1944.

Vader, John. "The Fall of the Philippines." *History of the Second World War*, Part 31, n.p.: 1972, 856–63.

Whitman, John W. "Delaying Action in the Philippines." *World War II*, November 1998, 42–48.

Wolf, Stewart, and Herbert S. Ripley. "Reactions among Allied Prisoners of War Subjected to Three Years of Imprisonment and Torture by the Japanese." *American Journal of Psychiatry*, September 1947, 180–93.

Woodhall, Jeffery W. "The 26th Cavalry in the Philippines." *Armor*, January–February 1983, 8–16.

Books

Allen, Francis J. *The Concrete Battleship: Fort Drum, El Fraile Island, and Manila Bay*. Missoula, MT: Pictorial Histories, 1988.

Armstrong, Alan. *Preemptive Strike*. Guilford, CT: Lyons Press, 2006.

Bartsch, William H. *December 8, 1941: MacArthur's Pearl Harbor*. College Station: Texas A&M University Press, 2003.

———. *Doomed at the Start: American Pursuit Pilots in the Philippines, 1941–1942*. College Station: Texas A&M University Press, 1992.

Belote, James H., and William M. Belote. *Corregidor*. New York: PEI Books, 1980.

Best, Antony. *British Intelligence and the Japanese Challenge in Asia, 1914–1941*. New York: Palgrave Macmillan, 2002.

Bilek, Tony. *No Uncle Sam: The Forgotten of Bataan*. Kent, OH: Kent State University Press, 2003.

Black, Jeremy. *The Age of Total War*. Lanham: Rowman & Littlefield, 2006.

Boyt, Gene. *Bataan: A Survivors Story*. Norman: University of Oklahoma Press, 2004.

Bradley, James. *Flyboys: A True Story of Courage*. New York: Little, Brown and Company, 2003.

Breuer, William B. *MacArthur's Undercover War*. New York: John Wiley & Sons, 1995.

Broch, Fred, and Daniel Martinez. *Kimmel, Short, and Pearl Harbor: The Final Report Revealed*. Annapolis: Naval Institute Press, 2005.

Bumgarner, John R. *Parade of the Dead*. Jefferson, NC: McFarland & Company, 1995.

Burton, John. *Fortnight of Infamy: The Collapse of Allied Airpower West of Pearl Harbor.* Annapolis: Naval Institute Press, 2006.

Callahan, Raymond. *The Worst Disaster: The Fall of Singapore.* Newark: University of Delaware Press, 1977.

Cameron, Robert S. *Mobility, Shock, and Firepower: The Emergence of the U.S. Army's Armor Branch, 1917–1945.* Washington, DC: Center of Military History, 2008.

Cave, Dorothy. *Beyond Courage: One Regiment Against Japan 1941–1945.* Las Cruces, NM: Yucca Free Press, 1992.

Coffman, Edward M. *The Regulars: The American Army 1898–1941.* Cambridge: Harvard University Press, 2004.

Connaughton, Richard. *MacArthur and Defeat in the Philippines.* Woodstock, NY: Overlook Press, 2001.

Connaughton, Richard, John Pimlott, and Duncan Anderson. *The Battle for Manila.* Novato, CA: Presidio Press, 1995.

Conroy, Robert. *The Battle of Bataan: America's Greatest Defeat.* London: Macmillan, 1969.

Coogan, Andy. *Tomorrow You Die: The Astonishing Survival Story of a Second World War Prisoner of the Japanese.* New York: Random House, 2012.

Cray, Ed. *General of the Army: George Marshall.* New York: W. W. Norton & Company, 1990.

Daniels, Robert C. *1220 Days: The Story of a Marine Edmond Babler.* Bloomington, IN: AuthorHouse, 2011.

Davis, Kenneth S. *FDR: The War President 1940–1943.* New York: Random House: 2000.

Daws, Gavan. *Prisoners of the Japanese: POWs of World War in the Pacific.* New York: William Morrow and Company, 1994.

Decker, Malcolm. *From Bataan to Safety.* Jefferson, NC: McFarland & Company, 2008.

Devlin, Gerard M. *Back to Corregidor: America Retakes the Rock.* New York: St. Martin's Press, 1992.

Dower, John W. *War without Mercy: Race and Power in the Pacific War.* New York: Pantheon Books, 1986.

Drea, Edward. *Japan's Imperial Army: Its Rise and Fall, 1953–1945.* Lawrence: University Press of Kansas, 2009.

Dyess, William E. *The Dyess Story: The Eye-Witness Account of the Death March from Bataan.* New York: G. P. Putnam's Sons, 1944.

Edmonds, Walter D. *They Fought with What They Had: The Story of the Army Air Forces in the Southwest Pacific, 1941–1942.* Boston: Little, Brown and Company, 1951.

Edwards, Bernard. *Blood and Bushido: Japanese Atrocities at Sea 1941–1945.* New York: Brick Tower Press, 1997.

Eisenhower, Dwight D. *Crusade in Europe.* New York: Doubleday, 1952.

Falk, Stanley L. *Bataan: The March of Death.* New York: Modern Literary Editions, 1962.

Fenberg, Steven. *Unprecedented Power: Jesse Jones, Capitalism, and the Common Good.* College Station: Texas A&M University Press, 2011.

Ferguson, Ted. *Desperate Siege: The Battle of Hong Kong.* New York: Doubleday, 1980.

Frank, Richard B. *MacArthur.* New York: Palgrave, 2007.

Frazier, Gleen D. *Hell's Guest.* n.p.: eGen Co., 2007.

Gay, George. *Sole Survivor: Torpedo Squadron Eight—Battle of Midway.* Naples: Midway, 1980.

Goldstein, Donald M., and Katherine V. Dillon, eds. *The Pacific War Papers: Japanese Documents of World War II.* Washington, DC: Potomac Books, 2004.

Gole, Henry G. *The Road to Rainbow: Army Planning for Global War, 1934–1940.* Annapolis: Naval Institute Press, 2002.

Gordon, John. *Fighting for MacArthur: The Navy and Marine Corps' Desperate Defense of the Philippines.* Annapolis: Naval Institute Press, 2011.

Hamm, Diane L., ed. *Military Intelligence: Its Heroes and Legends.* Honolulu: University of the Pacific, 2001.

Haney, Robert. *Caged Dragon.* Momentum Books, 1991.

Hank, Karl, and Kevin Blackburn. *Did Singapore Have to Fall? Churchill and the Impregnable Fortress.* London: Routledge, 2004.

Harries, Meiron, and Susie Harries. *Soldiers of the Sun: The Rise and Fall of the Imperial Japanese Army.* New York: Random House, 1991.

Harris, Sheldon H. *Factories of Death: Japanese Biological Warfare 1932–1945.* New York: Routledge, 1994.

Hartendrop, A. V. H. *The Santo Tomas Story.* New York: McGraw-Hill, 1964.

Haushofer, Karl. *Japan Baut Sein Reich.* Berlin: Zeitgeschichte-Verlag, 1941.

Hilsman, Roger. *American Guerrilla: My War Behind Japanese Lines.* Washington, DC: Potomac Books, 2005.

Hokins, William B. *The Pacific War: The Strategy, Politics, and Players That Won the War.* Minneapolis: Zenith Press, 2008.

Holmes, Linda G. *Guests of the Emperor: The Secret History of Japan's Mukden POW Camp.* Annapolis: Naval Institute Press, 2010.

———. *Unjust Enrichment.* Mechanicsburg, PA: Stackpole Books, 2001.

Holmes, Richard. *Acts of War: The Behavior of Men in Battle.* New York: Free Press, 1985.

Hoyt, Edwin P. *Japan's War.* New York: Da Capo Press, 1986.

———. *Warlord: Tojo Against the World.* Lanham, MD: Scarborough, 1993.

Hubbard, Preston J. *Apocalypse Undone.* Nashville: Vanderbilt University Press, 1990.

Ind, Allison. *Bataan: The Judgment Seat.* New York: Macmillan, 1944.

Jacobsen, Gene S. *We Refused to Die: My Time as a POW in Bataan and Japan, 1942–1945.* Salt Lake City: University of Utah Press, 2004.

Jordan, Jonathan. *American Warlords*. New York: NAL Caliber, 2015.

Kawai, Tatsuo. *The Goal of Japanese Expansion*. Tokyo: Hokuseido Press, 1938.

Keegan, John. *The Mask of Command*. New York: Viking, 1987.

Kerr, E. Bartlett. *Surrender and Survival: The Experience of American POWs in the Pacific, 1941–1945*. New York: William Morrow and Company, 1985.

Knox, Donald. *Death March: The Survivors of Bataan*. New York: Harcourt Brace Jovanovich, 1981.

Kubek, Antony. *How the Far East Was Lost*. Chicago: Henry Regnery Company, 1963.

Kwiecinski, Stephen A. *Honor Courage Faith: A Corregidor Story*. Manila: Anvil Press, 2012.

LaForte, Robert S., R. E. Marcello, and Richard L. Hummel, eds. *With Only the Will to Live: Accounts of Americans in Japanese Prison Camps 1941–1945*. Wilmington, DE: SR Books, 1994.

Lord, Walter. *Day of Infamy*. New York: Henry Holt and Company, 1957.

Lukacs, John D. *Escape from Davao: The Forgotten Story of the Most Daring Prison Break of the Pacific War*. New York: Simon & Schuster, 2010.

Maalikowski, Edward. *A Brother's Hero*. West Chester, PA: 2012.

MacArthur, Brian. *Surviving the Sword: Prisoners of the Japanese in the Far East, 1942–1945*. New York: Random House, 2005.

Maga, Timothy P. *Judgment at Tokyo: The Japanese War Crimes Trails*. Lexington: University of Kentucky Press.

Mallonee, Richard C., ed. *Battle for Bataan*. Novato, CA: Presidio Press, 1980.

Manchester, William. *American Caesar: Douglas MacArthur 1880–1964*. Boston: Little, Brown and Company, 1978.

Manning, Paul. *Hirohito: The War Years*. New York: Bantam, 1989.

Martin, Adrian R. *Brothers from Bataan: POWs, 1942–1945*. Manhattan, KS: Sunflower University Press, 1992.

Martin, Adrian R., and Larry W. Stephenson. *Operation Plum: The Ill-fated 27th Bombardment Group and the Fight for the Western Pacific*. College Station: Texas A&M University Press, 2008.

McCoy, Melvyn H., and S. M. Mellnik. *Ten Escape from Tojo*. New York: Farra & Rinehart, 1944.

McElvaine, Robert S. *The Great Depression: America, 1929–1941*. New York: Time Books, 1993.

McGee, John H. *Rice and Salt: A History of the Defense and Occupation of Mindanao during World War II*. San Antonio: Naylor, n.d.

Messimer, Dwight R. *In the Hands of Fate*. Annapolis: Naval Institute Press, 1985.

Michno, Gregory F. *Death on the Hellships: Prisoners at Sea in the Pacific War*. Annapolis: Naval Institute Press, 2001.

Miller, E. B. *Bataan Uncensored*. Long Prairie, MN: Hart Publications, 1949.

Miller, J. Michael. *From Shanghai to Corregidor: Marines in the Defense of the Philippines.* Washington, DC: Marine Corps Historical Center, 1997.

Mills, Scott A. *Stranded in the Philippines.* Annapolis: Naval Institute Press, 2009.

Miner, William D. *Surrender on Cebu: A POW's Diary—WWII.* Paduch, KY: Turner, 2001.

Morison, Samuel E. *The Rising Sun in the Pacific: 1931–April 1942.* Boston: Little, Brown and Company, 1984.

Morris, Eric. *Corregidor: The American Alamo of World War II.* New York: Cooper Square Press, 2000.

———. *Corregidor: The End of the Line.* New York: Stein and Day, 1981.

Morton, Louis. *Strategy and Command: The First Two Years.* Washington, DC: GPO, 1962.

———. *War in the Pacific: The Fall of the Philippines.* Washington, DC: Center for Military History, US Army, 1953.

Mosley, Leonard. *Hirohito: Emperor of Japan.* Englewood Cliffs, NJ: Prentice-Hall, 1966.

Murr, Dan. *But Deliver Us from Evil.* Florida: Murr, 2008.

Nash, Grace C. *That We Might Live.* Scottsdale: SHANO, 1984.

Nelson, Clarke. *The Fighting Douglas MacArthur.* New York: Dodd, Mead & Company, 1965.

Nitobe, Inazo. *Bushido: The Soul of Japan.* Boston: Tuttle, 2001.

———. *The Way of the Samurai.* London: Arcturus, 2011.

Nordin, Carl S. *We Were Next to Nothing: An American POW's Account of Japanese Prison Camps and Deliverance in World War II.* New York: McFarland & Company, 2004.

Norman, Elizabeth M. *We Band of Angels: The Untold Story of American Nurses Trapped on Bataan by the Japanese.* New York: Random House, 1999.

Norman, Michael, and Elizabeth M. Norman. *Tears in the Darkness: The Story of the Bataan Death March and Its Aftermath.* New York: Farrar, Straus and Giroux, 2009.

Parkinson, James W., and Lee Benson. *Soldier Slaves: Abandoned by the White House, Courts, and Congress.* Annapolis: Naval Institute Press, 2006.

Pearson, Judith L. *Belly of the Beast.* New York: New American Library, 2001.

Perry, Mark. *The Most Dangerous Man in America: The Making of Douglas MacArthur.* New York: Basic Books, 2014.

Pogue, Forrest. *George C. Marshall: Ordeal and Hope.* New York: Viking, 1965.

Prange, Gordon W. *At Dawn We Slept: The Untold Story of Pearl Harbor.* New York: Penguin, 1981.

Ramsey, Edwin Price, and Stephen J. Rivele. *Lieutenant Ramsey's War: From Horse Soldier to Guerrilla Commander.* Washington, DC: Brassey's, 1990.

Reel, A. Frank. *The Case of General Yamashita.* Chicago: University of Chicago Press, 1949.

Ricks, Thomas E. *The Generals*. New York: Penguin Books, 2012.

Roberts, Andrew. *Masters and Commanders*. New York: Harper, 2009.

———. *The Storm of War*. New York: Harper, 2011.

Romulo, Carlos P. *I Saw the Fall of the Philippines*. New York: Doubleday, Doran & Company, 1943.

Ross, Steven T. *American War Plans 1890–1939*. New York: Frank Cass, 2000.

Salecker, Gene E. *Rolling Thunder Against the Rising Sun*. Mechanicsville, PA: Stackpole Books, 2008.

Schaefer, Chris. *Bataan Diary: An American Family in World War II, 1941–1945*. Houston: Riverview, 2004.

Schaller, Michael. *Douglas MacArthur: The Far Eastern General*. New York: Oxford University Press, 1989.

Schultz, Duane. *Hero of Bataan: The Story of General Jonathan M. Wainwright*. New York: Harcourt Brace Jovanovich, 1981.

Scott, James M. *Target Tokyo*. New York: Norton, 2015.

Shirly, Craig. *December 1941*. Nashville: Thomas Nelson, 2011.

Sides, Hampton. *Ghost Soldiers*. New York: Doubleday, 2001.

Sloan, Bill. *Undefeated: America's Heroic Fight for Bataan and Corregidor*. New York: Simon & Schuster, 2012.

Small, Charles S. *Rails to Doomsday: The U.S. Army's Corregidor and Manila Bay Railroad*. Canton: Railhead Publications, 1998.

Snow, Philip. *The Fall of Hong Kong: Britain, China and the Japanese Occupation*. New Haven: Yale University Press, 2003.

Spector, Ronald H. *Eagle Against the Sun: The American War with Japan*. New York: Free Press.

Stewart, Sidney. *Give Us This Day: The Survivors of the Bataan Death March*. New York: Popular Library, 1958.

Tanaka, Yuki. *Hidden Horrors: Japanese War Crime in World War II*. Boulder: Westview Press, 1996.

Taylor, Lawrence. *A Trail of Generals: Homma, Yaamashita, MacArthur*. South Bend, IN: Icarus Press, 1981.

Taylor, Vince. *Cabanatuan: Japanese Death Camp*. Waco: Texian Press, 1985.

Taylor, William M. *Hell Ships: Voyages of Japanese Prison Ships, 1942–1945*. Oxford: Mississippi State University, 1972.

Tenner, Lester. *My Hitch in Hell: The Bataan Death March*. Washington, DC: Brassey's, 1995.

Thomas, Evan. *The War Lovers: Roosevelt, Lodge, Hearst, and the Rush to Empire, 1898*. New York: Back Bay Books, 2010.

Tokarz, Stanley. *Silent Tears: Lest We Forget*. Clinton, MA: Clinton Offset Press, 2000.

Toland, John. *But Not in Shame: The Six Months after Pearl Harbor*. New York: Random House, 1961.

Toll, Ian W. *Pacific Crucible: War at Sea in the Pacific, 1941–1942*. New York: W. W. Norton & Company, 2012.

Tooze, Adam. *The Deluge: The Great War, America and the Remaking of the Global Order, 1916–1931*. New York: Viking, 2014.

Tsuji, Masanobu. *Japan's Greatest Victory—Britain's Worst Defeat*. New York: Sarpedon, 1993.

Utinsky, Margaret. *"Miss U"*. San Antonio: Naylor Company, 1948.

Villarin, Mariano. *We Remember: Bataan and Corregidor*. Baltimore: Gateway Press, 1990.

Volckmann, R. W. *We Remained: Three Years Behind the Enemy Lines in the Philippines*. New York: W. W. Norton & Company, 1954.

Weintruab, Stanley. *Lear Harbor Christmas: A World at War, December 1941*. New York: DeCapo Press, 2011.

Welch, Bob. *Resolve: From the Jungles of World War II Bataan*. New York; Berkley Caliber, 2012.

Whitcomb, Edgar D. *Escape from Corregidor*. Chicago: Henry Regnery Company, 1958.

White, W. L. *Queens Die Proudly*. New York: Harcourt Brace, 1943.

Whitman, John W. *The Bataan Campaign, 1942*. New York: Hippocrene Books, 1990.

Whitney, Courtney. *MacArthur: His Rendezvous with History*. New York: Alfred A. Knopf, 1956.

Wilbanks, Bob. *Last Man Out: Glen McDole, USMC, Survivor of the Palawan Massacre in World War II*. Jefferson, NC: McFarland & Company, 2004.

Williams, Denny. *To The Angels*. San Francisco: Denson Press, 1985.

Young, Donald J. *The Battle of Bataan: A History of the 90 Day Siege and Eventual Surrender of 75,000 Filipino and United States Troops to the Japanese in World War II*. New York: McFarland & Company, 1992.

———. *Final Hours in the Pacific: The Allied Surrenders of Wake Island, Bataan*. New York: McFarland & Company, 2011.

Yuki, Tonaka. *Hidden Horrors: Japanese War Crimes in World War II*. Boulder: Westview Press, 1996.

Unpublished Manuscripts

Hillius, William J. "Assuming Rape: The Reproduction of Fear in American Military Female POWs." MA thesis, University of Washington, 2012.

"Japanese Prisoner of War Camps During World War II, 1941–1945." Medical Research Committee of American Ex-Prisoners of War, January 1980.

"List of Hellship Voyages in Chronological Sequence of Departure Date." http://www.west-point.org.

"Mukden (Hoten) Timeline." http://www.mansell.com.

Nelson, Jim. "The Causes of the Bataan Death March Revisited." n.p.: n.d.

"POW Camps in Japan Proper." http://www.powresearch.jp.

"Prisoners of War of the Japanese 1939–1945." http://www.forces-war-records.co.uk.

Wainwright, Peter S. "Memorial Address of November 11, 1996." Walla Walla, WA: November 1996.

Woodall, James. "General George Moore." Unpublished manuscript, College Station, TX, 2013.

Texas A&M Books and Documents

Adams, John A. Jr. *Keepers of the Spirit: The Corps of Cadets at Texas A&M University, 1976–2001*. College Station: Texas A&M University Press, 2001.

———. *Softly Call the Muster*. College Station: Texas A&M University Press, 1994.

———. *We Are the Aggies*. College Station: Texas A&M University Press, 1979.

Adams, John C., ed. *The Voices of a Proud Tradition: A Collection of Aggie Muster Speeches*. Bryan, TX: Brazos Valley Printing, 1985.

Association of Former Students. *Alumni Quarterly*, April 1916 to February 1920.

———. *Directory of Former Students*. College Station: 1976.

———. *Directory of Former Students of the A&M College of Texas, 1876–1949*. College Station: 1949.

———. *The Texas Aggie Magazine*. College Station: 1930–1950.

Battalion. College Station: 1930–50.

Dethloff, Henry C. *A Centennial History of Texas A&M University 1876–1976*, vol. 2. College Station: Texas A&M University Press, 1975.

Dethloff, Henry C., and John A. Adams Jr. *Texas Aggies Go to War*. College Station: Texas A&M University Press, 2009.

Evans, Wilbur, and H. B. McElroy. *The Twelfth Man*. Huntsville, AL: Strode, 1974.

Johnson, Pamela W. *The Corps: The Corps of A&M*. College Station: Texas A&M University Press, 2005.

Leftwich, Bill J. *The Corps at Aggieland*. Lubbock: Smoke Signal, 1976.

Longhorn. College Station (annual yearbook): 1904–46.

Perry, George S. *The Story of Texas A and M*. New York: McGraw-Hill, 1951.

Rollins, Joseph G. *"Aggies! Y'all Caught That Dam' Ol' Rat Yet?"* San Antonio: Naylor Company, 1970.

Smith, Edna M., ed. *Aggies, Moms, and Apple Pie*. College Station: Texas A&M University Press, 1987. Introduction by John A. Adams Jr. '73, xiii–xvii.

Woodall, James. *Texas Aggie Medal of Honor*. College Station: Texas A&M University Press, 2010.

———. *12 Texas Aggie War Heroes: From World War I to Vietnam*. College Station: Texas A&M University Press, 2015.

INDEX

Note: The letters f, t, and n indicate that the entry refers to a page's figure, table, or note, respectively.